The
Second Vatican Council
and the
New Catholicism

The Second Vatican Council and the New Catholicism

by

G. C. BERKOUWER
Professor of Systematic Theology
Free University of Amsterdam

translated by

LEWIS B. SMEDES
Associate Professor of Bible
Calvin College

WILLIAM B. EERDMANS PUBLISHING COMPANY
GRAND RAPIDS, MICHIGAN

Printed in the United States of America.
Library of Congress catalog card number 64-8581

Translated from the original Dutch edition
by special arrangement with
J. H. Kok
Kampen, The Netherlands

Translator's Preface

It is safe to say, I believe, that no Protestant theologian is better qualified to write this book than its author, G. C. Berkouwer. Known in the English-speaking world through the translations of his series of *Dogmatic Studies* and, perhaps even better, through his brilliant analysis of the theology of Karl Barth in the book *The Triumph of Grace in the Theology of Karl Barth,* Berkouwer is equally recognized in Europe as one of the outstanding participants in the ongoing Catholic-Protestant dialogue. He was invited by Pope John XXIII to be an official observer at the Second Vatican Council, a fact that is striking because Berkouwer represents a minority Reformed Church in the small country of Holland. His earlier works on Catholicism have demonstrated his unique ability to think and speak from within the mind and spirit of the Catholic Church.

Berkouwer stands in a line of conservative Dutch Reformed theologians that includes such men as Herman Bavinck and Abraham Kuyper. But he is an ecumenical theologian in the most profound and at the same time the most universal sense of the word. I have translated this volume on the theological background to the Second Vatican Council in the hope, not only that it would bring Berkouwer to a wider audience in this country, but that it

5

would demonstrate how genuinely a Protestant theologian whose only real concern is the accurate translation of the gospel of Jesus Christ can enter into a true and sympathetic dialogue with the Roman Catholic Church. It is my hope that it may also contribute to a deeper understanding of their own communion and tradition on the part of Catholics, and encourage Protestants to enter the dialogue that, though slow in starting, is taking place in this country as well as in Europe.

I have taken a few liberties in translation that I should acknowledge. For the sake of the English reader, I have eliminated some footnotes, particularly those that referred the reader to Dutch periodicals that largely are unavailable. Here and there I have also translated the sense rather than the words, though without sacrifice to Berkouwer's style or content. The bulk of the citations from the councils and encyclicals are from Roy J. Defferrari's translation of the Thirtieth edition of H. Denzinger's *Enchiridion Symbolorum,* published under the title *The Sources of Catholic Dogma* by B. Herder in 1957. The source of other translations are noted in the text, and where not noted they are my own.

—LEWIS B. SMEDES

Preface

When the full history of the Second Vatican Council is written, it will have to match in size Granderath's great three-volume history of the First Vatican Council. The present study is obviously not meant to be an account of the council in any historian's sense. My purpose is limited to a discussion of the single aspect of the council that is indicated by the title of this book. I have judged that this purpose can be achieved even though the council is not yet completed. For the relationship between the new theology that has risen within the Roman Church and the Second Vatican Council is one that has put its stamp on the whole council in all of its discussions. The new theology forms part of the background to the council, both in the books of theologians and in the life of the church. And it comes to the foreground at the council in almost every debate. We have limited ourselves to a few themes that are intimately involved in the entire Catholic situation; a discussion of any one of them brings the reader into contact with some of the most crucial problems of the current council. No one can pretend to understand either the Vatican Council or the Roman Catholic Church today without an acquaintance with these issues, which have come to life *via* the new theology.

—G. C. BERKOUWER

Contents

The Unexpected Council

THE SECOND VATICAN COUNCIL HAS CREATED UNMISTAK-able tensions within the Roman Catholic Church of the twentieth century. Since Pope John XXIII unexpectedly called the council on January 25, 1959, people every-where, within and outside of the Catholic Church, have asked themselves what the Pope's real intent was, and what the council would mean for the Catholic Church itself and for its relationship to other churches. The questions were under-standable, for the Vatican Council of 1870 ended without a hint that another council would be needed at any time. Pope John's decision to call a council was utterly unexpected. Moreover, with the final formalizing of the doctrine of papal infallibility in 1870, the Church seemed to have placed its own future into the guar-anteed guidance of "the Vicar of Christ." What, then, could have been intended with the calling of a new and ecumenical council?

The answer is closely tied to the person of Pope John, the man who surprised the world by his new plans for the Church. John XXIII was born on November 25, 1881, and so had already passed eighty when the council was opened on October 11, 1962. With rare vitality and enormous élan for a man of that age, he personally took direct leadership in preparations for the council. This unusual man took everyone by surprise. When Pius died on October 9, 1958, the choice of Roncalli to succeed to the papacy was generally taken to be a decision for an *interim* pope. But, as someone has said,[1] "the new pope captured by storm the sympathy of the world" with his great goodness and unconventional manners. He broke with empty customs and restored meaningful traditions. He appeared often in the city of Rome, visited prisons, hospitals, and schools, projected a synod for the bishopric of Rome — and proclaimed a new council. Before his ascension to the papacy, John XXIII had already lived a full life in the Roman Catholic Church. After his stint as sergeant in the Italian army (1915-1916) he was, to mention a few facets of his life, teacher of church history, patrology, and apologetics, president of the National Committee of the Association for the Propagation of the Faith, apostolic legate in Turkey, then papal nuntius in Paris. He was made a cardinal in 1953, and finally was selected to be Patriarch of Venice. In the conclave held October 25-28, 1958, he was elected Pope. On his election he declared that he had no right to look a long way ahead. But during his pontificate the idea of a council gradually ripened from a pious vision to a concrete plan.

The character of the man and the idea of calling a council are intimately intertwined. He once said in Venice: "Since my childhood, I have wanted nothing other than to be a common pastor." He was, in the words of a biographer, the shepherd of Venice, a man with a warm heart and a priest with a crusading zeal for souls.[2] Every description of John XXIII calls attention to this single ambition: he wanted first of all and genuinely to be a pastor. To be shepherd of the flock meant for him, of course, only to be pastor of the Roman Catholic Church. But this did not keep him from looking out through the windows of Rome to the divided churches and to a divided world. The parable of the Good Shepherd who was concerned with His "other sheep" and who saw only one flock under one Shepherd — this was the parable that possessed the mind and heart of John XXIII. He said that from this parable "rays of heavenly light break forth and shine to all people who are not yet Christian, and they proclaim the dayspring of the coming ecumenical council which has already aroused a

---

[1] Cf. the Introduction to *Ad Petri Cathedram,* June 29, 1959.

[2] In a speech given to the Roman Synod on January 27, 1960, he said: "We view it as the most important and precious grace that the portrayal of Christ as the Good Shepherd has exercised a strong fascination for us from the time of our youth until our old age."

mysterious expectation and an anxious longing in Christian people the world over."

Everything John said about the council breathed a universal concern. He expected the attention of "all people" to be fastened on the council, and during the interim between the first and second sessions he thought he could hear a "broad echo" of response. He was sure the council was an event that spread its power, not only over all Catholics, but over the whole world. It would be an echo of something said about the Divine Redeemer: "He died for our sins, and not for ours alone, but for the sins of the whole world."[3] This world-wide vision characterized John XXIII throughout his brief pontificate.

Who will ever know precisely what he meant when he called his an "ecumenical" council? In any case, John was always concerned with the calling of the Church in this world. Opposed to all world-denial and world-flight, he was deeply convinced that the responsibility of the Church was not simply for man's salvation, but for the "increasing needs of mankind and for the cares and burdens of this mortal life."[4] His concern for the whole of human existence raises the question of the role his council was intended and was able to play in this concern. After the Pope called the new council, people began asking whether he really meant to wage a full-scale offensive toward reunion in the manner of the Council at Lyon in 1274 and at Florence in 1439, where the divisions between East and West were at the center of interest. Was there a connection between John's "ecumenical" council and the ecumenical movement? And was the background of John's surprising plan actually the vision of the One Shepherd and the One Flock? The council understandably evoked such questions, and the fact that its proclamation awakened new interest for the visible unity of the Church is not surprising. Reunion was indeed one of the perspectives and visions that captured Pope John's imagination. Doubtless, he saw in the very fact that the council was being held a tremendous appeal for unity. And from the inception of his pontificate he gave repeated and moving expressions of his hope for unity. His decision to establish a Secretariat for Church Unity was simply part of his vision.[5]

[3] In the letter *Mirabilis ille* of January 6, 1963.

[4] In the encyclical *Mater et Magistra* (*Christianity and Social Progress*) of May 15, 1961.

[5] On May 30, 1960, John XXIII mentioned the establishment of a special secretariat "which will make it possible for separated brethren to follow the work of

But, nonetheless, we would be mistaken if we saw this council as a reunion council. This is clear from the fact that John, in his first encyclical about the council, remarked that the council would be first of all pre-occupied with the internal problems of the Roman Church.[6] With this he meant to indicate that the Church's thoughts about itself would lead the way to the wider perspectives that would embrace the vision of the unity of all Christians. In John's mind there was a close connection between the *internal* life of the Church and the future reunion of the churches. He explained the connection in these words about the coming council: "It will be a glorious display of truth, unity, and love. And, we trust, those who have been separated from the apostolic chair shall be led by this display to feel themselves moved to seek and to realize the unity which Jesus Christ invoked so passionately from His heavenly Father."[7]

John was fond of recalling that the Church was the one body of the Lord, the cloak without seam. He called non-Catholics brothers and sons. He set high hopes on the unity that he thought would be made visible in the council. With John, this was not simply a pretentious summons for all non-Catholics to return to the one exclusively saving Church. Nor was it a mere repetition of the claim that the only unity of the Church was that already existing in the Catholic Church. It was a vision which summoned the Roman Church itself to new responsibility. Characteristically for John XXIII, the ecumenical perspective was never dissociated from the internal problems of his Church. In the minds of other popes, the line of thought was indeed simple: the one Church, the single body of Christ, is here and now an irrefutable fact. So the answer to the problem of Church division was clear: it was the route back to Rome, the return to the one flock of Christ. John saw the situation as being far more complex than this. He believed that the Church was obliged to submit to a renewal of its own inner reality so that it would be more credible in the eyes and judgment of the separated brothers. The mere fact of the one Catholic Church was not the point of departure for simple and pretentious

the Council and thus to make easier their reunion in the one fold of Christ." Cf. A. Bea, *The Unity of Christians*, 1963, p. 50; cf. pp. 161ff.

[6] *Ad Petri Cathedram.* Cardinal Bea said emphatically that the Pope meant by the term "ecumenical" a council of all bishops of the inhabited earth who are bound to the chair of St. Peter. Cf. Bea, "Die Bedeutung des 2. Vatik. Konzils für die Einheit der Christe," *Stimmen der Zeit*, 1961-62, p. 243.

[7] *Ad Petri Cathedram.*

conclusions; instead John called that church to renewal and sanc-tification.[8] But this did not hinder him from bearing witness to his own longing for unity. To non-Catholics he said: "Allow us, in our intense longing, to call you brothers and sons; allow us the hope that, with fatherly love, we cherish for your return." Again, he used the words of Augustine in his appeal to non-Catholics: "Whether they will to be or not, they are our brothers. They will cease being our brothers when they cease praying 'Our Father.' "[9]

John made it clear that he was not enamored of a vague romanticism regarding unity or an oversimplified irenicism. His passionate longing for the visible unity of the Church did not rise from any inward doubt about the house that is already built, the Catholic Ecclesia. He sometimes made use of the word "return" without the modesty that surrounds the phrase these days. He liked to speak of the eternal youth of the Catholic Church, point-ing to it as an "ensign raised among the nations." When, in 1961, he issued an encyclical about Leo the Great as Pope and Teacher of the Church, he left no room for misunderstanding as to the "doctrinaire stand of the Catholic Church." Nothing cryptic or watered-down was heard when he spoke of the visible unity of the Church that was given an inexpendable support in the ultimate and infallible teaching authority with which Jesus Christ endowed Peter as the head of the apostles.[10] At the same time, he constantly underscored Christ's "prediction"[11] of the one flock and the one Shepherd. And so he reflected often on the place, the function, and the calling of the Church on its way to that divinely predicted reality.

The decisive motif in John's thoughts as we have briefly de-scribed them gives a special character to John's activity before and at the council. This comes out sharply in his repeated remind-ers of the theme of the one Shepherd throughout his brief pontifi-cate. Without trying to see church history in terms of personality, we can say that John wanted to make it clear in his own manner of life what was necessary for the Church truly to be the Church. In a speech to the cardinals on October 28, 1958, at the time he

[8] This is strikingly suggested in the title of a book by Hans Küng, *Konzil und Wiedervereinigung. Erneuerung als Ruf in die Einheit,* 1960 (*The Council and Reunion: Renewal as a Call to Unity*).

[9] *Ad Petri Cathedram.*

[10] In the encyclical *Aeterna Dei* of November 11, 1961. Cf. also *Ad Petri Cathedram* on the basis for firm unity that Christ gave to His Church lest His work should remain uncertain and given over to chance.

[11] *Aeterna Dei.*

took on his office, he said: "I shall be called John." He wanted to bear the name of the Baptist who was not himself the light, but only bore witness to the light, as well as of the other John who at the last supper rested his head on the heart of Jesus and there was filled with Christ's great love.[12] His personal ways fascinated the world. The history of the Catholic Church makes it terribly hard, even for the serious Catholic, to recognize the real Shepherd and Servant in the words and deeds of some popes. So the distinction between "person" and "office" has to be brought in to calm the soul troubled by the muddy waters. This is the tension inherent in a church that remains holy "in spite of the unholiness and fallibility of its human members, even of men in highest offices and orders." [13] For Catholics and non-Catholics as well, nothing of this tension and paradox was apparent in the figure of John XXIII. By word and act, he made it clear that he wanted to be nothing more than the "servant of servants." And his ideal was that *everyone* in the Church should work and live so that the character of Jesus Christ would be visible in the Church, and that thus by the renewal of the Church the way could be blazed to unity in Him. This is the vision that defined his thoughts about the "ecumenical" council.

Closely related to what we have said is John's frequent talk about the position of the Catholic Church *vis-à-vis* "the others." We can summarize John's views by saying that this position should not be principally antithetical. He was convinced that the council should not come out with new pronouncements, but with a new and appealing and positive witness, with a word of love and mercy. "In our time, the Bride of Christ may make better use of the healing instrument of mercy than of the weapons of discipline."[14] Such statements do not betray a lack of respect on John's part for the antithetical judgments the Church has made in the past. He spoke favorably of the Council of Chalcedon, which condemned various heresies. His stress on the healing powers of mercy are not to be mistaken for a spirit of vague toleration and indiffer-

---

[12] In the encyclical *Vocabor Johannes.*

[13] A. Rademacher, *Seine Reden und Aufsätze,* 1940, p. 163. Cf. in a wider connection H. de Lubac, *Méditations sur l'Eglise,* 1953, pp. 213ff. Cf. also the views of Karl Adam on the tragedy of the conflict between the real and the ideal in connection with the fact that the "extraordinary popes" are exceptions, and also his remarks about the "wounds" in the body of Christ (*Das Wesen des Katholizismus,* pp. 259ff.).

[14] In the encyclical *Gaudet Mater Ecclesia* on the occasion of the opening of the Second Vatican Council, October 11, 1962.

ence. But before and during the council he continuously expressed his belief that the Church should have a positive message, that the Church is not simply *against* things, but passionately for things. He said the Church was supported by the same Lord who, in His own world-oriented concern, came *into* the world as the concrete manifestation and reality of the love of God. This helps explain why John insisted that the council should have less concern for the exposition of the teaching about the Church than with the *"power"* of the teaching." [15] That is, the council has to see that the Church stands with a heart open to the needs of the world, with a will ready to serve the world as the Shepherd serves the flock with guidance and support in the world's confusion. The Church should not become worldly in serving, but it should manifest to the world what the Church in essence is. John also sought to find ways to demonstrate to the world the real unity of humankind, to provide the earthly city with the example of the heavenly city whose King is truth, whose law is love, and whose measure is eternity. [16]

John XXIII marks the end of the frequently negative and anti-thetical posture of the Roman Catholic Church. Though it was true that both thesis and antithesis were present in John's approach, the positive side, the thesis, came to have a heavier accent than ever before; the emphasis was laid on the witness of Him who was sent into the world, "not to condemn the world, but that the world through Him might be saved" (John 3:17).[17]

The words of John were also remarkable for their optimistic tone. His optimism was not, however, out of touch with the hard realities of his times. During the Cuban crisis he appealed to the peoples of the world and to their leaders to "listen to the frightful cry of inno-cent children and the aged, of individuals and societies, as it sounded over all the earth and reached up to heaven: Peace, Peace!" [18] But the realities of a world in danger could not stifle his optimism. He expressed his pained surprise at those who in spite of their religious zeal "see nothing other than decline and disaster

[15] *Gaudet Mater Ecclesia.* This thought comes to expression in various ways, as for example when he said that the council is not an academic conference. This was said in a speech at the conclusion of the first session of the Central Commission preparing for the council, June 20, 1961.

[16] *Ibid.* Cf. as well the encyclical *Mater et Magistra* of May 15, 1961, and *Pacem in terris* of April 11, 1962.

[17] Pope Paul VI also noted this text at the time he reopened the council. It was quoted in connection with the message of friendship, salvation, and hope that Christ brought to the world.

[18] From a radio broadcast titled "Seigneur Ecoute," October 25, 1962.

in our day." [19] "We find it impossible," he wrote, "to agree with these prophets of doom who can see the future only as bleak, as though the end of the world were around the corner." In days of crisis he seemed to have an eye for the mysterious ways of Divine Providence, which gains its purposes "through man's works and then mostly in ways beyond his expectations." This faith had implications for the Church and for the council, as he saw them. He was reminded of the Spirit of God brooding over the waters, "above the limitless, orderless, and still chaotic horizon of creation." [20] In this vein he waited for the appearance of a new Pentecost in which the kingdom of Christ would blossom anew on earth. [21]

Such hopefulness was, for John XXIII, inseparably bound up with *repentance*. On July 1, 1962, he devoted an encyclical to contrition as an incitement to penitence on behalf of the success of the council. [22] He saw a clear relationship between the success of the council and faith, penitence, and prayer, a relationship that brought with it a grave responsibility. On prayer, he spoke a word of warning to the spiritual leaders of the world. [23] He reminded them of the great drama played off in the Revelation of St. John, in which the angel with the golden censer was given incense to mingle with the prayers of all the saints on the golden altar before the throne (Revelation 8:3-5). He recalled that the angel then filled the censer with fire and threw it on the earth, causing peals of thunder, loud noises, flashes of lightning, and an earthquake. The point was clear: the lifting of prayer from earth called for an answer from heaven. The Pope saw in this apocalyptic vision the great power that prayer in the goodness of God worked "upon the course of events and history." In this way, again, he sought to awaken the people to a sense of great expectation for the council.

The council and its outcome were, for him, neither automatic nor self-evident, as though the Church could control it by a routine ecclesiastical technique. The council depended on the great Hearer of prayer. The Book of Revelation portrays surprising and breathtaking results of prayer. And this corresponded with John's thoughts about the council. The drama of the Apocalypse was not

[19] *Gaudet Mater Ecclesia.*

[20] From the Christmas message of 1962.

[21] From the speech "Prima Sessio" given at the conclusion of the first session of the council, December 8, 1962.

[22] *Paenitentiam agere (On Doing Penance for the Success of the Second Vatican Council).*

[23] *Sacrae Laudis (The Divine Office for the Council)*, January 6, 1962.

cited simply to show that great things were possible. The prayer that John was urging was not capricious or abritrary; it had a responsible context. Though it did not rule out surprise, it was clearly a prayer with a national purpose. Prayer had to be directed to the possibility of the *renewal* of the Catholic Church, not in self-glorification, but in the creative power of the Lord. The blazing forces and tremendous energy that break loose in the drama of the Apocalypse are seen by John as the possibility of a new possibility for the Church itself. In that connection he speaks of a "new era" that the Church has entered."[24]

Was Pope John's intense interest in the unity and reunion of the Church implicitly subverted by the Catholic *a priori* insistence that the Roman Church *is* the one Church? This question is made the more difficult in John's case by his desire that the council should occupy itself with the inner renewal of the Church with a view to making the Church itself credible. Pope John expressed himself emphatically on the unity of the Roman Catholic Church. The Redeemer, he insisted, has built His Church on the foundation of this unity, a unity lacking in any other association of Christian people. Catholic unity is visible to all, for it is marked by three attributes: unity of doctrine, unity of order, and unity of worship. He was, then, logical in saying that the task of the Church was to bring all the sheep of Christ into the one fold and "under the care of one Shepherd." "In this unity all men are called to the one Father's house that is built on the foundation of Peter."[25]

This is the Catholic *a priori* that raises questions as to whether the council can really open the door to new perspectives for the visible unity of the Church. Is the council a genuine attempt to open up new possibilities for ecumenicity, or is it meant as a summons to the departed to return to the only unity there is or can be, the unity that is not a thing to be sought, but only to be recognized as the unity of the Roman Church? Must not all Catholic attempts at renewal be dominated by the certainty that the one and only Church is the Catholic Church? And must they not all be shaped by the conviction that the Catholic doctrine is the unchangeable truth?

The Pope mentioned a few points in which there is room for discussion. There are some things that are not absolute. "There must be unity in the essentials, freedom in the doubtful, love in

24 *Ibid.*
25 *Ad Petri Cathedram.*

everything."[26] Of course, the question centers on what the "essentials" consist of. On the question of "unity in the essentials," many Protestants have doubted whether, in the present situation, any essentially new contribution to ecumenicity can be discovered. Most agree that the *personal* relationships between Rome and Protestantism have improved, but many doubt whether any "essential" changes can be expected or even, given the Catholic structure, be imagined. But in the face of Protestant skepticism Roman Catholics stubbornly insist that new and hopeful perspectives of ecumenicity have been opened. Whether in fact such perspectives are to be seen in the Second Vatican Council is a question of uppermost importance.

We could provide a great many citations from what we may call the "new theology" in the Catholic Church that witness unanimously to the new possibilities that exist for a truly ecumenical dialogue. These optimistic voices were heard long before a council was ever mentioned. Indeed, they had created tension within the Catholic Church because of the "ecumenicism" and "irenicism" they betrayed. They were strengthened and stimulated by the rise of John XXIII to the pontificate, and especially by the manner in which he, with the unchangeability of the Church as his base, addressed himself to the "separated brethren." These ecumenical interests were two-pronged, directed toward the Eastern Church on the one hand and toward Western Protestantism on the other. We Westerners are, of course, likely to think primarily in terms of the Rome-Reformation break. But the rupture of the Church into the East and West since 1054 is of equal concern to Catholicism, as is clear from discussion in the council[27] and more lately from Pope Paul's activities in the Holy Land. The particular attention given to the Eastern Church is attributable not so much to the greater length of the separation as to the consciousness of the many things that the Roman and the Eastern churches have in common.

The problems that lie in the way of unity between these two communions seem quite different from the barriers dividing the Reformation churches and Rome. The Eastern Churches have put heavy stress on the unchangeable decrees of the seven ecumenical councils. They have, moreover, an acute sense of the historical

[26] *Ibid.*
[27] In the schema "de oecumenismo" ("on ecumenicity"), the "special considerations of the Eastern Church" were discussed first and only thereafter were "the communions separated since the 16th Century" discussed.

legitimacy of their existence within the true succession and dogma.[28] These two matters, historical legitimacy and unchangeability of dogma, play a specially prominent role in the relationships between Eastern and Western Catholicism. The Roman Church has kept alive a strong hope of healing the separation, and has often expressed the conviction that the common inheritance of the faith and the power of a common piety will be the curative force. The schema on ecumenicity[29] says that the differences in theological formulations between East and West are complementary rather than contradictory. It wistfully recalls the Council of Florence of 1439, where an abortive attempt was made to heal the schism. There is no question but that Rome sets longing eyes Eastward in spite of the differences between them on the ancient "filioque" controversy as well as on Mariology. Rome's optimism about reunion with the East, however, is always under the shadow of one towering problem, the Primacy of the Pope, a matter that touches not only the dogma, but the entire spirituality of the two churches.

Pope John XXIII laid great stress on the Bishop of Rome as the heart of the visible unity of the Church in his encyclical about Leo the Great, which he issued in 1961 under the title *Aeterna Dei.* He discusses the famous 28th canon of the Chalcedon decrees, which refers to Constantinople as a competition to Rome, and he praises Leo for having resisted Constantinople's attack on the one apostolic seat. John's encyclical aroused a strong negative reaction in the Eastern Church and underscored again the fact that the Papacy was the roadblock on the way to reunion.[30]

[28] "No less than the Roman Catholic Church does the Eastern Church stand on the thesis of the unchangeability of the traditional inheritance of the faith" (A. Bea, *Stimmen der Zeit,* 1961-1962, p. 427). This conviction comes through clearly in the discussion by Florowski of the World Council assembly in New Delhi. For more background on the unchangeability of dogma in the Eastern Church, see E. Schlink, "Wandlungen im protestantischen Verständnis der Ostkirche," *Der kommende Christus und die kirchlichen Traditionen,* 1961, pp. 225ff.

[29] A *schema* is a draft report prepared in advance by appointed commissions and submitted to the council as the basis of its discussion on specific issues. The term "schema" is part of the Roman Catholic ecclesiastical jargon, and though in similar contexts it is not ordinarily used by Protestants, the word will be used regularly in this book. If one thinks of a report drafted by a study commission and submitted to a church assembly for adoption, he will have a sufficiently clear notion of what schema is in the Vatican Council. (Translator's note)

[30] Cf. N. Afanassief, N. Koulomzine, J. Meyendorff, and A. Schemann, *La Primauté de Pierre dans l' Eglise orthodoxe,* 1960.

The break within the Western Church is for Rome a far more complicated case. This split was widened by long and bitter controversy, with the *"damnamus"* of the Reformation writings facing the *"anathema sit"* of Trent. The issues have been defined sharply by later doctrinal developments. Roman spokesmen speak far more of the great difficulties in the way of reunion with Protestant churches than they do of possibilities for it. Paul VI has been only the most recent to speak of the obstacles on the road to the restoration of unity. The question is whether the history of the Church since the Reformation has not brought such complete estrangement and created such complicated divergencies between Reformation churches and the Roman Church that reunion must realistically be ruled out as an impossibility. Or is it possible that new ways can be found, new ways of thinking about each other free from caricatures, and new ways of meeting each other in Christ as the Lord of the Church?

Precisely at this point we encounter a most remarkable point of contact between the council and the theological discussions of our day. The first day of the council brought this matter into play by way of some provocative things said by the Pope. He spoke about the doctrine of the Church and about its unchangeability. This is what he said. "The certain and unchangeable doctrine, to which we must remain ever faithful, must be examined and expounded by the methods applicable in our times. We must *distinguish* between the inheritance of the faith itself, or the truths which are contained in our holy doctrine, and the way in which these truths are formulated, of course with the same sense and the same significance."[31] These sentences in themselves contain little that is sur-

---

[31] In *Gaudet Mater Ecclesia*. The Latin text reads: *oportet ut haec doctrina certa et immutabilis, cui fidele obsequium est praestandum, ea ratione pervestigatur et exponatur, quam tempora postulant nostra. Est enim aliud ipsum depositum Fidei, seu veritates, quae veneranda doctrina nostra continentur, aliud modus, quo eaedem enuntiantur, eodem tamen sensu eademque sententia.* Keen attention has been focused on these words of John XXIII. Some expressed surprise that so much attention was given them, as for example when *la Croix* published this single sentence on three different occasions. An interesting problem of translation has arisen in connection with the sentence. Someone spoke of a "tendentious and romantic translation." But, in regard to the words under discussion, the Pope quoted his own words on December 23, 1962, as they appeared in a previously criticized text. He accepted this translation as his own and thus removed it from debate. There were indeed problems of translation on this as well as other points. And the discussions about the translation only illustrate how seriously the words of John were taken. In respect to all this, see A. Wenger, *Vatican II, Première Session*, 1963, pp. 46-50.

prising. The unchangeability of doctrine still stands in the foreground. Moreover, the Pope went on to say that the truth of the Lord remains eternally the same in the face of all fluctuations in the thoughts of men and of all the heresies that disappear even as they arise, as new fallen snow melts under the rising sun. But the distinction that the Pope made between the *substance* and the *formulations* of the truth sparked immediate interest. The interest was only heightened by the Pope's call for the use of the distinction to meet the demands of our times. Clearly the unchangeability of truth — and of doctrine — is not in question.[32] But the question asked around council halls was what bearing the Pope's distinction would have for the general orientation of the council now that the Pope had made it part of the council's vocabulary.

It would be reckless to pull far-reaching conclusions out of Pope John's statement and to brand it with the mark of strong progressive theological outlook. His words suggest that they had been well considered, and they are marked by obvious caution.[33] Still, there is a clear association between this papal distinction and similar distinctions that Roman theologians of the new stripe have been making in the recent past. John may well have been intending simply to stress the pastoral aspect of doctrine. But this does not remove the existential element in his stress on the challenge of "our times." The papal caution did not keep many from seeing his words as of genuine ecumenical significance. After all, his distinction between the truth and its formulation seemed to open the door to new interpretations of church dogma. The possibility of a dialogue about the deepest motives that lie within and are distinguishable from the Church's formulations of doctrine seemed to be suggested. And the thought was perhaps implied that

[32] Cardinal Bea is very positive on this point. "What the Church has once for all declared as a matter of faith was declared under the guidance of the Holy Spirit as a divinely revealed truth, over which the Church can no longer in any way dispose" (A. Bea, *Stimmen der Zeit,* 1961-1962, p. 246). Cf. his attacks on false irenicism, compromise, and trimming of the truth.

[33] Cf. Th. Sartory, *Die Konfessionen und das II. Vatik. Konsil,* 1963, pp. 9ff. Sartory writes that John XXIII cannot be counted among the progressives. He says that French theologians, on the basis of his French *nuntiatur,* call him an *integralist.* He also points to elements in John's pontificate that seem to substantiate this impression, for instance, the encyclical on Leo the Great, the encyclical *Veterum Sapientia* — on Latin as the language of the church — and his relations with the Lateran University which has been antagonistic to the Biblical Institute. Cf. the fascinating article by Karl Rahner, "Ueber das Latein als Kirchensprache," *Schriften zur Theologie,* 1962, pp. 411-467, which, however, was not intended as a commentary on *Veterum Sapientia.*

the *formulation* of the truth could have, for various reasons, actually occasioned *misunderstandings* of the truth itself.

That John should have brought the distinction between truth and its formulation into the discussion at the very start of the council is the more striking because in doing so he seemed to be taking sides on a problem that has been involved in various doctrinal situations in times past. Pius XII, for example, took a very definite position against those who expressed a desire to disentangle dogma from elements that lie outside of revelation itself in order to "free dogma from certain formulations which the Church had long accepted." Pius, who discussed this matter in his encyclical *Humani Generis,* saw a close connection between these notions and what he termed "so-called ecumenicity." Along this way, he insisted, the Church would be led to an "assimilation of the opinions of dissenters into Catholic dogma." Pius XII could see in this tendency to criticize the terminology in which Church doctrine had long been formulated only a dangerous irenicism and a relativizing of dogma. The distinction that John XXIII made at the council alongside of *Humani Generis* makes a most interesting comparison. We are not eager to discover a difference between Pius XII and John XXIII, but only to underscore the vexing nature of the problem that has been placed on the agenda by John. The complexity of the problem appears from the fact that it persists in spite of the warnings of Pius XII as well as of Pius X in his encyclical *Pascendi Dominici Gregis* of 1907.[34] John's words are important precisely because they were spoken in full awareness that he entered the danger zone of Roman Catholic problematics. Nothing critical of the Church's formula is discernible in John's words; they were spoken in the context of a reaffirmation of the unchangeable character of Catholic truth. Still, he managed to make plain the legitimacy of the problem. Cardinal Bea had previously expressed the nature of the problem by saying that we must not lose sight of the fact "that many of our theological formulations, which do indeed express timeless and definite truths, must nevertheless be understood and appraised with reference to the ideological background of the times in which they developed."[35] Bea insists that we recognize the full importance of "this depend-

---

[34] This encyclical was directed against modernism and discusses the formulations of dogma in connection with modernism's charge that the Church "does not know how to distinguish the external formulations of truth from their religious and moral value."

[35] Cardinal Bea, *The Unity of Christians,* 1963, p. 97.

ence of dogmatic formulations on the historical situation and upon the intellectual climate of the times."[36] Hence, when we make a judgment on the dogmatic formulations we must make distinctions in any case and always reckon with the *historical conditionedness* of doctrinal definitions.

Protestants as well as Catholics immediately became interested in the words of John XXIII, regardless of how cautiously they were couched, for they affected the ecumenical possibilities of the council itself.[37] While Pius XII warned against putting distinctions between truth and formulations of the truth in the service of ecumenicity, Pope John set the distinction on the agenda with an eye to the needs of his own day. And it was bound to be caught up in the ecumenical dialogue at once, especially since it could now be used to remove misunderstandings about doctrines of the Church. Furthermore, Roman Catholics have been saying that the divisions of the Church cannot simply be laid at the doorstep of bad will, but that they are also clouded by polemics of a past era, which obscure for us the deeper intentions of the Church. All this explains why, since the opening day of the council, John's words about a distinction between truth and formulations of truth have been brought up whenever the real goals — explicit and implicit — of the council have been talked about. Whenever they were mentioned it was with the hope that perhaps now a new approach could be made to this age-old controversy.

The words of John XXIII and Cardinal Bea do not, of course, give us justification for supposing that a confessional watering-down or relativizing of dogma is taking place in Rome. There is no hint here that irenical and ecumenically minded men of our day are using the distinction between truth and its formulation to argue that there is no essential controversy between Rome and other churches. What is happening is that these men are intent on analyzing the possibilities that misunderstandings have occurred and whether, if the misunderstandings are removed, together we can discover where the *real* controversy lies. The placing of the

[36] *Ibid.*, p. 98. Bea speaks of explaining the formulations in terms of "circumstances and relationships within the history of thought" and sees a connection here with "a remarkable revival of a sense of history and the social structure of both thought and life" (*Stimmen der Zeit*, 1961-1962, pp. 248ff.).

[37] E. Schlink, for example, at a reception given by the Secretariat for Unity, called the statements of the Pope and Cardinal Bea of significance for the ecumenical dialogue. Cf. also E. Schlink, "Themen des zweiten Vatik. Konzils in evangelischer Sicht," in *Kerugma und Dogma*, 1963, p. 172. Cf. R. Kaiser, *Inside the Council*, 1963, p. 98; X. Rynne, *Letters from Vatican City*, 1963, p. 78.

distinction on the order of the day is no sign of a historicizing of truth, but it is the sign that the existence of a very real problem is being conceded. Clearly in John's mind such a concession can go hand in hand with an unmovable conviction that Rome is the one Catholic Church.

❋   ❋   ❋   ❋   ❋

The Second Vatican Council has been attended with certain tensions from its inception. These tensions are closely related to the problem that we have been discussing, and are often related to the presence of "conservative" and "progressive" elements within the Church. Both of these elements wondered aloud what the real significance of the council would be and how extensive would be the renewal of the Church. Did the renewal of the Church mean a renewal in the sense of a progressive sanctification of the Church, a renewal, then, concerning which there could be no difference of opinion between the conservatives and progressives? Or did the renewal to which the Church was then being called point to some different and deeper problem? This is the central question that dominated the council increasingly as it went on and that put its stamp on very wide-ranging discussions. Meanwhile, John XXIII followed the course of the council daily from his vantage point in the Vatican.

Pope John did not live to see the conclusion of the council. He discovered a great deal in the early period that strengthened him in his optimistic expectations for the council. He spoke of seeing his expectations surpassed in a way that reminded him of the first Pentecost and of the dayspring of the deeply desired day of the fulfillment of Jesus' prayer in John 17.[38] In the midst of preparations for the second session John XXIII died. In contrast to the voices that proclaimed his death a tragedy stands his own testimony that every day is a good day to be born and every day is a good day to die. As much as the council was in a sense *his* council, it was also a council of the Church, a fact that for him meant that the council could not be bound to his person. He would surely have smiled at Protestant Peter Vogelsander's statement that John's death must be seen as "conspiracy rising from the pit of darkness."[39] In any case, what had taken place in the first

38 In the letter *Mirabilis ille*, January 6, 1963.

39 Cf. *Johannes XXIII, Leben und Werke*, 1963, p. 117. A quotation from John's diary of 1963 is interesting in this connection. "Shall it be given me to see the end of the council? Then God be praised! Shall it not be given? Then in that case I shall experience the blessed conclusion of the council from heaven, to which the divine mercy shall have called me."

session was part of history and, in spite of John's removal from the scene, could not be undone. The plans for the second session were made in the shadow of strong memories of what was to have been only an "interim papacy." That the first session should pass without leaving a mark on the history of the Church is unthinkable. Too much was said, too many things were openly discussed, too much was explicitly criticized for that session to lapse as an unimportant and strange "incident" in the life of the Church.

* * * * *

John's council has become the council of Pope Paul VI. In his opening message, Paul associated himself immediately with his predecessor and repeated that the council had to be concerned, not with this or that article of the basic teachings of the Church, but first and foremost with the challenge of how the message of the Church could be proclaimed in a way that was understandable to our times. He spoke along the same lines as John did about Church authority being not simply a power to judge heresy, but the life-bringing power of the gospel of Christ. The change of popes in the midst of the council brought with it, understandably, a great many comparisons of the two men. There was a realistic awareness that nothing human is foreign even to Vicars of Christ and that their personality and character affect the way they fill the papal chair. The feelings of Paul VI were analyzed in statements he had made prior to being chosen Pope in an effort to diagnose his ideals for the council. The haunting question was whether he belonged to the more progressive or the more conservative wing as each had become apparent in the council.

Such a question as this need not detain us in this study, partly because speculations and guesses about it could only hurt the effort to make a responsible analysis of the council. We need only concern ourselves with the data that is available to us.[40] There is the first time that Cardinal Montini intervened in the council session of December 5, 1962. Here it was clear how deeply Paul shared in the ideals of John XXIII and how he wished these ideas to come to expression in the process of the discussions.[41] More important still are the ways in which Paul made his attitude clear after becoming Pope, particularly his opening speech at the reconvening of the council. It was clear from this speech that

---

[40] For the life and work of Paul VI, see Paul Lesourd, *Qui est le pape Paul VI?*, 1963.

[41] Cf. X. Rynne, *Letters from Vatican City*, 1963, pp. 227f.

John's thoughts about the renewal of the Church were also Paul's thoughts. He set this subject emphatically on the agenda as one of the primary purposes of the council for, as he said, the Church could show its true self to the world only through self-renewal. Christ wills the Church to manifest its beauty to the world. More than ever, the Church must make itself known to the world as it really is. At this point, the problem of ecumenicity arises. Paul VI addressed himself to this problem extensively, speaking of the council working toward "complete and universal ecumenicity." He was speaking here in the spirit of his predecessor. But where John had still talked of the return of the separated brothers, Paul spoke of "the sheep which are truly and wholly of Christ's fold and whom Christ calls, counts, and keeps with the sheepfold, holding the door open for the many sheep of Christ who do not yet belong to the one fold, and calling them with loud voice and waiting eagerly for them to come in."[42] Paul VI, it is clear, is not possessed by a romantic ecumenicity that waters down the Roman Church's conviction of itself as the only true fold of Christ. He has shown himself to be a realistic Pope in this regard. There is optimism, to be sure.[43] But he admits difficulties on the way to unity; he talks about ecumenicity as a problem that is not ready for solution. Thus, he says, we shall have to be patient while we wait for the great moment of complete reconciliation. His realism came out clearly in an audience that he gave to non-Catholic observers to the council on October 18, 1963. Here he talked on the "great dialogue" whose end no one is able to foresee in view of the many unsolved problems. We do not expect, he said, any miraculous and immediate solutions; we shall have to wait for the fruit to ripen in its own time, seizing on every sign that augurs the breaking of a new day in the coming together of those who are nourished by the same gospel.[44]

*   *   *   *   *

Without going into the more profound implications of the word

[42] *Salvete.* An English translation is found in *The Pope Speaks,* Vol. II, No. 2, 1964.

[43] *Ibid.:* "Today the hope, tomorrow the reality."

[44] Reported in *L'Osservatore Romano* of October 19, 1963. In a message to the Pope, Prof. E. Skijdsgaard expressed his satisfaction that the sober and realistic words of Paul VI at the reconvening of the council demonstrated that he was not captive of a naively optimistic and superficial ecumenicity (*L'Osservatore Romano, ibid.*).

"ecumenical"[45] in *this* context, we may note that the ecumenical *problem* of the council focuses on the Roman Catholic certainty that it is the one and only *Ecclesia Christi,* the exclusive Church of Christ. This is not a personal pretension. It is not a conviction that arose with John XXIII or Paul VI. It is a *religious* conviction implicit in the faith of the Roman Catholic. For this reason, the question that besets us is whether we can really expect a genuine ecumenical encounter and an open dialogue from Rome. Many Protestants have responded to the calling of the council by saying that while there can be a personal ecumenicity of love toward the separated brethren and prayers for the miracle of reunion, the Roman *a priori* allows for no genuine ecumenical dialogue. This opinion is bolstered by the way that Roman leaders like to talk of separated "brethren" but never of separated "churches." Hence, while the personal good will and openheartedness of Catholic leaders is accepted with gratitude, many fail to observe any principal difference between the present situation and the age-old posture of Rome in regard to the other churches.

We have hold of one of the most profound problems hovering over this ecumenical council. Everyone must agree that the personal relationships between Roman and Protestant men have undergone a radical change, a change whose potential should not be underestimated. The estrangement between the churches has often occured on a personal level; theological differences have often been made the more extreme and vexing because personal alienation has stimulated caricatured portraits of each side and this in turn has made understanding of each other terribly hard to achieve. Sometimes the élan of Protestant anti-Catholicism still seems to derive from caricature. But this kind of anti-Catholicism bypasses the real controversy and in the end is doomed to fruitlessness. Anti-Catholicism is a slippery phenomenon, hardly susceptible of definition, but it does have this characteristic, that it is unreceptive to any corrections in the caricature that it fights because it fears that correcting the caricature will mean a weakening of its own negative position. Anti-Catholicism, with all its apparent emotional force, is powerless to make a contribution to the controversy between Rome and the Reformation. We need not

[45] Cf. H. v. d. Linde, *Wat is Oecumenisch?;* A. F. N. Lekkerkerker, *Enige Overwegingen bij de Voorlopige Aankondiging Wan een Oecumenisch Concilie,* 1959; S. Lindbeck, "Evangelische Katholizität," *Kerugma und Dogma,* 1960, pp. 209f.; finally, a book important for many ecumenical questions, E. Schlink, *Der kommende Christus und die kirchlichen Traditionen,* 1961.

guess as to the psychological background to anti-Catholicism with its caricatures, but we can say that it offers a weak response to the challenge since it refuses to understand the opponent by means of an objective analysis. Anti-Catholicism usually concentrates on certain practices of the Roman Church, without keeping in mind other practices of other churches, and tries to get at the essence of the Church through observation of these practices. Anti-Catholics therefore are *a priori* skeptical of any talk of attempts at renewal of the Catholic Church.

The emotional anti-Catholic feels uncomfortable in a new situation in which by means of new confrontations and new investigations into exegesis and dogmatics the controversy is stripped of its simplistic forms. Many Protestants suspect that by taking these confrontations seriously, we may water down the differences and lose some of the old convictions of the struggle. These people forget that the Reformers expressed their convictions in earnest religious discussions by means of which they sought to set the controversy clearly within the actual situation. Responsible encounter is not a sign of weakness; it is rather a recognition of the seriousness of the division of the Church. Aware of the seriousness of the situation, we can follow the progress of the council with intense interest and take full account of all efforts at renewal going on in the Roman Church. To count all this as worthless because of the unchangeability of Catholicism would be irresponsible.

We must also note that Roman Catholics are busying themselves today with borderlines of Catholicism that do not coincide with those surrounding *all* who would follow and serve Jesus Christ in love and faith. The problem has been growing in a dynamic historical process for a long time, and came up anew on the conciliar level by the presence at the council of non-Catholic observers and by way of the conversations that took place between them and Catholic representatives.[46] There is a remarkable difference on this point between the first and second Vatican Councils. We are not thinking only of the famous Stroszmayer incident,[47] which occasioned a judgment by the Reformers, but of the invitation given to Protestants to attend the council of 1870. Formally, one could find similarities between this invitation with its crass pretensions and the terminology used by John XXIII and Paul VI

---

[46] Specifically, in the weekly discussions between the Secretariat for Unity and the Protestant observers, whose judgment was requested on the schemata for the council as they appeared.

[47] See Chapter II.

about the one Catholic Church and the one sheepfold of Christ. But a second look reveals that the situation has changed a great deal. The invitation to non-Catholics to attend the First Vatican Council carried no hint of a genuine ecumenical concern. It was actually not an invitation at all, but rather a proclamation that the Roman Church is the one, holy, Catholic and apostolic Church, built on Peter and clothed with all power, the Church that has faithfully preserved the inheritance of the faith and remains and shall remain unmoved and unchanged until the end of the age. The proclamation acknowledged that many "religious societies" existed outside of the Catholic Church, but that these by themselves or together in no sense are the Church that Christ has founded and in no sense form a part of the Church. These "societies" lack the living authority in matters that touch on eternal salvation, and therefore they will never transcend their flux and instability. In view of this, these "societies" were called to seize the opportunity that the council afforded them to forsake their status, in which they can never be sure of their own salvation.[48]

Here we observe a way of thinking that reasons simply from the "fact" of the Catholic Church and concludes that the only way to solve the problem of separation is for Protestants to come back into Rome and accept the unproblematic unity of the Church existing there. The element of Catholic renewal as a "Call into Unity," which is prominent today, played no observable role in 1870. The *a priori* conviction that the Catholic Church is the only true Church has not changed. But we must observe a change in spiritual attitude that transcends merely personal congeniality in ecumenical form. Only by making a serious effort to understand this change within the total context of the council with all its *a priori* convictions and its inner tensions can we gauge its real significance.

✿　✿　✿　✿　✿

We would be going at things badly if we tried to suggest that the tensions within the Catholic Church today are the real business of the council. To do this would smack of a simplistic anti-Catholic effort to demonstrate that the unity of Catholicism is basically only a matter of appearance. But there are inner tensions that are of great import for the final achievement of the council. These tensions exercise influence on the various Catholic visions of

---

[48] *Ab eo statu se eripere studeant, in quo de sua propria salute securi esse non possunt* ("They are seriously called to release themselves from this state, in which they are not able to find certainty of their salvation.") (Denzinger-Schönmetzer, 2999).

ecumenicity. This appears from the way in which the very word
ecumenical is interpreted. Some Catholics use the word to express
their optimism in the present situation for church unity. Others
who use the word feel strongly that clear and consistent exposition
of the Church's teachings is the most fruitful way to approach the
"separated brothers." For they must be made to understand most
clearly that they are estranged and divorced from the Catholic
Church.[49] Both views were evident at the council. But the call to
self-examination and penitence, and the need for a new "credibility" for the Church found a sympathetic hearing among the
council fathers, who were concretely confronted with the problems
when the schemata "On the Unity of the Church" and "On Ecumenicity" were placed before the council.

Nothing is more difficult to define than ecumenical dialogue.
To some council members even the term "dialogue" suggested a
threat of relativism. The trouble with fear of dialogue is that its
alternative is *monologue*. And monologists are usually people who
are afraid to let the gospel lead them into a genuine encounter
with others. Hence, the Second Vatican Council, not willing to
accept monologue as its habit, was faced with the challenge of
determining what the purpose of a dialogue could be. Protestants
as well as Catholics have an interest in this question. For after
the Vatican Council is over the non-Catholic churches must still
answer their own questions as to the way in which the Church
would walk as well as answering the Roman Catholic claim that
the New Testament knows of no plurality of churches. If only for
this reason, it is clear that Protestants cannot view the council as
an event having no implications for their own position, as an
event they can view from a distance in mere curiosity. Much
rather, the Vatican Council carries a challenge to the Protestant
churches to examine their own faithfulness or lack of it to the
gospel to which they have given witness since the Reformation in
a most varied and many-colored form. When today's Roman Catholic Church is called by its theology as well as by John XXIII
and Paul VI to question its own credibility — to attest its own
genuineness by means of true renewal — the fact that there is also
a problem of the credibility of the Reformation should not escape
the Protestant world. The Roman Catholic Church today puts before both the Reformed and Eastern churches some of the most
pressing questions of their existence. As the council becomes

[49] This attitude plays a part in various publications of the so-called "maximalists" in regard to Mariology. See Chapter VIII.

history, the way in which the Church of Christ must walk in faith and life, in new tasks and new responsibility, is going to become clearer. And then the question will be whether the Church has understood and now understands the prayer that Christ offered for the unity of the Church in the Father and Son, "*so that* the world will believe, that thou hast sent me" (John 17:21). The time will bring the Church to a clearer decision as to how it will live in view of what John XXIII called a prediction that "there shall be one flock and one Shepherd" (John 10:16).

The Changed Climate

2 THE SECOND VATICAN COUNCIL WAS CALLED AND HAS worked in a new climate of life and thought in the Catholic Church. It cannot be understood unless this is kept in mind and unless a real effort is made to probe this change. Everyone agrees that the climate has changed; few agree on a phrase that could capture the character of the change. The phrase that most interests us is "open Catholicism"; this phrase is meant to indicate that Catholicism is no longer pre-occupied with itself, that it has thrown open the windows of its concern to the whole world and all the problems and dangers that vex it. One Catholic publication uses the phrase "new breadth" to pin-point the change. Pulled out of isolation after a long period of self-defense, the Church has become conscious that the antitheses that had meaning in the past no longer fit our times. Facing the problems of the world and the churches more realistically, it senses that the Church must be possessed by a new humility and sense of calling, by an honest awareness that God loves the *world* and calls the Church to serve the world. Hans Urs von Balthasar recalls the disciples of Jesus closing doors in fear of the Jews, while Jesus Himself walked through the closed doors of the Church (John 20:26). The doors that swung open to Peter

(Acts 12:7) and the doors that changed things in the churches
of Philippi (Acts 16:26) suggest parables to von Balthasar for the
opening of the Church's doors to the world.[1] They are parables of
the newly opened Catholicism, opened not to compromise the rich-
ness of the Church, not to watering down the mystery of the
Church, but to the possibility that the full treasure of the Church
may become fruitful for all others in a world-wide vision. Simply
put, it is the perspective of Pentecost come alive again — "to the
ends of the earth" (Acts 1:8).

The way, it is understood, is full of hazards, including the danger of sacrificing depth for the sake of breadth. But it is also understood that this way, including its hazards, is the only way for the
Church of Jesus Christ to travel.[2] The change of climate is mirrored in many statements of Pope John XXIII, including that in
which he spoke about the bride of Christ who has come to prefer
the healing hands of mercy above the condemning finger of judgment. The Pope was not holding a brief for vague tolerance or for
relativizing the certainties of the Church and its faith. He was
pleading for a shift of accent within the certainty of faith, for a
new consideration of the question of what the doctrine, the witness of the Church, must signify for those standing outside the
Church.

The change of climate, then, has to do with the Catholic attitude towards those others, towards the missionary character of
the Church, as over against a self-assured apologetic, with a biblically defined offense instead of a rigid self-defense. The "others"
are no longer merely or in the first place viewed as a threat to the
Church, but as objects of a dutiful concern. This view is strengthened in a time of decline for the Church. And the secularization
and estrangement of our time is no longer attributed simply to
pride and enmity, but is seen in connection with the failure of the
Church in the past and present. For this reason, "the others,"
those outside the Church, have come to be seen in a new light;
they are no longer people whose unbelieving reactions and errors
are looked down upon with surprise and offense. Now they are
seen as those in whose lives are agitating questions that live in the
hearts of believers also, even though the believers find an ultimate
answer in the Lord.

The phenomenon of open Catholicism has sounded as a clear
rap at the door of the Church, has become a persistent probing of

[1] H. Urs von Balthasar, *Kerk en Ruimte*, 1961, pp. 13-19.
[2] Cf. K. Rahner, *Die Chancen des Christentums heute*, 1952.

the truth and assurance, and a reminder of the servanthood and the calling of the Church. No one should think of it as a kind of incipient revolt within the Church by those who have become mildly estranged from it. It is a collision with introverted traditional forms, with woodenness and closed-heartedness, with judgments made *about* others that were made too fast to be true and too quick to act as genuine appeals *to* others. It is a protest against the Pharisaism that haughtily condemns the crowds and, in the appearance of holiness, pretends to serve God, but does so in a way catastrophic for others (John 16:2). Thus, there are those who want to lead Catholicism into new experiences and new encounters. They are not interested in exchanging certainty for doubt, but in discovering a new kind of certainty that is not colored by so much self-assurance.[3] This call to a renewed insight and a changed attitude could work explosively because it makes its appeal to the essence of the gospel of grace and its inherent challenge. It appeals to the center of the gospel where one discovers that the Church allows no one to boast save in the Lord.

A spirit of anti-triumphalism is abroad, not only among laymen, but also among many of notable offices.[4] A search is on for a harmonious marriage between being the Church (this particular Church) and the warning that is given to the Church to be girded with humility, since "God withstands the proud, but gives grace to the humble" (I Peter 5:5). This word — from Peter, by the way — calls to mind the Shepherd of the Church girded with the servant's towel, washing the disciples' feet and insisting that this was an example for them to follow (John 13:14).

An open Catholicism has many implications. Whenever anyone stops closing himself from others in a judgmental rejection of them, he opens himself to self-correction and also to a correction of the caricatures he has made of others. This has happened in the case of the Roman Catholic image of the Reformation. What is being

---

[3] Cf. Henri Fequet, *Le Catholicisme Religion de Demain?*, 1962. This is a robust protest against the caricatures made of doctrine, particularly the doctrine of assurance. Though boasting and pride have always been condemned (I Corinthians 1:29; II Corinthians 10:17) the life and speech of the Church can transgress the distinction between boasting in the Lord and all other boasting with the result that the boasting in the Lord has a false ring about it, in spite of a protest that the Church is only boasting in the Pauline sense (cf. II Corinthians 10:8). Regarding the radical clarity with which the Bible speaks about boasting, see Kittel, *Theologisches Wörterbuch zum Neuen Testament*, III, pp. 648ff.

[4] Cf. Chapter VII for an extensive discussion of anti-triumphalism.

said about the Reformation today would have been unheard of in other times. At this point, it is interesting to recall a famous incident that occured at the First Vatican Council. In the session held on March 22, 1870, Stroszmayer protested against the notion that almost all modern errors, such as rationalism, pantheism or materialism, could be traced to the "revolution" of the Reformers. He insisted that this was not only historically inaccurate, but that it did injustice to many Protestants who truly loved the Lord and who erred in good faith. Stroszmayer's last words, drowned out in the council's negative outburst, were: "I protest . . . ."[5] The council was brutally insensitive to the lonely voice of Stroszmayer. For the council was still prisoner of a view of the Reformation that could see only a causal connection between the "revolt" of the sixteenth century and the then current threats to the Church. Its fears kept it from an honest apprasial of the motivations which brought on the Reformation, just as it could not recognize the actual situation in the Roman Catholic Church of the sixteenth century which occasioned the Reformation protest.

The council's position had its reflection in our century in the Borromeüs encyclical of 1910, in which the Reformers were judged as "proud and tumultuous men, enemies of the cross of Christ who were in love with earthly things." The Reformers, the encyclical went on, had no wish to better the moral life of people, but only to overthrow the teachings of the faith. "They created only chaos, blazed a trail of lawlessness for themselves and others, throwing off the authority and the guidance of the church." Such a judgment as this was part of a tradition that was hard to break through, a tradition according to which the intentions as well as the doctrine of the Reformers were prejudged. Within this tradition, the Reformation could be seen only as a great revolution in which no ray of good could be seen, a judgment that was reflected in Leo XIII's branding of the sixteenth-century Reformation as "Luther's rebellion."

Since then, a gradual change has taken place. The origin of this tradition was recognized and with it the tradition itself fell under a cloud. It was seen that the traditional view of the Reformation simply took over a critique made by Cochlaeus in 1549. Cochlaeus at that time had delivered an erroneous and destructive judgment of Luther, a judgment which Adolf Herte has described as a

---

[5] Cf. C. Butler, *Das 1. Vatik. Konzil,* 1961, pp. 149ff.

poisonous injection into the confessional life.[6] Herte explains that at that time men had closed their eyes to the deepest motives of the Reformation and could therefore brand it as rebellion in the most negative and antithetical sense. Recalling this traditional view of the Reformation, one can better appreciate the change that has taken place in the climate. A radical change has occured in the way that Catholics judge the Reformation.[7] Now, more than ever, the strong religious motives of the Reformation are acknowledged. This does not mean, of course, that Catholics are about to admit the legitimacy of the break from Rome, but they do emphasize that the religiously defined Reformation can be understood only against the background of the great guilt of the Roman Catholic Church.

In the sixteenth century, the Dutch Pope Adrian VI (1522-1523) recognized the fault of the Roman Church, but insisted that it belonged not so much to the people as to the rulers of the Church. Along with this, voices gradually have come to speak of the Reformation less as a revolutionary movement than as a crusading movement to bring the Church back under the gospel. Without trying to pin-point the birth of the changing atmosphere in our day, we can point to a few things that herald the change. One of these is Yves Congar's book *Divided Christendom*.[8] In this book Congar calls attention to genuinely religious motives in Luther which have been severely misunderstood for a long time. Karl Adam speaks in Congar's spirit about the admirable gifts possessed by Luther's heart and spirit, about Luther's genial perception of what is truly essential in the Christian faith, his radical rejection of all that was unholy. Adam goes on to say that had Luther dedicated these great gifts to the keeping of God's garden,

---

[6] Cochlaeus, *Commentarius de actis et scriptis Martini Lutheri*, 1549. Herte tells us that Cochlaeus' work went through 150 printings and, in his judgment, had a negative influence "without parallel" in Germany, France, Italy, Belgium, and Holland (A. Herte, *Das Katholisches Lutherbild im Banne der Luther-kommentare von Cochlaeus*, 1963, Vol. III).

[7] This does not mean that caricatures are now out of the picture. The difference is that Catholics are now warning against them lest the "great purification" of the atmosphere be jeopardized. In this connection, see E. Iserloh's sharp criticism of R. Weyenborg's study of Luther in the *Antonianum*. Cf. E. Iserloh, "Lutherkritik oder Lutherpolemik?" in *Festgabe J. Lortz*, Vol. I, pp. 15ff. (1958), particularly his remarks about the use of "falsely indicated sources."

[8] Y. Congar, *Chrétiens désunies. Principes d'un Oecuménisme catholique*, 1937. Along with Congar, J. Lortz must be noted. Cf. his *Die Reformation in Deutschland*, 1939. Cf. also his *Die Reformation als religiöses Anliegen heute*, 1948.

he would have come to stand equal in line with Thomas Aquinas and Francis of Assisi.[9] Adam recognizes Luther's protest and, to a point, honors the religious quality of the man. However uncalled for the break from Catholicism was, the issue of its legitimacy was complicated by the guilt of the Catholic Church and by the religious motives of the Reformers. The black and white interpretations of the Reformation have been rejected. There is a great deal of historical research into the actual writings of the Reformation giving added objective basis to the changed attitude about the origins of the Reformation movement.[10] This has brought about a more open mindedness toward the Reformation which in turn has created a far better possibility for dialogue than has been known since the sixteenth century.

All this is reflected in a semantic shift. For instance, we hear these days about misunderstandings that must be removed and, instead of rebellion and revolution, we hear about the drama and tragedy of the Reformation. What is called the "joyless tradition" of the Counter-Reformation is said to have been broken for the first time in our own day now that students are really serious about reading the writings of the Reformers. The protective dam that Ignatius of Loyola tried to erect against the storm of the Reformation without having read "a single writing of the German Reformers," and having neither insight into the situation of the Reformers nor a desire to "get inside the problems" surrounding the movement, has been abandoned.[11] The past, of course, was not completely void of understanding of the Reformation. There were exceptions. Contarini is contrasted to Ignatius Loyola because of his

[9] Y. Congar, *op. cit.*

[10] This change is the more to be respected in view of the difficulties inherent in any analysis of Luther's theology. Consider the various themes that have to be part of a Luther study: law and gospel, the two kingdom idea, the *deus absconditus*, and many others — themes that have led to divergent interpretations among Protestants. Very relevant here also is the study of the relationship between Luther and Occam, a lasting issue for Catholics. We need point here only to the significant historical study by H. A. Oberman, *The Harvest of Medieval Thought. Gabriel Biel and Late Medieval Nominalism*, 1963. The second volume of this work promises a study of the relationship between Luther and nominalism specifically, but even the first volume offers quite a different picture from that found in Roman Catholic literature as is indicated by the very word "harvest" rather than "autumn" in the title. He also sees a triangle: Medieval thought — Catholic Church — Protestantism, not allowing for a simple identification of Medieval and Catholic thought.

[11] H. Wolter, "Gestalt und Werk der Reformatoren im Urteil des hl. Ignatius von Loyola," *Festgabe J. Lortz*, pp. 53, 65.

respect for the religious motives of the Reformation. Contarini, at the confrontation at Regensburg in 1541, exclaimed: "Praise be to God. Yesterday, the Catholic and Protestant theologians came to agreement on the doctrine of Justification."[12] Alongside of Contarini, there was Seripando, whose doctrine of twofold righteousness "betrayed a far-reaching influence by Reformation thinking."

But these were exceptions, and the tradition that took root adopted another mind.[13] This tradition gradually became hardened, but at the same time became increasingly difficult to maintain as history went on. That it is falling apart under the growth in understanding of the complexities of the sixteenth century can only lead to better understanding of the real controversy. Roman Catholics are putting increasing emphasis on the new possibility of an existential encounter between Rome and the Reformation. Van de Pol, for example, while recognizing the Reformation as a temporary historical phenomenon, on the other hand rejects the traditional black-white picture and speaks of the *providential* task that the Reformation shall one day fulfill.[14]

Another indication of new terminology is the reference to "integration" in which a new possibility for the unity of the Church is recognized. What is meant by the word integration is hard to define with precision. But what is clear is that a recognition of a more inclusive vision of the truth is involved in it. Reformation Christians, it is said, live from a portion of revealed truth that can be useful as a corrective agent in the faith-outlook of Catholics. Catholics in turn have allowed some aspects of revealed reality to lapse into the background of their faith. Obviously, to speak of a simple "return" to the Mother Church does not fit well with this. Rather, we hear of a "growing together toward the fullness of Christ." If the Reformation arose as an honest effort to reclaim certain aspects of faith that had been lost to experience, the Catholic Church by making the Reformation protest superfluous can open the way to a new rapprochement. The gospel in its fullness can lead the way to integration, and this would involve the acceptance of the Reformation's

[12] *Ibid.* Cf. in regard to Contarini: *Pastor-Geschichte der Päpste*, V.; L. Ranke, *Die Römischer Papste in dem letzten vier Jahrhunderte*, pp. 104f.; J. Lortz, *Die Reformation in Deutschland*, 1940, II, 232.

[13] H. Rückert, *Die Rechtfertigungslehre auf dem Trident. Konzil*, 1925, pp. 227 ff. Rückert was accused of being infected with Luther's theology. Cf. Stakemeier, *Der Kampf im Augustin auf dem Tridentium*, 1937, and his *Glaube und Rechtfertigung*, 1937, p. 20; H. Jeden, *Girolamo Seripando. Sein Leben und Werken*, 1957; and G. C. Berkouwer, *Verdienste of Genade?*, 1958.

[14] W. H. van de Pol, *Het getuigenis van de Reformatie*, 1960, pp. 279 ff.

contribution to the unity of the Church and to the fullness of Catholic truth.[15]

More than a respect for the religious *intent* of the Reformation is involved here. For the intent was crystallized in concrete matters and accents that must be understood and accepted by Rome. Many writers among Roman Catholics witness strongly to the idea that there is a Catholic *sola fide-sola gratia*. In view of the fact that the *sola fide-sola gratia* (along with the *solo Christo* and *sola Scriptura*) have always been assumed to be exclusive Reformation properties precisely in opposition to Rome, these Catholic witnesses are the more noteworthy. The question arises, then, whether the phrase *sola fide* still can function as a critical and helpful distinction between Rome and the Reformation. That is, does a sharper analysis reveal that the old distinction between Rome with its "by faith *and* works" and the Reformation with its "by faith *alone*" fails to get at the real situation? Catholic theologians are insisting urgently that Catholic theology refuses to sacrifice *sola fide-sola gratia* to the Reformation, that Catholicism too seeks to preserve the truth of the complete gratuity of grace. Van de Pol wrote a paraphrase of Paul that illustrates this. "Without a single merit on the part of the believer, his sins are forgiven and the righteousness of Christ is given him in place of them — given him completely through grace. For if merit is brought in, then grace would no longer be grace." And he adds: "This is precisely the teaching of the Catholic Church."[16]

Meanwhile, Catholics are continually reminding us that Rome has rejected synergism. Kreling fully recognizes the value of Calvin's

[15] A. Fiolet, *Verdeelde Christenen in Gesprek*, 1960, p. 100, 143. According to Fiolet the Catholic Church does not demand an "unconditional return or a capitulation of one side to the other, but a growth toward and a reciprocal enrichment of each other." Cf. Fiolet, *Onvermoed Perspectief op de Oecumene. Poging tot Integratie van het Katholiek en Reformatorisch Relijden*, 1963. In the same vein, Karl Rahner writes that the Catholic Church shall not have brought to full and actual manifestation the Catholic truth unless "divided Christendom (and all the pagan world as well) finds its home in the Church as in the Father's house and there brings to full Christian realization what it can realize in full measure only on the basis of its ethnic, historical, cultural character." The present non-Catholic "Christendom" cannot, in Rahner's view, be likened without qualification to the heretics and schismatics of the age of the fathers and pre-Reformation tradition (K. Rahner, "Die Gliedschaft in der Kirche nach der Lehre der Enzyklika Pius XII, 'Mystici Corporis Christi,'" *Schriften zur Theologie*, II, p. 31).

[16] W. H. v. d. Pol, *Karakteristiek van het Reformatorisch Christendom*, 1952, p. 348.

intention in maintaining his doctrine of the sovereignty of grace against the self-righteousness of men.[17] Hans Küng is foremost among those pre-occupied with this matter at present. He concludes that there is no essential disagreement between Rome and the Reformation on the two cardinal points of *soli deo gloria* and *sola fide*. On this matter, "The time of antithesis is over." Catholics must frankly and without reservation agree with the Reformation on this point: the "complete incapacity on the part of man for any kind of self-justification."[18] Justification is not partly the work of God and partly the work of man, for "what have you that you have not received?" Küng attacks pharisaical doctrines of merit and morality by recalling the phrase that appeared prominently in Reformation writings — including the confessions: "unworthy servants" (Luke 17:10).

All of this is related to the Council of Trent and the interpretation of its decree concerning justification. Men like Küng are not without deep commitment to the Church's tradition. They are convinced that the Church itself, specifically at Trent, has never intended anything other than to confess the full gratuity of grace, a thesis which is said to be clear from Trent's attacks against all forms of moral pride. They recall Trent's decrees which definitively declare Roman doctrine against anything that would minimize the glory of God and the merits of Christ.[19] The changed perspective on the Reformation and its religious concern to uphold the glory of God and the completeness of grace goes hand in hand with a revised interpretation of the Catholic, Tridentine doctrine of justification.

In this regard, attention has also been centered on the question of the assurance of salvation and whether even at this point we can speak of a radical contradiction between Trent and the Reformers. Here too we are told that Trent did not in the least mean to deny the possibility of assurance as such, and that to understand what Trent said we must recall the position that the men of Trent

---

[17] G. Kreling, *Genade en Kerk*, 1953, p. 16.

[18] H. Küng, *Rechtfertigung*, 1957, p. 244.

[19] Cf. Denzinger, *The Sources of Catholic Dogma*, 1957, 843, Canon 33. "If anyone shall say that because of this Catholic doctrine of justification . . . there is some degree of detraction from the glory of God or from the merits of Jesus Christ our Lord, and that the truth of our faith, and in fact the glory of God and of Jesus Christ are not rather rendered illustrious: let him be anathema." Trent also explains that no Christian may find reason in himself to boast, and refers to I Corinthians 1:31 and II Corinthians 10:17 just as the Reformers did.

were combating.[20] The question is whether some clarification of the real controversy can come out of a recognition on one hand of the genuinely religious motives of the Reformation and the deepest intent of Trent. Specifically, the newer interpretation contends that Rome was not supporting a superficial motion of human merit and was not teaching that believers cannot be sure of salvation as Protestants have often been inclined to suppose. Does this historical clarification change our notion of the character of the long controversy?[21] Karl Barth, who has attacked the Roman doctrine of justification as bitterly as anyone, wrote in his introduction to Hans Küng's book on justification that *if* Küng's interpretation of Trent is correct, the basis for the controversy, at least on this point, has evaporated.[22] Barth asks of Küng, "How must we explain the fact that this has, within and outside of Catholicism, remained hidden for so long?" Barth's question underscores a problem of interpretation that is of no mean significance.[23]

But we would be mistaken if we were to conclude that this new interpretation is really a "discovery" that is forced on Trent by revised notions about justification itself. There is always a temptation to revise historical opinions about older confessions to make them agree with one's own revised ideas. But the danger of this temptation is always limited by the availability of the texts themselves. Historical research into a council could bring about a clearer image of the divergences that existed there and thus face theologians with the task of revising their historical judgment and interpretation of the council's intention. W. F. Dankbaar has

[20] Cf. H. Manders, "Certitudine fidei cui potest subesse falsum" (*Concerning the certitude of faith, which cannot admit any error*), *Werkgenootschap van katholieke Theologen in Nederland*, 1962, pp. 52ff., and St. Pfürtner, "Die Heilsgewissheit nach Luther und die Hoffnungsgewissheit nach Thomas von Aquin," *Catholica*, 1959, pp. 182ff. Both of these discuss the question of whether the doctrines of assurance are truly divisive as well as the necessity for a revision in Catholic interpretations of this controversy.

[21] The problem of (un)certainty of salvation played a large role in Reformed reaction to Trent. Cf. the Confession of Saxony of 1551 on *doubt* as being "Gentile imagination." Harnack said that if the Tridentine decree on justification had been issued a half century earlier, the separation of the church would have been unnecessary. Stakemeier agrees with Harnack on the score that Trent leaves room for the spirit of Luther's assurance of salvation. Cf. A. Stakemeier, *Das Konzil von Trient über die Heilsgewissheit*, 1947, p. 175.

[22] In his *Foreword* to Küng's *Rechtfertigung*, p. 11. Cf. K. Barth, *Kirchliche Dogmatik*, IV/1, p. 697ff.

[23] H. Küng, *op cit.*, p 12. Here Barth says that it is not easy for him to find in the text of Trent – "as we all have it before us" – what Küng writes about freedom, grace, and justification.

pointed out that when Calvin replied to the first seven decretals of Trent, he was not informed on the backgrounds and motives in the discussions that lay behind the decretals — which in any case were secret — and thus had to confine himself to the published text.[24] Later, by means of historical research, the background has come increasingly to light, opening up the possibility that revised analyses of the real intent of Trent may be required in the light of the historical developments that lay behind the final definitions.

For our púrpose, it is important that we are facing such a revised interpretation at the present time. Quite apart from the question of whether a revised consensus concerning the intentions of Trent will be possible now, we are in fact witnessing a shift of opinion which cannot be overlooked. The issues of old controversies are not as obvious as they used to be. For though the new interpretations of Trent are received with official reservation, no one has suggested that *what Küng claims to read in the intention of Trent is unorthodox.*[25] Many Catholics insist that no interpretation of Trent is valid which suggests that Rome meant to minimize the sovereignty of grace or that there is in Roman doctrine any competition between grace and merit. This is why they are asking whether the *sola fide – sola gratia* scheme can serve to express the Reformation alternative in the controversy with Rome.[26]

Historical research, with its disclosures of sources and official records, sometimes brings about important new understanding of

[24] W. F. Dankbaar, "Calvijn's oordeel over het concilie van Trente," *Nederlandse Archief voor Kerkgeschiedenis,* 1962, p. 82. Cf., besides Calvin's tract on Trent (*Acta Synodi Tridentinaecum Antidoto,* in *Corpus Reformatorum,* VII, pp. 473ff.), his harsh judgment in the Dedicatory Epistle of his *Commentary on Acts.* According to Dankbaar, Calvin, though only sparingly informed of all that went on at Trent, hit on the ultimate significance of Trent's decree on justification (*op. cit.,* pp. 82, 111). A statement in the Erlauthaler Confession is remarkable in this connection: "We receive with joy the Tridentine doctrines of justification, faith, and works (Müller, *Bekenntnis Schriften der Reformierten Kirchen,* p. 323). Cf. Barth's comments in this connection about "superficial readers" (*Kirchliche Dogmatik,* IV/1, p. 697).

[25] See the discussion of Küng's book in K. Rahner, "Fragen der Kontroverstheologie über die Rechtfertigung," *Schriften zur Theologie,* 1960, IV, 238, in which he says that there is no doubt as to the "orthodoxy of Küng's summary of the Catholic teaching on justification." Cf. also W. Joest, "Die tridentinische Rechtfertigungslehre," in *Kerugma and Dogma,* 1963, p. 412.

[26] The studies of W. Stählin still have significance for this question. Cf. Stählin, *Allein. Recht and Gefahr einer polemischen Formel,* 1950. Cf. also E. Wolf, "Sola Gratia?" *Peregrinatio,* 1954, pp. 113ff., and A. F. N. Lekkerkerker, "Notities over de rechtvaardigingsleer bij Luther en Trente," *Kerk en Theologie,* 1958, pp. 147f.

and new approaches to ancient controversies. In the present case, this does not mean that Protestants are forced to abandon their convictions on the necessity of the Reformation, but it does mean a call to honesty and genuineness. In this connection, we must ask why and on what grounds the works of the Reformers were so sharply condemned by Trent. We ought to know here whether the delegates at Trent were completely informed of the works of the Reformers and whether they were really condemning what the Reformation really intended to teach. Roman Catholics themselves are approaching this very question with more open-mindedness today than ever before. Catholics do not suppose that Trent's analysis of Reformation "heresy" was made under the charism of infallibility. It is recognized that the antithesis that Trent posits between itself and Luther proceeded from certain presuppositions about the Reformation and that these assumptions in turn played a large role in the Counter-Reformation.

One of the central items of this questionable Luther-image is the notion that Luther taught a purely "external" justification of man as sinner and had no concern for the real change in the inner life of the sinner through grace. Much of the traditional Catholic polemic against Luther is based on the false assumption that Luther taught only an external verbalism (the word of pardon) expressed in the slogan that the Christian man is "at once sinner and justified." More lately, Catholic scholars have wondered whether Luther's doctrine of justification has not been misrepresented by attaching too much importance to this cliché. Küng, for instance, has been very honest in insisting on asking "whether Luther actually taught a pure extrinsicism."[27]

Another item in the newer Catholic interpretation of the Reformation involves the frequent and long established accusation that the Reformation rejected the meritoriousness of good works in its

---

[27] H. Küng, *op. cit.*, p. 215. The relationship between Luther and Melanchthon further complicates this problem. Cf. H. Rückert, *Die Rechtfertigungslehre auf dem Trident. Konzil*, p. 103. Rückert calls Salmeron's criticism of Melanchthon typical of the way in which Trent judged Luther. It is clear that the Reformation was judged without an eye for nuances within it. A more extended reflection of the *justus et peccator* motif is found already in R. Grosche, "Simul peccator et justus," *Catholica*, 1935, pp. 132-139. Grosche analyzes Luther's formulation (by way of Luther's commentary on Romans) and concludes that "a completely orthodox sense" can be given to it by the Catholic person. He approaches Luther differently from the usual Catholic interpreter of his day.

insistence on the absolutely exclusive activity of God in salvation. According to this notion the Reformers left no room for significant human activity in laying the basis for salvation. This idea has been given extensive and able defense by Erich Przywara, who sees in it the fundamental difference between the Reformation and Rome: *exclusive* divine action versus *total* divine action. Catholic critics of the Reformation have emphasized this antithesis ever since. It creates the impression that the Reformation doctrine of justification implies an annihilation of all human activity in view of the overpowering divine transcendance. But it has now become ever clearer that this kind of annihilation of the human element in salvation did not play the slightest role in the Reformation. The religious insight into the greatness of divine majesty was falsely transposed into a sort of "ontology" of annihilation by later interpreters.[28]

It has become clear that Rome's interpretation of the Reformation forms a crucial point in the controversy as it took shape at Trent. Equally crucial at present is the question of what Trent really wanted to reject when it rejected the Reformation doctrine of *sola fide*. It is especially crucial in view of the present tendency on the part of Catholics to insist that Catholicism also teaches a *sola fide*. The answer to this question is related to the estimate that Catholics have had of the Reformed notion of faith as *fiducia*.[29] From the Tridentine decree on justification it appears that *fiducia* was understood to be an empty and vain *confidence*. The acts of the sixth session condemn the "vain confidence of the heretics" in which they boast themselves of forgiveness and seek rest in it

[28] Cf. Przywara, *Ringen der Gegenwart,* 1929. For a discussion of Przywara's analysis, see G. C. Berkouwer, *Barthianisme en Katholicisme,* 1940, and *Verdienste of Genade?,* 1958. Cf. M. Fr. Marlet, *Grundlinien der Kalvinistisch Philosophie der Gesetzesidee als Christlich Transzendentalphilosophie,* 1954. Marlet says that Calvinism tends to absorb mediate causes into the ultimate cause. This is in line with Przywara's analysis, in which Calvinism tends toward divine monergism. Cf. Przywara, *Gespräch zwischen den Kirchen,* 1956, p. 11, in which he terms the "God only" motif as basic to the structure of Reformation theology. The weakness of this analysis is evident in his conclusion that the Reformation sets the theology of grace *alone* against the theology of works.

In honesty, it must be said that Protestant writers give credence to this misunderstanding when they say that the prime interest of Reformers was in the "exclusiveness of divine work." Cf. E. Brunner, *Dogmatik* II, p. 46. Brunner endangers the biblical concern for human freedom and responsibility.

[29] Cf. H. Jedin, *Geschichte des Konzils von Trient* II, 1957, Chapters 5, 7, and 8, in connection with the complexities surrounding the phrase *sola fide*.

alone.[30] But now a Catholic consensus is forming that this was a false way of stating the implication of the *fiducia* doctrine. Küng and others as well, such as Stakemeier, have questioned it, and Stakemeier has asserted that Luther had no intentions of "commending a self assured presumption of the possession of grace."[31]

* * * * *

Thus, as the climate has changed all sorts of new and important questions have been set on the agenda about traditional Catholic interpretations of the Reformation and about the real intention of the Council of Trent. The seriousness of these questions gives them an urgency that cannot be avoided. They have to do with the way certain historical doctrinal decisions are understood by Roman Catholics. And this understanding, in turn, is affected by a vigorous historical study stimulated by the recent publication of the *Acts of Trent*. These historical studies into Trent have had a bearing on Catholicism's newer and more profound insights into what really motivated the Reformation.[32] The parallel to this in Protestantism is a more determined effort to interpret its own confessions in a historical sense. Polman, for example, says we must "interpret the confession by means of the past" because no confession can be isolated "from the ... thinking of theologians at the time of its origin."[33]

With this arises an all-important question that is part of the change in climate. Whoever comes into contact with current problems of interpretation within Roman Catholic theology, especially with its reassessment of the traditional interpretation of the Reformation's *sola fide* and *sola gratia* doctrines, is forced to wonder whether the possibility exists of the Roman Catholic Church mak-

[30] Denzinger, 802. The judgment is as unclear as it is surprising. It is made after Trent itself first explained that one must believe that his "sins are neither forgiven nor ever have been forgiven, except gratuitously through divine mercy.

[31] Cf. A. Stakemeier, *Das Konzil von Trient über die Heilsgewissheit*, 1947, p. 175. Stakemeier says that Trent's statement in Session VI, canon 9, does not touch Luther's teaching. In his judgment Trent was opposing "overly refined formulations of Luther" which were misused by his disciples. The council did not stick to the task of searching out the "relationship of ideas" in Luther "according to the sources." *Ibid.*, p. 92.

[32] The opening up of the Acts of councils always leads to a more profound historical study, as was the case when the Acts of the First Vatican Council were opened by Leo XIV. W. Köhler speaks of "a scientific boon by Leo XIII which cannot be sufficiently praised" (*Katholizismus und Reform.*, 1905, p. 19).

[33] A. D. R. Polman, *Onze Nederlands Geloofsbelijdenis*, I, p. 89. Polman's entire work proves how unfounded is the antithesis between simple confessions and complex theology.

ing a new confession of justification by faith. If we were to insist that such a new confession is out of the question in the face of the Catholic dogma of infallibility we would be extracting illegitimate conclusions from the notion of infallibility. For the possibility of a new confession would not, in the view of the newer interpretations, be a retraction of the essential dogma of Trent, but a statement of the *real intentions* of Trent abstracted from Trent's antithetical judgments of the Reformation, judgments which were tainted by the historical circumstances of that day. From the Roman Catholic viewpoint, the possibility would exist of expressing the unchangeable dogma in a way that it would do justice to the evangelical intentions of Trent to say that grace is completely free, that men are saved by grace alone and faith alone, and that the Catholic doctrine of merit only echoes the New Testament promise of rewards. A new statement would elevate the real doctrine above the complex question of how to interpret Trent. One Dutch Catholic, W. F. Dankbaar, contends that the Tridentine decree of justification needs "not merely a new interpretation, but a genuine revision and if not this, the doctrine of Trent will have to be replaced by a completely new definition."[34]

If a new Catholic confession were possible, we would be able to get some clarification in our discussion: at least the Catholic doctrine would not be formulated to oppose the "vain and empty confidence" that Trent read into the Reformation. Such a confession, in Roman Catholic thinking, could validate the contention that a Catholic *sola fide* is a meaningful option and that the Catholic doctrine of merit is nothing more than the New Testament doctrine of reward. It could demonstrate that Catholicism is free from any intent to minimize the freedom of sovereign grace. The unchangeability of dogma would not be sacrificed. For the Church's deepest intentions would simply be brought to clearer expression in a new formulation.

One problem that the doctrine of infallibility raises here is the interesting one of the so-called "dogmatic facts." These are not the facts of salvation history; they are the facts involved in the Church's censorship of heresies. The question is whether the censure of the Reformation doctrine of justification forms part of the infallible censorship of the Church. Put another way, the question is: Does a judgment by the Church of a given position carry with it the assumption that its *analysis* of the postion under judg-

---

[34] W. F. Dankbaar, *Ned. Archief van Kerkgeschiedenis*, 1962, p. 112.

ment is necessarily accurate? The problem is illustrated in the Church's judgment of Jansenism. In 1653, five theses from Jansen's *Augustine* were condemned.[35] But Jansenists contended that these five theses were not accurate representations of the book. The Pope (Alexander VII), however, declared that the theses were taken from Jansen's book "in the sense that the writer intended them." So the Pope's *analysis* of Jansen's book was part of the truth of his condemnation of certain views.[36] This is an example of the problem of the "dogmatic facts." Must these "facts" — the *analysis* of a condemned idea — be considered part of infallibly proclaimed truth? Or is it possible that the analysis may later be seen as mistaken even though the intention of preserving a truth may have been valid? Can we distinguish between the Church's positive intention to confess a truth and its analysis of an "error" so that the constructive intention could be admitted without imply-ing that the analysis of the "error" was correct? The infallibility of "dogmatic facts" is frequently defended on the grounds that they are *implied* in the positive statements of the Church. Moreover, if it were conceded that the Church could be mistaken in "dogmatic facts," people would lose confidence in the Church's censorship of error and hence in the Church's preservation of the faith.

Catholics are generally aware, however, that the "dogmatic facts" are indeed influenced by historically limited insight, and it is clear that the newer judgments concerning the Reformation have in fact led to a shifting of ground within Catholicism. From the Roman Catholic standpoint this altered view of "dogmatic facts" need not bring the assertions of the Church into uncertainty. The Church has been constant in *truth at its deepest intent*, even though it has not been elevated above historical relativity in its *analysis of the rejected errors*. Further developments will prove whether the changed climate and the altered insight into the moti-vations of the Reformation offer the possibility that Rome can indeed bring itself in an act of self-criticism to a new statement of faith. Such a statement of faith could also be seen as a religious challenge to those non-Catholics who are convinced that Rome has never done justice to the sovereignty of divine grace.

Some of the consequences of the one-sided and, in many senses,

[35] Denzinger, 1098, 1099, 1350.
[36] Even if these theses taken from Jansen's book were found there word for word, the problem of his intention would remain. The use of quotations is never conclusive, for there is always the question of how a sentence is related to the non-quoted context, including the immediate and the broader context of the entire book and even of the whole scope of the author's thought.

reactionary Counter-Reformation may possibly be undone by this route. The fruits of historical research — should the Church wish again to speak antithetically — could pay off in new clarity as to why the Reformation must be evaluated as an impoverishment of the Church's treasure of faith. Clearly, this has nothing in common with false irenicism. Rather, it could be a helpful clarification of the controversy, a clarification which would bring an even greater responsibility to both parties.[37] This would especially concern issues which many consider to have been gradually obscured (the Protestant and Catholic views of *sola fide*, for example). The two parties would have to meet each other, not at their respective weak points, but at their strongest points at which each is wholly convinced that it truly translates the voice of the gospel.[38] As the end of the Counter-Reformation is proclaimed by Catholic scholars and as the present council moves away from Counter-Reformation toward internal reformation,[39] a very serious analysis of this historical event in Church history is an absolute imperative. For we are dealing with questions that have long divided people who call themselves Christians and who are not ready to deny the use of that name to the others.

✻   ✻   ✻   ✻   ✻

The fact is noteworthy that repentance is emphasized very strongly as a condition for Church unity. Filthaut, for example, calls repentance "the inexpendable presupposition for true ecumenical action."[40] For a concrete illustration of confession of guilt he points to Adrian VI's well known admission of the guilt of the Catholic Church in the persons of its officials. Adrian in this case did not single out the guilt of Protestants, but pointed his finger inward. Such honest self-accusation is possible only as one seriously analyzes the history of schisms in order to discover the errors of one's Church and not as a means to hide one's own community's sins behind the faults discovered in others. The serious

---

[37] Paul VI, in his message opening the second session on October 11, 1963, applauded the work of the "separated brethren" in getting at the original sources of the faith and he urged a deeper study of "our teachings" and "of our history and religious life" by Catholics.

[38] Cf. the important article by E. Schlink, "Pneumatische Erschütterung?" *Kerugma und Dogma*, 1962, pp. 221ff.

[39] Cf. H. Fries, "Das bisherige Konzilgeschehen und die Wiedervereinigung im Glauben," *Catholica*, 1963, p. 108, and L. Jaeger, "Vigilia Concilii," *Catholica*, 1962, pp. 161f.

[40] T. Filthaut, "Die Busse und die Einigung der Christen," *Catholica*, 1961, p. 83.

student of Church history "will be satisfied to discover his own part in the guilt of the Church. His own and not the sins of others will he confess."[41] Filthaut does not suppose that this sort of honest historical awareness implies a sacrifice of the truth of his own convictions. He feels free to speak of the necessity of the "return" of the separated brethren because he is convinced that a return to the gospel means a return to the Catholic Church. Filthaut's use of the idea of repentance is clear. The Church is obliged to recognize its own guilt as a human institution within the complexities of history, while at the same time holding to its conviction of its being the one Church. The fact that it is almost impossible to recognize the real fold of Christ in the visage of the sixteenth-century Roman Church has dug deep in present Catholic consciences. The black-white antithesis between Rome and the Reformation is not tenable once one admits that the human, sinful side of the Catholic Church shares responsibility for the break that occured.

These same questions about the relation of unity and penitence were raised in the Second Vatican Council by Paul VI when he said in his opening speech: "If we are in any way to blame for this separation, we humbly beg God's forgiveness and ask our brothers' pardon for any injuries they feel they have sustained from us."[42] The Pope's intention was not perfectly clear here in view of his conditional approach ("if" — *si quae culpa*). But we may also note his words to non-Catholic observers when he reverted to the subject by saying: "You were present at our discourse on September 29 when we asked the pardon of Christians, reciprocally if possible." He ended by citing Horatio: "We give pardon and ask for reciprocation." That human guilt can be interwoven with the mystery of the unchangeable Church is another hint of how complicated the situation is. No one would suppose that words about admission of guilt are going to bring about the solution for the ecumenical problem. After admitting guilt in general, we get into an extremely sensitive area of the particular sins for which guilt is confessed. Moreover, confession — and very earnestly meant confession — is made by churches that meanwhile still insist on going their own ways. Confession in the ecumenical context can have real significance if it has to do with more than personal and individual guilt — "for we all make many mistakes" (James 3:2). It must involve an awareness of how our darkening of the truth and

41 *Ibid.*, p. 93.
42 *Salvete*, in *The Pope Speaks*, Vol. 9, No. 2, 1964.

our crippled way of walking in the truth has hampered the Church's search for unity.

We are faced with something far more complex than the picture of one Church pitting the one true doctrine against all others. We are dealing with the truth of the gospel, which can be made believable only in the total life of the Church, in its preaching and witnessing, its acts and its avoidance of acts, its song and its works, its service and its sacrifice. Here a burden of guilt encounters us, a guilt which is entrenched and which continues to establish itself in the life of the churches, with the effect that the alienation between churches now appears almost incurable. To say this is not to minimize differences in doctrine, but it is to admit that doctrine and truth are really understood and made understandable when they become transparent in the real life of the Church, and that, failing to gauge the connection between truth and life, we betray our failure to understand either doctrine or truth, both of which demand first of all that we *walk* in them.[43]

* * * * *

We will do well to be extremely careful not to lose ourselves in the illusions and pretensions that are easily created by the divisions of the Church. We are called to avoid a superficial cure for our troubles and to turn a deaf ear to the call for peace "when there is no peace." In the face of unrealistic common denominator types of unity, which always disappoint in the end, it is imperative to resist superficiality, and to let the many lessons of history warn us on this score. Pope Paul has also warned against reconciliation in appearance only, the kind of reconciliation which only submerges problems instead of solving them. He was realistic when he asked: "Watchman, tell us of the night."[44]

Reflecting on the realism that is evident in Protestant as well as Catholic circles, we are also reminded of the opposite attitude which sees attempts at unity as a visionary grasp for Utopia. In respect to Roman and Reformation relations, some people fail to see any genuine reason for hope, even though they are aware that personal relations are better and that there is a better mutual understanding. Ecumenical realism and this pessimistic view, which sees hope as Utopian vision, are not at all the same. In

---

[43] Cf. III John 3, 4. Also II John 1 where we find: knowing the truth (v. 1), truth and love (v. 3), a command to love (v. 6), acknowledging the coming of Christ (v. 7), and the doctrine of Christ (v. 9) all in the same context.

[44] Paul VI in *Salvete*. Cf. Jeremiah 6:14; 8:11, 21.

view of a realistic survey of history, to be sure, there are many reasons for pessimism in regard to the future of Catholic and Protestant rapprochement. It is not merely Protestant negativism that asks whether the Roman Catholic Church, taken with utter seriousness, can ever shed its pretensions and its exclusiveness. There is reason to wonder whether the changes that have occured since the sharp criticism of the ecumenical movement in the encyclical *Mortalium animos* of 1928 are *essential* changes, even granting the startling fact that Pope John sent five observers to New Delhi and cordially invited non-Catholic observers to the Vatican Council. An almost irresistible logic informs this sort of question. Rome genuinely believes that it recognizes the presence of the Holy Spirit in its own Church life. It is buoyed by a conviction that its doctrine alone is the true continuity of apostolic truth, doctrine elevated above all historical change because it is guaranteed by the charism of infallibility. Does not this imply that an approach of the churches toward each other must be an approach only from one side?

These are not questions that stem merely from anti-papistic Protestantism. They are questions asked by Catholics themselves even more importunately, especially when they dampen ecumenical optimism by recalling such once-for-all established doctrines as the immaculate conception, the ascension of Mary, the primacy and infallibility of the Pope.[45] What is remarkable is that Catholics also contend that the logic of the anti-Utopians itself fails to take realistic account of the actual situation. What is involved here is a new concern for the more profound *intentions* and tendencies of the infallible teachings of the Church. Far from admitting that ecumenical bridges can be built only at the price of watering down the truth, this group of Catholics seeks to get around the caricatures each side has drawn of the other by means of a fresh interpretation of the Church's confessions. Thus, they are bringing into the arena of discussion today new insights into the Catholic doctrines of justification, Scripture and tradition, the infallibility of the Church and so forth. We contend that we are observing a new interpretative phase of Roman Catholicism. All the problems that are engaging the attention of Catholics in dialogue with Protestants are connected with a new and wholly conscious effort at reinterpretation of old confessions.

The problem of interpretation opens up many possibilities. One

---

[45] H. Fries, "Einigung der Christen eine Utopie?" *Catholica*, 1961, pp. 121ff.

possibility is to keep the past alive by giving it new forms of expression in a new time. But there is also the possibility that this could lead to a *radical revision* of the confession that is meant only to be interpreted. The tensions within Catholicism could be characterized as basically a tension between these two possibilities. Outside of the Roman Catholic Church there are those who see the new theological thinking more as a revision than an interpretation of Catholic dogma. Now and then one gets a hint of suspicion that an element of dishonesty is afoot here. Coming mostly from those who have their own narrowly traditional and closed portrait of Rome, there is a suspicion that the newer theologians are going off on their own independent paths of interpretation while they are formally committed to Roman dogma; meanwhile they torture the official doctrines to make them fit their own new ideas. New ideas within Catholicism are said to be retrojected into the Church's past and made out to be the real intent of the Roman fathers. Herein lies what some suspect to be an element of dishonesty.

In my judgment such suspicions are as baseless as they are fruitless. They can only block our way to an understanding of what is preoccupying the Roman Church today. The possibility always exists that theologians may introduce their own novel opinions into the old doctrines of the Church. This is as true of Catholics as it is of Protestants. We all run this danger whenever we come to new insights and begin to think along new paths that simply were not within the range of our fathers and then attempt to assimilate the old confessions into a new day. When this happens we always experience tensions. We have had tensions in facing the results of natural science and the progress of biblical scholarship, in both of which certain traditional ways of looking at things have been broken through. In such matters we try all sorts of ways to harmonize the new ideas with the old teachings, unless we have become so individualistic that the relationship of our thinking to the Church's teaching is no longer a problem. Among those who feel a responsibility for the Church, we usually find a genuine and careful effort to avoid conflict between the old and the new. And the more responsible we are, the more severe are the tensions we experience.

A very relevant example of such tensions is the Catholic Church's response to Catholic modernism. In this case, Catholic modernism was afoot on a way diametrically opposed to that on which the Church was going. But even here there were moments of hesitation, and there was a willingness temporarily on the part of the modernists to subject themselves to the judgment of the Church. Alfred Loisy said after his book was condemned in 1903: "Of course, I disclaim and reject all errors which could be read into my book." Again, after his next book was condemned, Loisy subjected himself to a similar judgment and accepted another condemnation. But then he added that in spite of his acceptance of the Church's judgment, he could not personally throw over his convictions as an historian. Of course, the existential problem of life that Loisy faced in this could not be permanently settled by his easy distinction between himself as historian and himself as Catholic. He tried to find another way out, sacrificing a coveted appointment to the Sorbonne in order to return to his birthplace to work out a reconciliation between his two loyalties. He never came to a resolution of his conflict, and to this day Loisy illustrates the very personal dimensions of this tension between intellectual convictions and religious loyalty to the Church.

Galileo offers a similar example of the same tensions. When the storm broke over his head and he was called to decide whether or not he believed the Bible when it so clearly said, in Joshua's command: "Sun stand thou still over Gibeon and thou moon over the valley of Ajalon" (Joshua 10:12). Galileo retired into silence. When he was hauled before the inquisition in 1632, he agreed to swear that he renounced his previous convictions and to betray his disciples to the inquisition. He accepted his penance, three years during which he would pray the seven penitential Psalms each week and imprisonment for an undetermined period in the Holy Office. Later critics have been hard on Galileo for his concessions to the Church. But actually he was part of a situation that had been gradual in the making but in which Galileo, like most others of his day, was caught to the very depth of his existence. He was a victim of the inescapable tensions of Church life at the dawn of a new age. Such tensions occur when new scientific discoveries seem to contradict the teachings of the Church; they can also exist when theologians resist the direction that doctrinal development is taking.[46] But in all of them we have phases in which the Church's leaders are obligated to grope their way

[46] Recall the condemnation of Berenger of Tours (1000-1086) at the synods of 1059 and 1079 and Berenger's recantation. Harnack refers to an "external subjection" to the church. Seeberg indicts Berenger as lacking "greatness of character."

through interpretations of the Church's teaching toward a resolution of the tension.

Whenever the tensions between older formulations of truth and newer insights into reality are overcome, it is made possible by the Church's willingness to reject a hidebound traditionalism that closes its eyes to reality and at the same time rejects any easy accommodation of its faith to conform to new trends of scientific theory. The newer Roman Catholic theology has not been marked by a spirit of accommodation; its clear dissociation from modernism is what makes its efforts at reinterpretation of dogmatic formulae significant. When the new theology accepts the doctrine of infallibility, it is not making public concessions to orthodoxy against its deepest conscience. It thinks wholly in the context of a conviction that the Holy Spirit guides and keeps the Roman Church and for this reason feels it is incumbent on the Church to be fearless in facing the new questions that science and biblical research have placed in its path. The reinterpretations that it makes are matters of debate. But what is clear is that the new theology is not a neo-modernistic movement. It is not revisionist. Nor is it twisting the old dogmas to fit the new thoughts. It is trying honestly to read and interpret the dogmas of the Church within the framework of their historical context and the conditionedness of their formulation. Its aim in this is to rediscover what the Church, led by the Spirit, really wanted to express in its historical formulations.

The work of the new theology has helped create the changed climate in the Roman Church. It is the kind of movement in which the whole Roman Church and every church must be involved sooner or later. The unavoidable radical questions which face the Church of our time, not the charm of ecumenicity, creates the change of climate. They have achieved particular urgency in the Roman Catholic Church because of its dogma of infallibility. The last and unavoidable question must be whether that dogma, that the Church is infallible, is the one dogma whose formulation is lifted above all change and historical influence. Or is it like all the others involved in the possibility of reinterpretation? This is the central theme of the following chapter. The changeability and the unchangeability of dogma — can the Roman Church digest this very real problem or must it always remain an unresolvable paradox?

Unchangeability and Changeability of Dogma

THE VERY TITLE OF THIS CHAPTER BRINGS US TO THE
kernel of the problem. The unchangeability of Catholic
dogma does not constitute a problem, since it is integral
to the infallibility of the Church and its teaching authority. The big question, however, is whether and, if so,
how dogma can be understood as changeable with-
out creating an obvious contradiction. Rome means to say by its
notion of infallibility that the truth remains ever the same,
lifted above the changes of history. Therefore the Church views
its possession of the truth as an essential aspect of the Church
which is the Church of Him who is indeed the same yesterday,
today, and forever (Hebrews 13:8). The dogmas of the Reformation, too, it has often been noted, show a large measure of continuity and unchangeableness. No one in Reformed churches seriously
counts on his Church's recanting prior doctrinal decisions.[1] Roman
Catholics are quite prepared to defend the idea of doctrinal unchangeability; the identification of the Church with continuity of
doctrine is an article of faith, based on the fact that Christ is Lord

---

[1] The possibility of *gravamen* does not alter this fact, for we are speaking of
the way things have actually gone in Reformed churches. Think, for instance,
of the continuity of the christological and trinitarian confessions.

of the Church, and connected with His promise of the Holy Spirit's guidance of the Church into the way of the whole truth (John 14:13; 16:13).

* * * * *

Roman Catholics do not suppose they have the problem of dogma formation sewed up with their belief in unchangeability. They are very aware that the life of the Church is not frozen into static sameness, showing the same expression in every era, unaffected by the continuous process of growth and variation in history. History with its irresistible mutations has set its stamp on the Church as it has on all institutions. Every era of history is mirrored in things done and things left undone, in the speech and the silences of the Church. We need only recall once again the condemnation of Galileo, the changed attitudes toward Church-state relations since the publication of *Unam Sanctum* in 1302, the attitude of the Church on Bible reading, the many pronouncements by the biblical commission since 1902, and, to mention one more, the gradual shifting of ground on the idea of natural evolution. None of these instances imply a retraction of the Church's infallible utterances, but they all have to do with attempts to lead the Church on its path through the modern world.

We come to the real question when we ask whether the dogma of the Church is also subject to the influence of historical variation. Does dogma stand alone as the one unchangeable and untouchable rock within the waves of history, transcending the law of changeability? Or does dogma participate in the law of historical change? Currently, as they have never done before, Catholic answers to this question suggest that even dogma does not altogether escape subjection to time. The forms in which faith is expressed manifest many idiomatic characteristics of their time. This is, of course, true of Protestant confessions as well as of Catholic. For example, the passing of the Reformation into post-Reformation scholasticism created striking changes in Reformed thought. Then, again, we find "new Reformations" of thought. Even the jargon suggests flux; we speak of old and new Protestantism, old and new Lutheranism, and old and new Calvinism. But the terms underscore continuity, even while suggesting that a lasting idea is applied in new form to new times. Windelband's remark that "to understand Kant is to go beyond him" has been quoted in connection with many theological situations in which continuity amid change is observed.

Those who accept the necessity of change always insist that they are not unfaithful to the past; they seek only to understand the deeper meaning of the past in order to press its relevance for the present actuality.[2] Clearly the adjectival "neo" carries with it fascinating problems that evoke what are often very emotional discussions among those who have roots in a given tradition. There are always those who see in every change of form a betrayal of the past. While some churchmen have urged renewal in the face of new situations and new problems, there have always been those who observed these developments with profound unrest, fearful that the Christian faith itself was being twisted to meet the times, and fearful that Christianity itself become a *cultural* phenomenon subject to the same relativity and changeability as everything else. This is a problem that meets us everywhere in the Church's history and in the history of theology. That not even the Roman Catholic Church, where the notion of continuity is made into an absolute, should escape the awareness that the Church's speech is historically conditioned, should not be surprising. The fact of actual shifts and changes was too obvious to be ignored.

Catholic concern about change and continuity in doctrine has focused on the problem of the evolution of dogma. The Church of the present compared with the Church of the past betrays so many changes and developments that the Church can no longer be thought of as merely *preserving intact* the truth once for all delivered to it.

Cardinal Newman's study of the evolution of dogma was stimulated by the question of how the process of development had taken place and of the factors that had influenced it, a question which for Newman was most existential. He came to the conclusion that a genuine evolution had taken place in the development of dogma, while the *truths* of revelation were not really affected by the historical process. Evolution of dogma was not a development of truth,

2 The examples are countless. Herman Dooyeweerd criticizes Abraham Kuyper's "metaphysical doctrine of the Logos" and his failure to extricate himself from the scholastic, Aristotelian tradition, but agrees fully with Kuyper's "basic religious perspective," a perspective which, according to Dooyeweerd, must now be developed more consistently than Kuyper himself succeeded in doing. Herman Bavinck talks of the need for theology to relate itself to the "mind and spirit of the era in which it speaks" (Bavinck, *Modernisme en Orthodoxie,* 1911, p. 35). A. Kuyper wanted to bring Reformed theology into contact with "human consciousness as it had developed at the end of the nineteenth century," and he spoke of bringing one's confession awareness to the "level of the modern consciousness," *Encyclopaedie,* I, 1908, Foreword, and II, 552. Kuyper frequently talked of the need for bringing the *forms* of orthodoxy into harmony with the thought forms of modern times. Cf. his *Conservatisme en Orthodoxie,* 1870, pp. 21ff.

but a development of the Church's *consciousness of the truth*. The question of the unchangeability and the evolution of dogma has challenged Catholic thinkers increasingly since Newman. While no unanimity has been gained on how the evolution occurred, most Catholics agree that the evolution was a consistent development from implicit to explicit doctrine. The dogma of the Church was clarified by factors like the Church's need to express itself against heresy. And the notion that evolution of dogma was only a consistent development from lesser to great clarity of expression and understanding distinguished *this* evolution from all other developments of thought that involved an assimilation of one idea with another. Unlike Harnack, who sees the very formation of dogma as a rationalistic betrayal of the simple gospel of Jesus, Roman Catholics have believed that dogma developed consistently with the growth of that simple gospel in the Church's consciousness.[3] The Catholics did not admit a possibility that a real break occurred anywhere in the evolutionary process. This evolution did not have in it the elements of conflict between thesis and antithesis. In the Catholic conviction, however, there has often been a hint of overzealousness to protect the dogma from evolutionary influence. In spite of their willingness to come to grips with the complexities of the evolutionary process and in spite of their willingness to admit the influence of historical factors in the formation of dogma,[4] Catholics have tended to inject their own apologetics for Catholic truth into the problem.[5]

The harmonistic approach to the evolution of dogma has not been the only one to appear in the Catholic Church. The modern-

[3] Cf. Marin Sola, *L'Evolution homogène du Dogma catholique*, I, 268, and J. van Ginkel, *De Evolutie van het Dogma*, 1926, pp. 33ff. Of the great number of studies on the evolution of dogma, a few of the more important works are: K. Rahner, "Zur Frage des Dogmenentwicklung," in *Schriften zur Theologie*, 1954, I; G. Meuleman, *De Ontwikkeling van het Dogma in de Rooms-Katholieke Theologie*, 1951; F. W. Kantzenbach, *Evangelium und Dogma. Die Bewältigung des theol. Problems der Dogmengeschichte im Protestantismus*, 1959, and *Zur Deutung der kontrovers-theologischen Problematik*, 1963.

[4] Newman was convinced that the development of dogma was not simply a "logical sequence." He recognized a "power of assimilation" in dogma (*An Essay on the Development of Christian Doctrine*, 1845, pp. 171ff.).

[5] "The problem of the development of dogma consists in the task of showing the possibility that the formulations of faith as they developed later are really identical with the apostolic formulations of the revelation which came in Christ and in specific instances to demonstrate their identity" (*Kleines theologisches Wörterbuch*, Rahner-Vorgrimler, p. 76 — this is a Catholic dictionary published in Germany).

istic wing of the Church had another view; it was convinced that the Church's dogma had developed in a way that was open to criticism and correction. Catholic modernism was not a defensive, but an offensive movement, critical of traditional elements in the process of dogma evolution, critical of what it felt to be the Church's failure to keep pace with the development of knowledge in other spheres. In response to the modernistic movement, the Church became even more cautious about the evolution of dogma and began to emphasize the *unchangeability* of its truth. But the problem of change was never successfully shoved aside. In an off-shoot of the modernist movement, several anonymous books appeared from Catholic writers carrying severe criticism of the Church's posture toward the development of science. Some of these books called for a radical reduction of church dogma.[6] Since then the problem of change has been of mounting concern in the minds of many Catholics. At the time of the anonymous publications, what is now commonly known as the "new theology" of Roman Catholicism was just beginning.

The new theology does not lend itself to a precise description. Karl Rahner wrote in 1958 (along with Schlier) that all that is meant is a scientific theology. "We are concerned simply with theology, not with a 'new theology,'" he wrote.[7] Rahner is obviously trying to avoid the suggestion that the new theology is a new school. We feel free to use the term *new theology* since several common traits are visible in the work of an identifiable group of contemporary Catholic theologians whose work has, in Europe at least, come to be identified as the "new theology." These thinkers are having a broad influence in the Church and, specifically, at the Vatican Council.

The term "new theology" has gradually gained a clearer meaning. It has come to stand for the need to free theology from abstractions and from isolated intellectualism, and for theologians to involve themselves in the living reality of the Church in the world, with what John XXIII called the "life of doctrine." Moreover, the new theology has a strong sense of the humanity and the historical conditionedness of the Church as it responds to the revelation of God. Even where theological differences exist within the group of new theologians, the members share a common openness and hon-

---

[6] Cf. the publication in 1937 of *Der Katholizismus, sein Stirb und Werde, Von Katholischen Theologen und Laien.* After considerable criticism of this book, another appeared called, *Der Katholizismus der Zukunft,* in 1940.

[7] K. Rahner, *Ueber die Schriftinspiration,* 1958, p. 5.

esty in confrontation with the questions of our day. They are not content to *augment* the "real" dogma of the Church with a practical or kerugmatic theology, but are addressing themselves to the need for an existentially relevant theology which, while not rejecting tradition, will discard any traditional schematization of doctrine which has actually kept people from an insight into the gospel.

The new theology had its origin in a new confrontation with the problem of change. This confrontation, unlike the modernist movement, occurred within the context of a conscious acceptance of the entire dogma of the Church. Yet, we would be minimizing the importance of the movement were we to conclude from its acceptance of Catholic dogma as it stands, that the new theologians were merely trying to defend the notion that doctrinal evolution is a homogeneous and logical development of truth. Actually, the evolution of dogma was construed as a far more complex affair than was previously imagined.[8] An analysis of the new theology can well begin with H. Bouillard, who, in 1941, pointed to a distinction between the unchangeable "affirmations" and the changeable "representations" of truth.[9] This distinction has been used frequently in the new theology, and the distinction that John XXIII made at the opening of the council has been viewed by many as a clear indication that he wished the considerations begun by the new theology to be given continued study.

*   *   *   *   *

Bouillard pointed out that theology always expresses the truth by making use of the concepts, terms, and images typical of the intellectual climate of a given era. This is true indeed of all that the Church says and not only of theology. Since the expressions of truth bear an historically conditioned character, the Church must keep in mind, as it seeks to understand a given dogmatic definition, that the truth is never expressed in an absolute, wholly adequate, and irreplaceable form. A given formulation is never the only form the content of that truth may take. Bouillard, while accepting the unchangeability of what the Church affirms, insists that what the Church affirms is expressed in variable form. The philosophical

[8] As, for an example, by Bossuet. Owen Chadwick gives a reliable account of Bossuet's notion of continuity in his *From Bossuet to Newman. The Idea of Doctrinal Development*, 1957. Chadwick shows that Bossuet believed that doctrinal development involved only a wider ramification of the one truth. Bossuet had no real feeling for a genuine noetic evolution.

[9] H. Bouilard. *Conversion et grâce chez Thomas d'Aquin*, 1941. The part of this book that came to play a large role is found on pages 220, 221.

thought of any era puts its stamp on the forms of dogmatic truth in a special way. For example, the Church made much use of Aristotelian concepts during the late Medieval period. But Bouillard insists that the Church was not canonizing Aristotelian concepts when it made use of them; the Church was not binding itself to the philosophical inclinations of a given period, but was only finding the most suitable form available at the time to give its unchangeable truth a meaningful expression. The form is not opposed to content; but it is only form, a time-bound utterance of the truth. Another age brings with it new and different concepts in which the unchangeable truth can be expressed, again without touching the continuity of the Church's life. The truth never changes; new representations of the truth merely reveal the truth in other dress.

Bouillard's approach makes it possible to speak of a certain sort of relativity in dogma. This relativity must be distinguished from the critical relativism that accepts no norm of truth. The normative truth remains the same, in Bouillard's construction, amid the movement and the dynamic of thought forms and structures. But a certain doctrinal relativity must be accepted simply in view of the fact that the Church and its theology are temporal, part of the living stream of human thought. This fact makes it possible for the preaching of the truth to cast off old, traditional, and in many senses fossilized and unintelligible forms as times change. Only as they are willing to change can theology and preaching be a living reality in the Church of today's world.[10]

Obviously, an outlook on the evolution of dogma which, like this, combines the relativity with the absoluteness of truth, does not regret the influence of changing thought forms on abiding dogmatic truth. Evolution is inherently necessary because no human words, concepts, or propositions can possibly contain or adequately express the inexhaustible truth of God. This inadequacy of concepts and words frees the Church from slavish marriage to expressions of the past. It allows apostolic missionary theology to remove the obstacles to understanding that Western thought forms have erected for the Eastern mind.[11]

Precisely because divine truth is at stake here, it must be in-

---

[10] Cf. *ibid.*, p. 219, where he insists that an *irrelevant* theology is a *false* theology. Rahner says that it is *heresy* to suggest that a theology of revelation "created only dangers, and that everything has already been set in theological concepts" (K. Rahner, *Schriften zur Theologie*, I, 13).

[11] J. Daniélou, *Dieu et Nous*, 1956, p. 203. Cf. also Daniélou, "Les orientations présentes de la pensée religieuse," *Etudes*, 1946, pp. 5f.

carnate in the forms suitable to every age so that it can speak to the age with its own communicative power. As the Church passes into new eras and opens itself to the totality of life with its science and culture, it must take care not to sacrifice its unchangeable truth to historicism, but it must also, without fear, make clear to the world that it cannot and does not pretend to fathom the whole truth. The Church must not retreat into a past age for fear of accommodation to modernity; it must make clear that it gladly accepts the ever renewed responsibility that rests on those who are given the truth.[12]

       ❉   ❉   ❉   ❉   ❉

Roman Catholics these days like to remind their readers of Paul's statement that we see as through a glass darkly, and that our knowledge is incomplete (I Corinthians 13:12). The incompleteness of our knowledge plays a large role in their discussions, indicating their sense of the immeasurable terrain of truth on which men are privileged to set foot. The modesty apparent here suggests that modern Catholics are taking seriously Paul's warning against the knowledge "that puffs up." Paul is not against knowledge; he is against an exaggerated sense of one's own achievement of knowledge. The Church must be open to all truth; it must be ready for the truth that reaches us and surrounds us as grace. In readiness for a new and surprising witness the Church, we are told, must be willing to abandon all of yesterday's formulae whenever they fail to serve the purpose of effective witness, regardless of how well they served the truth in former generations.[13]

The distinction between dogmatic truth and its expressions, affirmation of truth and representation of truth, invariables and variables in the Church's witness, is of fundamental significance to Hans Küng.[14] The truth of revelation comes to us on the level of our human understanding and there, in the answer faith gives to revelation, is given formulation. Küng points out that the one faith receives various formulations even in Holy Scripture. Truth and its formulations are simply not identifiable, and a change in formulation need not mean that a break from faith has occurred somewhere. Küng considers this of utmost importance for any ecumenical contact. For in real encounter all participants must have a sense "of the incompleteness and imperfection, the fragmented

---

12 Danéilou, *Dieu et Nous*, p. 203.
13 H. Urs von Balthasar, *Theologie der Geschichte*, 1952, p. 65.
14 H. Küng, *Strukturen der Kirche*, 1962, p. 347.

character of their own formulations of faith."[15] He does not mean to say that previous formulations have to be despised; he does mean that Christians must strive "to discover a single faith within the varied and contradictory formulations, so that each will be prepared, in openness and readiness to understand, to grant to the others the right for their formulations so long as they have the same faith."[16] A viewpoint like this stems naturally from an awareness of the imperfection of all human formulae. It is what Karl Rahner calls the tendency of "all formulae to transcend themselves . . . , not because they are untrue, but just because they are true."[17] Every formulation of divine mystery is the beginning, never the terminal. Formulae are not sufficient for knowledge, as though they contained and condensed the truth and reality of divine revelation; they are pointers to the reality of God. Hence, every time the Church formulates its faith, it begins a movement, it starts on a new way and must be conscious of this. No formulation exhausts the truth; it can only be a means to help the Church listen anew to revelation tomorrow and the next day. And when the Church looks back on past deliverances, on its speech of yesterday, it must always remember that when it talked yesterday it set itself to the task of listening so that it could speak anew today.[18]

❊　❊　❊　❊　❊

A question of utmost importance — and with it is associated a criticism that has been levelled against the new theology — is this: what is the criterion for distinguishing between form and content, representation and affirmation? Where is the line beyond

---

15 *Ibid.*, p. 350.

16 *Ibid.*

17 K. Rahner, *Schriften zur Theologie*, I, 1954, p. 169. Rahner expresses this idea in an introduction to a discussion of Chalcedonian christology.

18 H. Küng, *op. cit.*, p. 352. Von Balthasar recalls the relationship between the human word and divine truth in the words of Jesus. Jesus, he says, adapts Himself to the "ability of His contemporaries to understand His concepts." "He weaves a new form of apocalyptic into the entire gospel, and the gospel then becomes the truth of that new form" (*Het beschouwende gebed*, 1962, p. 118). Karl Rahner also draws a distinction between "manner of expression" and "the truth of the expression." Heresy, he says, comes about when the "expression" is in conflict, not with the "manner of expression" the Church once used, but with the Scripturally grounded *content* ("Theol. Prinzipien der Hermeneutik eschatologischer Aussagen," *Schriften zur Theologie*, 1960, IV, 40ff.).

which the unchangeability of dogma is lost in relativism? The new theology cannot claim to have given a complete answer to this pressing question, though it has been intensely preoccupied with it. In spite of this area of uncertainity, the necessity of the distinction seems to have pressed itself on most Catholic thinkers, probably because the human side of the Church in both its witnessing to and formulation of the truth is undeniable. To accept the implications of the humanity of the Church is to deny that the vertical dimension of truth and revelation renders the horizontal dimension in which truth actually comes to incarnation essentially unnecessary.

Schillebeeckx notes that our growth in the knowledge of faith is part of the "essential historicity of our existence." He wants us to recognize that new "situations for thought arise as they are created by the ever renewed forms in which existence is experienced." For all its unchangeability, the truth "as known by us in faith participates in all the marks of humanity: in imperfection, the relativity and growth, or the historicity, of every human possession of truth." There is a "way of listening to the Word of God that is peculiar to its own time." And because there is only an imperfect human perspective of the truth of salvation, our knowledge is capable of growth and is in need for fulfillment.[19] Perspectives change as time changes. But since this fact could make everything seem relative and historicized, Schillebeeckx underscores the fact that it is in the growth dynamic that we mount above relativism.

The new theologians seem to have a constant sense of danger in their own renewal of theology; they are aware that a theological renewal is always capable of evacuating faith of permanent truth. But they also know that renewal can be an authentic enrichment of our understanding of unchangeable truth. For this reason, they are in a position to contribute a genuine new approach to the ecumenical dialogue. Heresy hunting is in flight before a con-

[19] E. Schillebeeckx, "De nieuwe wending in de huidige dogmatiek," in *Tijdschrift voor theologie,* 1961, p. 17. As to this humanity of all dogmatic speech, cf. the Reformed theologian H. Bavinck, who says that all of our thinking and speaking about God is temporal, limited, imperfect, not divine, but human and therefore inadequate. Bavinck says that "we are better able to say what God is not than what He is." That this does not make a relativist or an agnostic of Bavinck is demonstrated by his four large volumes of dogmatics. H. Bavinck, *Gereformeerde Dogmatik,* IV, p. 401, and *Modernisme en Orthodoxie,* 1911, p. 34.

structive dialogue.[20] This brings us to a contribution of the new theology which goes far beyond the value of personal contact that has already broken through the inner estrangement between the parties to the dialogue. For in this case we are dealing with the *humanness of the faith,* a fact that may never be neglected for fear that the absolute may be lost by admitting it. This approach to the evolution of dogma carries with it a basically new thrust. For now the changeability rather than the unchangeability is at the foreground of the evolution of dogma. Now Catholic theologians are taken up with the variable, the inadequacy of every era to define truth for future eras. Even while they give no hint of denying the unchangeability of truth itself they take a new approach to it, which is itself a sign of a shift of ground.

The entire problem of the evolution of dogma has been a real one for only a century. In the West, as in the East, the Church went for centuries without anyone seriously considering it at all. For the East this is more or less understandable in view of its strict subjection to the seven ecumenical councils and its protest against all further developments of dogma, as in the case of the *filioque* controversy and later Mariology.[21] Within the Roman Church the problem *had* to be faced, especially in relation to such matters as Mariology. It appeared in the form of the continuity of truth in the evolution of dogma in the nineteenth century, perhaps most famously in the role that this played in the conversion of Cardinal Newman to the Catholic Church. In our day, the same problem is given new form by the modern emphasis on the historicity of all human existence and the awareness of the temporally conditioned nature of dogma. The evolution of dogma can no longer be construed simply as a straight development of the explicit out of implicit truth. The implicit-explicit scheme has in fact been steadily losing favor as a

---

[20] Schillebeeckx is not saying that there is an absolute contradiction between condemning heresy and engaging in dialogue; it has to do with emphasis and prime concern. Cf. the important article by K. Rahner, "Ein Gestaltwandel der Häresie," *Gefahren im heutigen Katholizismus,* 1955, pp. 63ff.; also his "Was ist Häresie?" *Schriften zur Theologie,* V, 1962, pp. 527ff. Cf. also A. Kuyper's idea is that another may build on the same foundation as you do and still build in quite another style. Irenicism alerts us to "keep our eyes open for the common basis in all Christian religion in order to prevent our polemical zeal from boiling over into fanaticism" (*Encyclopaedie der Heilige Godgeleerdheid,* III, 436).

[21] See further, on the emphasis on "continuity" in the Eastern church, E. Schlink, *Der kommende Christus und die kirchlichen Traditionen,* 1961, pp. 236ff.

principle of explanation.[22] Today, such a rather intellectualistic explanation of the evolutionary process of dogma is considered out of keeping with the character of divine revelation. Revelation, it is said, is not a reservoir of intellectual propositions from which other propositions can be deduced. Revelation is a personal self-disclosure by God in which He encounters the total person and calls him to answer in faith. "Revelation is in the first place not a communication of a certain number of facts," but "an historical dialogue between God and man in which something really happens, and the communication of truth occurs in the Event, the Act of God."[23] The new Catholic theology is not herewith teaching a personalistic idea of revelation, but it is protesting against depersonalization of both divine revelation and human reception of the truth. If revelation bears a personal character, this fact is bound to affect the way dogma evolves. For evolution of dogma takes place, not in intellectual isolation, but in "a living contact with the material it is made of."[24] Hence, the growth of dogma cannot occur by way of deduction from revealed propositions.

Since the reality of revelation is the reality of God's presence in Jesus Christ, faith's answer to it can never consist in a completed "truth possession." Faith can give its answer only in finite expressions which reveal that faith itself must keep looking for fulfillment, rootage, and enrichment. The limitation of faith's answer does not mean that the answer is untrue. It only means that it cannot exhaust the truth and that it knows that it cannot. Because truth and revelation have a personal, human character, every formula of faith can be surpassed; on principle, it can be exchanged for another formula that says more and yet says the same thing. Even where we are definitely convinced that faith has a hold on truth, we cannot deny that its hold on truth is at "a finite, historical point" and that even faith's perspective can change.[25]

✻   ✻   ✻   ✻   ✻

All these ideas fermenting in the new Catholic theology are significant because of their relationship to the Church's dogmatic pronouncements on the faith. These too participate in the inade-

[22] Cf. G. E. Meuleman, *De Ontwikkeling van het Dogma in de Rooms-Katholieke Theologie*, pp. 31ff. When Paul VI calls attention to "how *logically*" Catholic teaching flows from the deposit of divine revelation" he is not taking sides on a theory of the evolution of dogma.

[23] K. Rahner, *Schriften zur Theologie*, I, 59.

[24] Cf. all of Rahner's article in "Zur Frage der Dogmenentwicklung," *ibid.*, pp. 49f.

[25] *Ibid.*, p. 55.

quacy of all human speech. The task of the theologian is to recognize the infallible *sense* and *truth* in the historical doctrinal pronouncement. These days we hear warnings against the so-called Denzinger-theology, by which is meant the notion that one knows the teaching of the Church when he has categorized them. In opposition the new theology insists that the Church's pronouncements can be understood only in their context and their orientation. A dogmatic formula is usually an answer to a heresy. The polemical situation from which dogma arises keeps it from expressing the full truth. The Church concentrates at a historical moment on the point at which the danger of heresy is most acute, and then "throws a searchlight on that dark corner" of thought. But a searchlight puts other corners in a darker hue. And this creates the danger of one-sidedness, of impoverishment of the scene as a whole, a situation that is true not only of theological reflection, but of the official pronouncements of faith.

An unmistakable limitation and even, in a sense, an overshadowing of the fullness of truth is created by the defensive and polemical character of dogmatic pronouncements. Thus, Trent judged the Reformation *sola fide* as a vain confidence, but failed to "delineate what could rightfully have been intended by the phrase *sola fide*."[26] The historical and polemical conditionedness of Church pronouncements must be respected. It seems both necessary and almost self-evident that previous pronouncements of dogma must be interpreted in this light. The interpretation need not bear the character of a revision which gives a new and different meaning to the dogma in order to make it acceptable to a new era. But dogma must be understood in the light of revelation and of the intention of the Church as that intention came to expression in a given period of history.[27]

*   *   *   *   *

Very early after the first phase of the new theology, reactions were forthcoming that signaled intense apprehension of this new way of thinking. Garrigou-Lagrange and Labourdette saw in it a false concept of truth, and both feared the worst for the Catholic doctrine of the unchangeability of dogma.[28] Their criticism was

[26] Küng, *Strukturen,* p. 354.

[27] For the discussion in the last paragraph, cf. Rahner, *op. cit.,* pp. 55f., and Küng, *Rechtfertiguing,* pp. 109ff.

[28] R. Garrigou-Lagrange asks in the title of an article, "La nouvelle theologie, où va-t-elle?" (Whither the New Theology?), and his answer is: *modernism. Angelicum,* Vol. XXIII, 1946, p. 143. Cf. his article, "L'immutabilité du dogme selon le concile du Vatican et le relativisme," *Angelicum,* 1949, pp. 309ff.

based on the judgment that the basic idea of the new theology — the distinction between form and content, and representation and affirmation — had been rejected in principle by the Church when it condemned modernism on the basis of the unchangeability of the truth. The danger of the new theology, it was suspected, was that theology and official Church dogma as well would be watered down to a reflection of human understanding under the influence of the results of science and a steadily influential historicism. The criticism of the new theology recalls the condemnation of Guenther in 1857 because of his relativizing of the truth of dogma by means of the relationship that he saw between the formulation of dogma and the state of science which existed at the time the dogma was formulated. In response to Guenther the Church maintained that truth is always one and the same.[29] In 1867, the First Vatican Council also condemned attempts to interpret the confessions of the Church in a sense that agreed with the progress of science.[30]

Roman Catholicism in the nineteenth century was alarmed at attempts to allow science to dominate faith. Fear that the changeable notions of science would destroy the unchangeability of dogma seized Church leaders at the time. It was evident in Pius X's attack against modernism in the encyclical *Pascendi dominici gregis* of 1907. Pius X associated the notion of the evolution of dogma with the immanence and vitalist theories of modernism. Modernists were characterized as those who "most boldly attack the Church as moving on a path of error because she does not distinguish the religious and moral force from the superficial significance of the formulae, and by clinging . . . to formula devoid of meaning, permits religion itself to collapse."[31] Such pronouncements as these were recalled by critics of the new theology in order to show that this new way of thinking had already been con-

[29] Cf. Denzinger, 1655. In the Brief, *Exiniam tuam,* we read that Guenther's work disturbs "the eternal immutability of faith, which is always one and the same, while philosophy and human studies are . . . not immune to a multiple variety of errors."

[30] Cf. Denzinger, 1818: "If anyone shall have said that it is possible that to the dogmas declared by the Church a meaning must sometimes be attributed according to the progress of science, different from that which the Church has understood and understands: let him be anathema."

[31] Denzinger, 2080. The encyclical says that modernists hold that dogmatic formulae not only can, but that they *ought* to change. This, says Pius, follows from their view that dogma really is an expression of the dictates of the heart. The modernists, the Pope declares, are blind leaders of the blind who turn "eternal truths" upside down.

demned by the Church. Besides, it was pointed out, the rejection of such thoughts was still *in force*.

A new phase of the discussion began with the publication of Pius XII's *Humani Generis* in 1950.[32] This encyclical is highly important for an analysis of present-day Catholicism because it definitely is involved with several new streams of Roman Catholic thought. It not only takes sides against irenicism and existentialism, but also against "those who weaken the significance of the dogmas of the Church by seeking to free them from concepts and formulations long held by the Church and to return instead to the language of the Bible and the fathers." The encyclical views such efforts as part of ecumenical tendencies to build bridges between Catholics and others by means of exchanging old concepts for new ones. It was directed against doctrinal relativism, against those who think that "the mysteries of faith can never be expressed adequately in concepts, but in concepts that only approach the truth and are always subject to change." The problem of formulation is at stake in this encyclical, as it sharply attacks those who are disdainful of the terminology and concepts employed by the Church. It admits that these could be refined and improved, but insists that they must be maintained since what the Church has constructed is built "on principles and concepts which are led out of the true knowledge of created things."

The encyclical concretely contends that some concepts were given official sanction by their use in general councils, and to reject older terminology and substitute for it "hypothetical notions and glib and vague jargon of a new philosophy turns the rock of dogma into a bent reed." *Humani Generis* has a remarkable parallel in Gregory IX's warning in 1228 against "novelties" in terminology which veered from the language of the fathers, rejecting such novelties as "rash" and "profane."[33] Pius XII's criticism in *Humani Generis* echoes that of Garrigou-Lagrange's view that the new theology has similarities with the older modernism in its subjectivistic approach to the truth of dogma. But the practical question then arose as to whether *Humani Generis* specifically placed the new theology under the suspicion of modernism. The question did not get an easy answer. The encyclical contains many ambiguities in its description of the views it was combatting, making it very

[32] *Humani Generis* (*Some False Opinions that Threaten to Undermine the Foundations of Catholic Doctrine*), Denzinger, 2305-2330.

[33] "Terminology and traditions must be the servants of theology" (Denzinger, p. 442).

hard to pin-point the objects of the Pope's rebuke. For instance, he spoke of a disdain for the terminology and concepts of scholastic theology and, moreover, about the derogation of the teaching authority of the Church by those who see in it a damper on the progress of science. The Pope said more specifically that some writers approached the doctrine of original sin without recourse to the definitions given at Trent. He warns against the argument that the doctrine of transubstantiation must be improved in a way "that would reduce the real presence of Christ in the holy eucharist to a kind of symbolism." Finally, he criticized those who did not want to be bound to the identification of the mystical body of Christ with the Roman Catholic Church.

Understandably, not many felt themselves hit by such general characterizations. It caused no such crisis for the new theology as the 1907 encyclical brought on for modernism. But there is one point in *Humani Generis* that demands and gets attention, for it poses a problem that is very acute within the new theology. This is the distinction between dogma and its formulation. Pius XII was fearful that the distinction between abiding truth and its historically conditioned formulation could lead to relativism in regard to the truth itself. So, he cautioned theologians about the danger of modernism and its use of the same distinction. It is clear, however, that the Pope's letter does not settle the questions raised by the new theology. Modernism did underscore the variability in the historical process and with it the distinction between unchanging truth and its dogmatical formulation. But this formal similarity does not prove a similarity between modernism and the new theology.

The encyclical of 1907 saw modernism in terms of agnosticism, vitalism, and immanentism, and chides modernism for reducing dogma to religious feeling. This cannot at all be said of the new theology. They do touch each other in a number of questions and problems that both throw on the table for discussion, problems that according to the new theology cannot be avoided simply because of their association with modernism. Hans Küng has said in this connection that it needs no long argument to show "that our remarks may not be taken in a modernistic sense."[34] In the present writer's judgment Küng is quite right. But it is also true that, given the present situation in the Catholic Church, the new theology has a most important responsibility to demonstrate clearly that its outlook on dogma has no relationship at all to that of modernism.

34 Küng, *Strukturen,* p. 349.

In my judgment, the influence that the new theology will have on Catholicism depends on how clearly it can distinguish itself from the modernist movement.

Should the new theology be seen in terms of a revived modernism and be associated with the rebuke administered by *Humani Generis,* the forces of traditionalism are likely to be concentrated in a revived *integralism.* The word integralism says nothing in itself, since all it denotes is a desire for integrity or purity of thought. But it has connotations in Roman Catholic history, especially in our century, that brand integralism as a strong reactionary movement, an antithetical attitude toward everything which is not *obviously* of the same voice as tradition. After the condemnation of modernism occured in 1907, integralism took the form of vigilante movements on the hunt for modernism revised in whatever forms. Everything that sounded new or untraditional was quickly suspected as being neo-modernism. Integralism was said to be "idealistic" in its zeal to protect the Church against everything that seemed to attack its fundamentals. But in fact integralism was goaded by, and its character was formed by, fear. And in its fear it was disposed to make many unfair judgments.

Integralism has been resisted within Catholicism for its lack of moderation and carefulness, its failure to exercise charity and justice in its unnecessary arousal of suspicions.[35] Some of the Catholic reactions against the new theology suggest the danger of a revived integralism.[36] Behind integralism, undeniably, there is heard a summons to the Church to preserve its faith. But the manner in which the call is given betrays a misunderstanding of the real problems that exist, and should an integralist reaction gain sway, it would endanger not only the Catholic Church's efforts at renewal of itself, but it would be a threat to the common concern that Protestants and Catholics exercise together for the very real problems of theology today. The error of integralism is not its zeal for the purity of the faith but its blindness to very profound problems that confront the Church in changing times. In-

[35] Cf. L. J. Rogier, *Katholieke Herleving,* for severe indictments of integralism. He uses such barbed words as: "sick," "an epidemic of after-thoughts," "acute desperation." Cf. the encyclical, *Ad Beatissimi Apostolorum Principis,* by Benedictus XV, in which the Pope calls for moderation and adds, with an eye to the integralists, that it is not necessary to demand oaths from people to demonstrate the genuineness of their Catholic faith.

[36] Spadafora's attack on the papal Biblical Institute in Rome and the anonymous attack on the new theology betrays this kind of reaction. We shall return to both of these in Chapter V.

tegralism is always marked by a negative, anti-modernistic way of setting up the problems, a stance which is rightly resisted by the proponents of the new theology.

Ratzinger is one person who has laid heavy emphasis on the changes that have taken place in our day. He points to the period between 1907 (and the encyclical of Pius X) and 1950 (the *Humani Generis* encyclical), calling the latter the "final lightning flash of the anti-modernist crisis."[37] Ratzinger makes no brief for modernism; he only seeks to lay to rest the fear and negation of that period and point the way to a new willingness to come to grips, in courage and fearlessness, with the new problems that rise from a new situation. His sympathy is with those who have set aside the cramped ways of anti-modernist struggles and seek to build something more than a theology of prohibitions. According to Ratzinger the question of whether the narrow anti-modernist spirit will dominate the Church or whether the Church is ready for "a revitalized encounter with its own origins, with its brothers, and with the world" is the question that forms the background to the Vatican Council. Here again the close connection between the council and theology is made clear. Those of Ratzinger's mind do not have a drop of modernism in their veins, but they do appreciate that the dangers facing the Church in our day cannot be met by avoiding the real problems, for if the Church avoids these, it will lose its influence, if not now then for the next generation.

The issue raised by the new theology is certainly not new, nor is it limited to Roman theology. It has lurked in the background of many controversies in connection with the various terms, concepts, images, and propositions that the Church has used to confess its faith. We meet it in the ancient Church when all sorts of complex and very unclear terms were used which later only created the need for further interpretation of them; for example, in the christological and trinitarian controversies, such words as consubstantial, hypostasis, person, nature, and many others. The terms often evoked misunderstandings, and different interpretations of them created conflicts of opinion. The Church has been at its most lucid in its condemnation of heresy. But no one can deny that its theses have needed constant interpretation and that in its assertions it has

[37] J. Ratzinger, *Die erste Sitzungsperiode des 2. Vatik. Konzils*, 1963, pp. 39ff. That *Humani Generis* is mentioned in this context is, it seems to me, correct. Remarkable is the fact that criticism is rather frequently levelled at this particular encyclical which warns against treating encyclicals too lightly. Pius XII had said that the words of Jesus: "He who hears you, hears Me," hold even for the ordinary (*not ex cathedra*) teaching authority of the Pope.

employed terms that have had to be explained again and again. The real intentions of the Church's language have had to be clarified within the total message of the Church. The use of the word co-essential in the Church's condemnation of Arianism in 325 is very illustrative. This word had previously been condemned at the synod of Antioch in 268 because *at that time* it was used in a Sabellian, anti-trinitarian sense. After 325 it was a shibboleth of orthodoxy, causing some to suspect the Nicene theology of Sabellian or modalistic heresy.[38]

The problem of semantics does not suggest that the confessions of the Church are of little value. Rather, it underscores the need for a continuous attempt to make the content of faith more completely unambiguous and understandable. This effort is surrounded with dangers, it seems, but it does express the very intention the Church had in making the confession in the first place. The Church can accomplish this only by a constant review of the gospel itself, the gospel that the Church had in view when it used the terms it did, terms that in themselves were never wholly above ambiguity and that therefore required further interpretation in the preaching and the living faith of the Church.[39] To recognize this is only to admit that terminology available to the Church for its witness is never adequate for the gospel. The Church's witness can find no guarantee against misunderstanding, for there is no special clarity inherent in the Church's vocabulary.[40]

From all this, it is easy to understand why the history of dogma has witnessed many efforts to distinguish between the faith confessed and the words used to confess it, between terminology and matter, between form and content. These efforts are largely motivated by a desire to protect the content of the faith from false interpretations that could be plausibly given to the words used by the Church. We speak these days of the substance of the truth, not to separate form from content, but to acknowledge a distinction be-

---

[38] Athanasius uses the word homoousious (same in substance) most sparingly in his *Orationes Contra Arianos* without veering an inch from the confession which insisted on the term as a test of orthodoxy. Cf. Berkouwer, *The Person of Christ*, 1953.

[39] Cf. Berkouwer, "Vragen rondom de belijdenis," *Gereformeerde Theologische Tijdschrift*, 1963, pp. 26ff.

[40] Cf. H. Bavinck, who refers to such terms as "essence, person, generation, spiration" that are used in the doctrine of the Trinity as being "only auxiliaries called to serve the church in protecting the truth of Scripture . . ." (Bavinck, *Modernisme en Orthodoxie*, 1911, p. 35). Cf. also B. Lohse, *Epochen der Dogmengeschichte*, 1963, pp. 61ff. on the problems bound up with terminology.

tween them. The same notion forms a background to the controversy between Calvin and Caroli at the time Calvin refused to sign
the ancient Church confessions as proof of his orthodoxy. Calvin
accepted the substance of these confessions, rejected the biblicistic
view that words foreign to the Bible should not be used and
insisted that any terms may be employed as long as they served
to clarify the truth of Scripture. The Church found it necessary to
use such words as trinity and person, as it did the much debated
word consubstantial. But Calvin is impressed with the complexities
involved in many terms, and he admires the modesty of these holy
men who admitted "poverty of human language to express so
great a matter" and still used such words as were available "not to
tell us how the Father, Son, and Holy Spirit were indeed one, but
because they could not keep silent about it," "not to express what
it is, but only not to be silent on how Father, Son, and Spirit are
three."[41]

The problem of semantics and modes of expression used by the
Church is a universal one that happens now to be forced upon the
Roman Catholic theology in a pressing way. That the doctrine of
infallibility causes peculiar questions in this regard is not surprising.
We are forced to make distinctions when we see that dogma cannot be understood in isolation from the full life of the Church and
particularly from its preaching. Statements of dogmatic faith cannot be preserved as a group of propositions sealed off from all the
pressures of interpretation that come from the dynamics of real
life problems in a modern world. But the necessity of making distinctions causes some people to wonder whether the simple faith
does not become a subtle and sophisticated affair, too complex for
the average believer. There is a constant temptation, in both Roman
and Protestant circles, to set the simplicity of faith over against
the complexities of theology, a temptation that causes, when yielded
to, an abstraction of theology from the real life of the Church and
faith. But the history of the Church teaches us that a tension between simple faith and sophisticated theology, and hence between
believers and theologians, is fictional. It rises from the false notion
that theology could be kept simple if only it were a set of clear
and simple sentences removed from the complex dynamics of faith
and life. In short, theology is complex because life is complex; a

---

[41] Calvin, *Institutes,* I, xiii, 3, 4, 5. Calvin says that one ought not be disdainful of the terms that were used, but adds: "I could wish they were buried,
if only among all men the *faith* were agreed on: that Father and Son and Spirit
are one God."

simple theology is always a theology abstracted from life, and gains simplicity at the price of relevance.[42]

In view of the little room that seems allowed within the Roman Catholic Church for elements of relativity, historical conditionedness, responsibility, the problems raised by the new theology have caused a great deal of tension there. There is a traditional Catholic notion that the formulations of the Church if not totally adequate, nonetheless satisfactorily and faithfully translated the truth. The impact of idioms peculiar to the day were not supposed to have influenced the formulations measurably. Garrigou-Lagrange appealed to Matthew 34:35 ("Heaven and earth shall pass away, but my words shall never pass away") to argue that truth does not depend on its conformity with the measure of human knowledge in a given day, but on its conformity to the reality of things as they are.[43] This argument obviously is no answer to the questions raised by the new theology. In view of the fact that Catholicism looks back to previous doctrinal decisions in which, as all agree, specific philosophical notions are implied, it should be utterly understandable that now theologians should ask what the real intention of the Church was in its use of these philosophical concepts and that, thus, a distinction would have to be granted between the form and content of the confessions. It was unavoidable, according to von Balthasar, "that the Church in controversy should make use of the terminology of certain schools of thought in a given epoch, with the result that those who come later and try to understand what the Church said will have to know the peculiar vocabulary of past centuries in order to get at the meaning of the Church's declarations."[44] It is no longer possible to speak

---

[42] One need only consider the enormous reservoir of biblical terms and their complex backgrounds to see through the fictional notion of verbal simplicity in the Bible. Cf. the treatments of the Septuagint and Greek backgrounds to New Testament words in Kittel, *Theologisches Wörterbuch zum Neuen Testament.* One example of the complexity of biblical semantics is the wide variety of interpretations of the word *nature* (*physis*) in II Peter 1:4 where we are told that believers have a share in the divine nature, and also the difficulties with that same word in christological discussions.

[43] Garrigou-Lagrange, "L'immutabilité du dogme selon le concile du Vatican et le relativasme," *Angelicum,* 1949, p. 313.

[44] Von Balthasar, *Karl Barth,* 1951, p. 266. We note again how universally the distinction between form and content is used. Cf. Vollenhoven's statement that the phraseology of Chalcedon is "most unfortunate." He accepts the *intent* of Chalcedon, however, while pointing out that Augustine got along very well without the use of this church terminology. D. H. Th. Vollenhoven, *Het Calvinisme en de Reformatie van de Wijsbegeerte,* 1933, pp. 146f.

naively of an obvious meaning. Ages after the Church has spoken, people will complain of the complexities of the terminology, and will ask whether it is not terribly difficult ever to get at the real intention of the Church. There is, however, something docetic in this complaint. Many very "simple" confessions generations later reveal how completely the simplicists had missed the mystery. The fact is undeniable that *form* is given to faith the moment the Church puts it into words. And the moment form is given to faith a hermeneutical problem arises that creates an honest need for consideration of the background and the orientation of a given confession. To insist that there is a direct, verbal clarity in the statements of the past, apart from historical context and the need for hermeneutical principles of interpretation, is to betray an ignorance of Church history. The more, then, must we attend to the efforts in Catholicism to give full weight to the historical character of the life of the Church, especially where that historical character touches the infallibility and unchangeability of the Church's dogma.

What are the consequences of the evolution of dogma for the Church, not only in its theology, but for its mandate to preserve the faith? We would underestimate the importance of this question were we to suppose that all that needs doing is to translate the verbal forms of another day into those of our own, and that this task of translation will be simply a matter of finding modern vocabulary for an ancient idea. We are not involved with a formal matter of translating an older vocabulary that bears the stamp of another day, but with the far-reaching fact that the Church in its historical and human existence always speaks out of a limited horizon of *knowledge,* a limitation which has to be kept in mind as we attempt to understand what the Church said in the past.[45] Here we touch on the relation between the evolution of dogma and the Church's limited insight into questions about man and his world. The case of the Church's condemnation of Galileo — even though "infallible" utterances were not made in his instance — underscores this limitation. The question rises at once as to the erroneous assumptions that lay behind the Church's speech at Galileo's time and how the limited scope of the Church's knowl-

---

[45] There is a close connection between these questions and Schlink's important chapter, "Die Struktuur der dogmatischen Aussage als ökumenisches Problem," in his *Der kommende Christus,* pp. 48ff. Schlink speaks of the anthropologically conditioned forms of knowledge in "various phases of the development of the human race," in all of which phases the *forms* of knowledge materially influence the *content.*

edge has to be related to its teaching authority. When the new theology raises this question, we can see that it is concerned with far more than the semantic problem of the Church's forms of expression.

Enough has been said to show that we are dealing here with a problem that transcends semantics. For we are dealing with the translation of doctrinal pronouncements made during a time of limited and erroneous assumptions, with a translation therefore that must distinguish between specific areas of limited knowledge betrayed in the pronouncement and the doctrine that was pronounced. We could say that the Church's dogma was materially affected by its limited knowledge about man and his world, so that the Church's statements are bound even as to *content* within the limitations of the day they were made. The question of the unchangeability and infallibility of dogma becomes intensely acute here, for if the material content within dogmatic statements were assimilated from the epoch in which dogma is formed, a far-reaching problem is raised as to our present understanding of the infallible dogma.[46] The new theology does not wish to go in this direction, but it does seek to clarify the *intention* of the Church as it witnesses to the truth of God in each historical era. The question of the teaching authority of the Church was therefore bound to become part of the discussion surrounding this effort. This was impossible to avoid in view of the Catholic conviction that the Church is never submerged in relativity in spite of all the changes in the philosophical and scientific assumptions underlying doctrinal statements. The question, then, is how the infallible authority of the Church can indeed function as the guide star through the shifting sands of time. Prior to the time that the evolution of dogma was recognized to be the complicated phenomenon that it is, the infallible teaching authority could function as the final guarantee for the Church's teachings against all new ideas which could threaten them. The decisive speech of the Church was the guarantee for the continuity of the Church's life.

The First Vatican Council could give no answer to the questions that are being asked today for the simple reason that they were not asked at that time. All that really interested the Church at

---

[46] Cf. U. Neuenschwander, "Die Unwandelbarkeit der Glaubens und seine geschichlichen Wandlungen in ihrem dialektische Verhältnis zu einander," *Theologisches Zeitschrift*, 1950, pp. 358-375. He makes a distinction between conceptual forms and religious substance, contending that it is now necessary to "formulate the (religious substance) in a form of myth."

that time was the definition of papal infallibility, ruling out essential or personal infallibility on the part of the Pope, and insisting that infallibility was not a matter of direct revelation or inspiration, but that it rests solely on divine assistance of the sort that excluded new revelations.[47] The assistance given by the Holy Spirit was limited to the once-for-all closed revelation and to the preservation of the faith. The teaching authority is provided for the fulfillment of this task and the continuity of the Church is guaranteed along with it.

In the mind of the First Vatican Council, the Holy Spirit provides a problemless guardianship by which the Church is led as by a light from heaven. The problematics of the temporal conditionedness of the Church's speech did not figure as of any real significance. Thereafter, the distinctions we have heard so much about recently came into view only in the anti-modernist period, and then the distinction only signalled a danger to the dogma of the Church and could not be taken seriously as a problem *within* the Church. Thus, all the emphasis was put on the *semper eadem*, the theme that Bossuet underscored so strongly, and one granting scant room for any historical variability in the Church's teaching.

In our day the changeability of dogma has been given much attention, though without denying the infallibility of the Church. Schillebeeckx lays a great deal of stress on the human character of all that the Church says, but he nonetheless talks of the "charismatic gift of infallibility" that belongs to the Church. We do not have a subjective assimilation of revelation in a *merely* human response; we have a process of ripening insight into truth which comes about under the leading of the Holy Spirit as the "final criterion of a faithful development of dogma."[48] While the Church with its dogmatic proclamations is not lifted above the thought structure and the forms of expression that belong to our human mode of existence in one or the other period of time, the Spirit remains its guide through all the inescapable changes. Herewith we meet one of the most fascinating sides of the new theology. For it faces the question of how, if the teaching authority of the Church is engulfed in the problematics of historicity even as is

[47] The Holy Spirit was not promised to Peter's successors "that they might make known new doctrines by His revelation, but rather, that, with his assistance, they might sacredly guard and faithfully explain the revelation handed down by the apostles and the deposit of faith." (Denzinger, 1836). The idea of guardianship appears frequently in the decrees of Vatican I.

[48] *Theologische Woordenboek*, I, 1104f.

everything else, it be explained that this single aspect is able to escape the changes that are inherent to everything historical.

The distinction between form and content of dogma, representation and affirmation of truth, involves proclamations the Church has made under the charismatic power of infallibility. Such distinctions have not led to a devaluation of the Church's teaching authority because of a strong conviction that it is founded in the eschatological situation of the Church as the people of God. Since the Church is the historical arena of God's gracious will in Jesus Christ and therefore is the decisive and inconquerable locale for saving grace, it is impossible that the Church should be affected by the variations of history in such a way that it would fall from the truth and the love of God. The infallibility of the Church "is bound up with the eschatological validity of the salvation situation."[49]

We shall have to return to this way of guaranteeing the Church's authority, since it touches on the entire mystery of the Church and its indefectibility. For the present we must look further at the eschatological perspective which is associated with the Church's authority in the new theology, a perspective essential to its whole approach to the Church's dogma. The charism of infallibility does not, in its mind, have any relationship with a "supernaturalistic" kind of charism that is identified with various forms of mysticism. Indeed, it is expressly said that this charism has nothing to do with "a miraculous production of special clairvoyance,"[50] as though the Church had access to secret sources or possessed a unique intuitive insight different from the ways in which the Church normally seeks and finds the truth in the divine revelation. In a supranaturalistic concept of the Church's authority, the Church would possess these special sources, and the guarantee of infallibility would be unambiguous and transparent.

But if the authority of the Church does not depend on a miracle, the question rises as to how it works within the changes and variations of terms and concepts, and within the limits of human knowledge. The association of the charism of infallibility with the complex evolution of dogma, with all its temporal aspects, can be understood only by way of an *a priori* vision of the Church. The new theology is not preoccupied with a kind of changeability-unchangeability dialectic; it is concerned with the *a priori certain* unchangeability *within* all the variations of history. From this it follows that an understanding of the Church's teaching cannot

49 *Kleines Theologisches Wörterbuch*, pp. 369ff.
50 *Ibid*, p. 370.

rest with the texts of dogma, apart from their historical context, but that such understanding is possible only in the knowledge of what the Church, led by the Spirit, *willed* in essence to confess. In that respect the Church cannot err, and in that respect the Church in its authority is the infallible guide of men's faith. This confession of the infallible teaching authority of the Church does not cut off all further discussion for the new theology, as though infallibility were a sort of supranatural addition to the Church's normal speech; rather, it stimulates further study as to the essential intention of the Church that was clothed in normally limited human speech.

In this situation there is an open door to an ecumenical perspective, because while the speech of the Church is not sucked into relativism, it is acknowledged that the Church's teaching can be recognized only in the temporal conditionedness of human speech, since the Church cannot lift its speech above its own limited scope of knowledge.

❋ ❋ ❋ ❋ ❋

The encyclical *Human Generis* suggested that talk of a distinction between form and content in the Church's dogma was a spurious form of ecumenical bridge building. But we would only confuse the issue if we tried to account for the new theology by way of this explanation. Surely the new theology has brought a creative new element into Catholic theology compared with the "always the same" theme of Bossuet, and this new element does suggest that the intense concern for the variability and historicity of the dogmatic formulations of the Church may offer a point of contact for deeper understanding of each other by both Protestants and Catholics. This possibility is the more interesting when we recall that considerable Catholic pre-Reformation criticism had been levelled at the scholastic form that the Church's dogma was then taking, a form that seemed to be opposed to the biblical character of dogma. Dogmatic indifference has nothing to do with the new theology's offering of a better hope of mutual understanding. We may recall Luther's reaction against the decisions of the Fifth Lateran Council of 1512-1517. This council repeated what the Council of Vienna had said in 1311, namely, that the soul is the form of the body.[51] Luther thought that the biblical view of man was threatened by this scholastic way of describing the soul and argued that the source of this evil lay in the philosophical terminology that the Church was using in this case, a terminology that could

[51] Denzinger, 481, 738.

only obscure the depths of Scripture.[52] Today's Catholic pleas are made for a freedom from scholastic terminology which would make it possible to treat such formulations as Vienna gave to the nature of the soul (soul as *form* of the body) as unessential and non-integral to the teaching of the Church, and, of course, in no sense to be considered an infallible expression of the truth. We must remember that the intention of the Church at Vienna was to controvert a dualistic view of man and to maintain the integral unity of man. It attempted to do this by using the terminology and concepts available to it at a given period without wishing to canonize this particular terminology. In the light of this Catholic probing of the intention of a council, we may add that Luther had no argument against the Church's intention to preserve the unity of human nature, a unity on which no one laid stronger emphasis than he did. Who spoke more convincingly than did Luther of the total man living as a unity under the face of God? What Luther criticized was the terminology which the Church felt obligated to use. We certainly do not mean to suggest that the problem can be solved by getting at the sense of a certain term. An analysis of Luther's opposition to scholasticism reveals that Luther was not concerned merely with a formal problem of terminology, but with what he discerned as the matter to which this particular terminology gave form. And what the thought was involved in it was nothing less than the freedom of grace. Nonetheless, we may ask whether the anti-scholastic polemic by the Reformers[53] does not establish a point of contact with the discussions carried on by the new Catholic theology.

There can be no doubt that we have an intensely absorbing problem on our hands when we ask what significance one must give to dogmatic formulae and how these are to function within the total life of the Church. It would be misleading if we were to assume that the problem of the distinction between affirmation and representation involves only Roman Catholic theology. In fact, it is a universal problem on the agenda wherever the Church confesses its faith in human terms. It has vexed Protestant theology for long. One need think at this point only of the problem of terminology in the controversy about the Lord's Supper at the time

---

52 Cf. C. Stange, "Luther und das fünfte Laterankonzil," *Zeitschrift für systematische Theologie*, 1928, pp. 339f.

53 Cf. Luther's *Disputatio contra scholasticam theologicam*, and B. Hägglund, *Theologie und Philosophie bei Luther und in der occamistischen Tradition. Luthers Stellung zur Theorie der doppelten Wahrheit*, 1955, pp. 100ff.

of the Reformation. The mystery of the sacrament was expressed in a wide variety of terms. For instance, the word "substance" was important to Calvin, and the fact that he was unwilling to give it up was due to his refusal to take flight into the spiritualistic understanding of the presence of Christ. Besides this, he saw in the word a possible means for arriving at a consensus with the Lutherans. Obviously we cannot laden this word with the associations surrounding the philosophical concept of substance. The passage from a concept of substance to a confession that utilizes the term *substance* shows how tense the matter of word usage can become when one is not willing to sacrifice a term, but does invest it with new meaning.[54] The tensions that surround the term *substance* as it was used by the Reformers forms a parallel with various problems that presently engage Roman Catholic theology. It would surely be unfair to grant to Reformed theology the possibility of a distinction between terms and their real meaning and then to suggest that similar Roman Catholic distinctions are a suspicious device to get around Church authority.

It is no simple matter to distinguish the intention from the formulation and the presuppositions that underlie it. It is possible that certain non-Christian philosophical (Platonic or Aristotelian) categories influenced the Church's understanding of the truth and that these categories, then, materially as well as formally took root in the life and theology of the Church. In any case, the distinction between form-giving and content is not a simple device to demonstrate how the *truth* of dogma is continuous within the evolution and change of the dogma formulations. No one would dare argue that the words of John XXIII about the truth and the way it was expressed in other days or that the distinction between affirmation and representation can be used as a magician's wand to clear up every burning question.[55] Much more, it must be admitted that

[54] The Gallican Confession, Art. 36, is alluded to here. At the Synod of La Rochelle objections were raised to the word *substance*. Cf. Berkouwer, *De Sacramenten*, 1954, p. 304. Cf. the objections raised by Peter Ramus to the use of the same word.

[55] E. Wolf warns with good reasons against the temptation to think of the distinction between form and substance as a "magic key" to all problems (Th. Sartory and E. Wolf, *Die Konfessionen und das II Vatik. Konzil*, 1963, p. 48). Dr. L. Vischer pointed this out in his "Bericht über das zweite Vatik. Konzil," *Document, Centrum Concilie*. Responding to those who made much of the distinction, he asks: "Is the matter really so simple? Are not substance and expression much more intimately related? Would not a new formula involve far more radical surgery than is commonly thought?"

this distinction can be used to undermine the confessions of the Church, reducing them to a mere reflection of the self-consciousness of the Church of a given time with the effect that theology becomes no more than a projection of anthropology.

Is it consistent with Catholicism to dissociate the Church from the forms which the Church has given to its faith in the past? Has not the Church identified itself irretrievably with the forms it took during the Middle Ages? This is not an easy thing to decide, but even those who insist on the intimate connection between content and the form it takes and who recognize that the formal aspect often puts its stamp on the totality of the Church's confession, will not be able to make good on the assertion that the new theology is bringing something radically different to Catholicism and that it has no point of contact with the traditions of the Church. And the authentic Catholicism of the new theology and its anti-scholastic tendencies raise many issues for discussion with the Reformation. The new theology has insisted that its interpretation is consistent with Catholicism and that Catholic history even demands the interpretations given to it today. There is, in the present writer's mind, no reason why the new theology should not be accepted as authentic Catholicism, and, from the Protestant point of view, no reason to suspect the new theology of a soft, watered-down ecumenical spirit that does not enter the dialogue as representative of genuine Catholicism.

The problematics of the new interpretations will become more and more apparent.[56] They have already aroused heated discussions which go far deeper than questions of terminology. There is a discernible distrust in some Catholic quarters of any explicit acceptance of the historicity and variability of the Church's speech, for fear that it will undermine the belief that the Church has an unchangeable deposit of faith. Those who suspect the new theology's outlook tend to fasten on Paul's cautionary words: "guard

---

[56] The Catholic discussions regarding the problem of interpretation throw light on several discussions within Protestantism. For example, the discussions between Dooyeweerd and contemporary philosophers about various motifs such as the form-content and the nature-grace motifs. Though the problem of Church relations does not enter into Dooyeweerd's distinction, he does make use of distinctions similar to those used by modern Catholics. We refer again to his distinction between A. Kuyper's basic religious perspective and his working notions, such as the Logos doctrine; Dooyeweerd is committed to the former, but rejects the latter. The question remains how far such distinctions are imposed upon the truth and in how far they are forced upon one by the character of a given truth.

what has been entrusted to you. Avoid the godless chatter and contradictions of what is falsely called knowledge, for by professing it some have missed the mark as regards the faith" (I Timothy 6:20). The caution displayed in such encyclicals as *Human Generis* will not quickly evaporate; for the matter of distinctions between form and content of faith still evokes vivid memories of modernism. The fear that relativism will subtly become master of dogma persists in spite of assurances that the new theology accepts the infallible teaching authority of the Church.

If we identify this fear with a "conservative wing" of the church, we must not lose sight of the fact that its criticism of the new theology has roots in a long tradition[57] and that it represents a very existential Catholic problem. At the same time, one cannot avoid the impression that criticism of it is strongly negative, and that those who make it have no real inclination to face the problems put on the agenda by the new theology. The critics are hesitant to recognize the very intimate involvement of these problems with the real life of today's Catholic Church and with the undeniable fact of the Church's continuous involvement in the human and relative process of history. When the Catholic Church condemned Guenther in 1853 — a condemnation approved at the First Vatican Council — it did so on the basis of the faith which is "always and ever the same," in contrast to the variability of philosophy and science. In condemning Guenther, the Church assumed the inflexibility of its formulations of its faith over against the "threat" of the rising sciences.[58] This was very possible in the middle of the nineteenth century. But now the complex nuances and relations between what the Church has said on specific matters and the results of science are recognized far more clearly. With this, discernible shifts are taking place that reach beyond the Vat-

[57] Problems similar to those with which the new theology is involved played a role in the Dominican, Petavius (1583-1652). Petavius, on the basis of his affinity for both the fathers and Scripture and in scepticism of scholastic distinctions, tried to revitalize theology in his day. Cf. F. W. Katzenbach, *Evangelium und Dogma*, 1959, pp. 45ff. Emotional complications arise in the problem of the distinction between form and content by the orthodox memory of its use by Unitarians and Socinians. The fact that they used it, of course, says nothing about its legitimate use.

[58] Denzinger, 1655-1659. On Günther, see also L. Scheffczyk. "Schöpfung und Vorsehung," *Handbuch der Dogmengeschichte*, 1963, pp. 140ff. Scheffczyk sees Günther's ideas as an attempt to understand the truth of revelation by means of his analysis of human self-consciousness. According to Scheffczyk, twentieth century Catholicism is the first to try to bring revelation into some relationship with biblical criticism and natural science (*ibid.*, p. 141).

ican Council and affect not only the *theology* of Catholic scholars, but the official, though not infallable, pronouncements of the Church as well. These are problems that were everywhere evident at the council. A climate was present which allowed the council to face the new problems of a new day out of a deep concern for the Church. The climate was evident not only in John XXIII's opening speech, but in his total awareness for *nostra tempora*. The questions faced are not new in every sense. The confrontation with vital questions involved Leo XIII, and John's description of Leo as that "amazing pontifact" was more than incidental.[59] Leo's concern for the social problem, but more his sense of the responsibility that the Church has with periods of great change to be ready for an inner renewal so that it can truly be relevant to the world, had an appeal for John. Basically, the Church faced the issue of whether it had the courage to face the dangers that relevance always involves. Schleiermacher's question is pertinent here: "How shall the alliances of history go: shall Christendom be joined with barbarism and Science with unbelief?" This is the question that has haunted the men of the new theology. It is the question that calls for a common response from those who are parties to an age-old controversy. Not least for this reason we shall have to follow the profoundly significant developments within the Roman Catholic Church and its theology with intense interest — an interest stimulated by the very dangers implicit in a fearless confrontation with Catholicism. John XXIII and Paul VI have both brought issues to the open forum that touch on the very holiness of the Church. But the holiness of the Church cannot be separated from honesty and genuineness. And so when these two Popes call their Church to self-examination and renewal, they have gone on record as wishing to lead it into an encounter with great decisions. And we must be aware that these decisions will not be confined to the internal affairs of the Catholic Church.

Among the non-Catholic observers at the council there was no feeling that the inner tensions of Catholicism were being repressed or minimized for their sakes. From their perspective, they were also aware that they had no reason for smugness as they observed a council and a theology wrestling with so many acute problems. For the very problems that vexed this council are in large part problems that belong to all of us. And perhaps the relationship of

59 In the encyclical, *La Vostra Presenza. Cf. Mater et Magistra.*

the divided Churches will be affected as they all recognize the depth and importance of problems they share. Von Balthasar made sense when he said that we face many theological matters together on which we can be hopeful, if only, on both sides, we can rise above the ancient judgments that each has hurled against the other and that provide each with plausible arguments that nothing can really be gained by a genuine encounter.[60] This has nothing to do with a common denominator relativism which would nullify the kind of realism for which Paul VI called, but with a common sense that faithfulness to the gospel is laid on us all amid the revolutions of our time.

[60] H. Urs von Balthasar, "Christlicher Universalismus," *Antwort. K. Barth zum siebziegsten Geburtstag,* 1956, p. 248.

Scripture and Tradition

4ANYONE PRESENT AT THE FIRST SESSION OF THE SECOND
Vatican Council will long remember the moving discussion about the sources of revelation.[1] It was an
unusually tension-filled debate. The obvious Catholic
teaching is that Scripture and tradition are the two
sources of revelation; both the Council of Trent and
the First Vatican Council declared that these two sources are co-
ordinate. Hence, the fact that the sources (rather than the source)
of revelation were discussed as it should have been in view of the
general understanding that tradition stands alongside of and possesses equal authority with Scripture. But, in view of this, the
surprising element was that the subject should have aroused such
a tension-packed debate. Given the official Catholic doctrine, how
is it possible that the "two sources" notion should have been as
intensely debated as it was? Answers to this important question
vary. Some delegates thought that the attack made on the doctrine
was indeed strange, ill-founded, and illegitimate, for the theory

[1] In the schema *Constitutionum et decretorum*, the first chapter dealt with
the sources of revelation and the first section of that chapter with the two-fold
source of revelation.

of two sources of revelation is simply the traditional Catholic teaching about revelation, solidified at Trent. Others thought that every reason was present for a sharp criticism[2] because the subject as introduced at the Vatican Council did not reflect the teaching of the Church, but only that of a single theological school.

Before going into the background of this debate, we will note the results of it. After a lengthy discussion a vote was taken on the question of whether the council should proceed to deal with the subject at all. The vote resulted in a large negative majority (1368 vs. 822). But the necessary two-thirds majority was not attained, and the discussion was to have been carried forward. It would have gone on as intended had not John XXIII intervened. He called the debate to a halt in view of the large majority of votes against it. Instead, he named a new commission to review the schema on revelation. The commission was made up of the Theological Commission, the Secretariat for Unity, with Cardinal Ottaviani and Cardinal Bea as co-chairmen. This unexpected intervention by the Pope was generally considered a victory for the more progressive wing of the council, for the group represented ideas very different from those of the schema turned in to the council.[3] The differences came to light in the discussion when the report was criticized as being far too scholastic and not sufficiently pastoral and ecumenical.

The council was reminded that the aim of John XXIII in calling the council was pastoral and ecumenical. The Pope had, to be sure, declared that the Church was called to follow the paths on which it had travelled for twenty centuries, but he also insisted that the primary task of this council was not "to discuss discrete points of doctrine nor to repeat extensively what had already been said by the fathers or by older and newer theologians."[4] In our day, the Pope said, the great need is for the Christian faith in all its fullness to be presented to all people of our time. The Pope was saying that he wanted the council to be pastorally oriented with a view to a translation of the gospel of salvation so that it can be understandably and relevantly pressed upon the needs of our present world. The Church, he said, must strive to show the true profile of

---

[2] H. Küng, in *Kerk in Concilie. Tussentijdse Balans*, 1963, p. 197, called the use of the plural (sources) by the theological commission "a forecast of trouble."

[3] Cf. A. Wenger, *Vatican II. Première Session*, 1963, pp. 114ff; R. Kaiser, *Inside the Council*, 1963, pp. 172ff. Kaiser quotes Gregory Baum as saying that the Pope's intervention "prevented the smaller party from imposing its will on the larger party."

[4] In his opening message of October 11, 1962. Cf. *Gaudet Mater Ecclesia*.

the bride of Christ to the world, as it takes its place in the midst of our time witnessing to and addressing real people, not the least those who have a grotesque caricature of the Church — a caricature for which, after all, the Church shares responsibility. The Church must also, the Pope insisted, recruit the separated brethren with the fullness of truth. "What our times demand is a pastoral approach demonstrating the love and kindness that flow from our religion."[5]

The Pope's words formed the background to the criticism that was directed against the report on the sources of revelation. This report, it was contended, made no effort to come to terms with the new insights which the exegetical and dogmatic labors of recent times had come upon, insights which had already been able to create a new dialogue with the separated brethren. Here again the close connection between theology and the council was evident. The feeling ran very strong that a new theology should never be constructed along side of the real life of the Church, but that any living theology had to be a biblically oriented theology with the power and relevance to renew and fructify the life of the Church.

The discussion in the council revealed the striking influence that the new theology was having in the Church. Prior to the council the new theology was written off by some as a small school of radical theologians with no real echo in the actual life of the Church. Now it appeared that the new theology was far more influential than most had realized. Not all who voted against the continuation of the discussion, and hence against the report for which the council's approval was being asked, voted with a keen insight into the significance of the new theology. Not everyone present was fully informed of the things being written in the French and German journals almost every day for the past several years. But many of these were impressed and encouraged by the voices of the new theology as they were raised in council meetings calling for a renewal of the Church and a reorientation to new streams of thought, along with a plea for greater pastoral and missionary concentration, to say nothing of more ecumenical contacts. In the midst of all these questions which touched so sensitively upon the spirituality of the Church, the acute problem of the sources of revelation arose and quickly became a point of intense concentration.

✣ ✣ ✣ ✣ ✣

The question of revelational sources was, naturally, not the only

[5] X. Rynne, *Letters from Vatican City*, 1963, p. 149. See Chapter I on John XXIII's motives.

one that created visible tension. The relationship between the primate and the episcopate created just about as much heat.[6] But the tensions surrounding it were anticipated since it had been debated long before the council met. The debate on Scripture and tradition came as a surprise to all parties. The theological commission had written the report in the firm conviction that it was merely repeating the universally held teaching of the Church on revelation. Following the discussion and after the Pope's intervention, commission members tried to show in various ways that the report was simply a reiteration of official Catholic teaching. Trape,[7] for instance, pointed out that the report contained absolutely nothing new, that it was directly in line with Pius XII's encyclical *Humani Generis* which also discussed the sources of revelation.[8] John XXIII, too, he noted, had said that the Church accepted everything that God revealed, with revelation coming through Scripture *and* tradition.[9] Has not the Church always taught, asked Trape, that the whole truth is revealed, not merely in Scripture, but in both Scripture and tradition?[10] Indeed, was this not the kernel of the Catholic conflict with the Reformation notion of *sola Scriptura?* He summed up by arguing that to oppose the plurality of revelational sources is to oppose the Catholic Church.

✷   ✷   ✷   ✷   ✷

In order to get the full impact of what was at stake in this discussion, we must resort to what the Council of Trent said about Scripture and tradition. Trent declared that the truth is "contained in the written books and in the unwritten traditions, which have been received by the apostles from the mouth of Christ Himself, or from the apostles themselves at the dictation of the Holy Spirit, (and has) come down even to us, transmitted as it were from hand to hand."[11] It was moreover declared that the Church receives the truth in equal veneration for Scripture and tradition, whether it is on a matter of faith or of morals, and accepts the truth as it was spoken by means of the unbroken tradition that has been preserved

[6] Cf. Chapter VI.

[7] A. Trapé, "De traditionis relatione ad S. Scripturam juxta Concil. Trident," in *Augustinianum,* 1963, pp. 280ff.

[8] *Humani Generis.* Here it is said that theologians must continually resort to the sources of divine revelation (*ad divinae revelationis fontes*).

[9] *Ad Petri Cathedram.*

[10] Trapé is surprised by the "new opinion" for "if the words of the popes do not teach two sources then words no longer have meaning" (*op. cit.,* pp. 280ff.).

[11] Denzinger, 783.

continuously by the Church. The big question is whether this decree in fact canonizes, clearly and unmincingly, the doctrine of two parallel sources of revelation. The same question can be asked of the First Vatican Council which, in reverting to Trent, speaks of a two-fold source of revelation.[12]

The course of events at Trent adds to the trouble we have in determining the exact mind of that council. A report was brought in first which must be interpreted as teaching two distinct and parallel sources of revelation. For it maintained that the truth was contained "*partly* in written books, *partly* in unwritten tradition." The opponents of the two-source theory argue that Trent supports their view by rejecting this first report as it stood. Trent revised by deleting the word "partly" and making it read: Scripture *and* tradition. Why did Trent revise the report? Attention has been called to the fact that the parallelism of Scripture and tradition was criticized at Trent by Nacchianti and Bonuccio, who felt that by teaching two equal sources of revelation the Church was undermining the unique authority of Holy Scripture. These men were not confessing a contempt for tradition's authority, but they were making a case for the authority of Scripture being of such unique character that it could not be placed on the same level with tradition. In view of this discussion at Trent, modern theologians contend that Trent consciously turned down the equal status idea when it revised the report, and that therefore Trent lends support to the conviction that the two-source theory of revelation is open to another than the traditional interpretation of it. All agree that both Scripture and tradition are accepted by Trent as sources of revelation. The issue is whether Trent left the matter of their mutual relationship an open question.[13]

* * * * *

More than anyone else, R. J. Geiselmann has been the man to

---

[12] This supernatural revelation is "contained in the written books and in the unwritten traditions" (Denzinger, 1787). The title that Denzinger gives to the section — *de fontibus revelationis* (On the Sources of Revelation) — is not part of the decree, anymore than the phrase *fontes revelationis* that is found in the index. Cf. E. Molland, in *Schrift und Tradition*, 1963, p. 90.

[13] Cf. J. N. Bakhuizen van den Brink, *Traditio in de Reformatie en het Katholicisme in de 16e eeuw*, 1952, pp. 24ff.; G. E. Meuleman, *De Ontwikkeling van het Rooms-Katholieke Dogma*, 1950 79ff.; E. Molland, E. Skijdsgaard, and G. Ebeling, *Schrift und Tradition*, 1963.

bring Trent's revision to the attention of present-day theologians.[14] He believed that the significance of the revision was forgotten almost immediately after Trent. Under the influence of Melchior Cano, the theology of the Counter-Reformation lapsed into the *equal status* notion or into other modes of expression that came to the same thing.[15] According to Geiselmann it was not until the nineteenth century that the mistake was recognized, and a new attitude toward the Tridentine decree was born. He mentions the Catholic theologians Möhler, Newman, and Kuhn,[16] but recalls that it was an Anglican theologian by the name of William Palmer who first cast serious doubt on the traditional interpretation of Trent. Palmer concluded that the final version with its simple "and" was intended to be a genuine alteration of the original draft, with its "partly Scripture and partly tradition" phraseology. Trent, then, did not mean to teach a theory as to two sources of revelation. Indeed, claimed Palmer, Trent actually came close to the position of the Thirty-Nine Articles of the Anglican Church which, in Article Six, states: "Holy Scripture containeth all things necessary for salvation, so that whatsoever is not read therein, nor may be proved thereby, is not to be required of any man, that it should be believed as an article of the faith or be thought requisite or necessary to salvation."[17]

Palmer judged, as did Geiselmann later, that Trent did not really have anything to say about the relationship between Scripture and tradition. Though Perrone said that he did not know where Palmer got his information, the ultimate publication of the Acts of the

14 R. J. Geiselmann, "Das Konzil von Trient über das Verhältnis der H. Schrift und der nicht geschriebenen Traditionen," in M. Schmaus, *Die mündliche Ueberlieferung*, 1957, p. 125; *ibid.*, "Die Tradition," *Fragen der Theologie heute*, 1957, pp. 69ff. and *ibid.*, "Scripture, Tradition and the Church, an Ecumenical Problem," *Christianity Divided*, 1961, pp. 39ff., and especially, *ibid.*, *Die Heilige Schrift und die Tradition*, 1962.

15 Melchior Cano is so completely convinced that Scripture and tradition are equally authoritative that he contends that it is self-evidently implied by Trent. Cf. Geiselmann, *Die Heilige Schrift und die Tradition*, pp. 113ff. The Roman Catechism of 1564 does not use the "partly-partly" expression, but it does use the equally bold phrase *"distributed* in Scripture and tradition" (*quod in Scripturam traditionesque distributum est*).

16 For Möhler, cf. his *Symbolik*, 1864, pp. 354ff.

17 For more on Palmer, see J. Beumer, "Die Suffizieuz der H. Schrift in der anglikanischen und katholischen Sicht des 19. Jahrhunderts," *Catholica*, 1961, pp. 209ff. Though Beumer thinks that Palmer brings Trent and the Thirty-Nine Articles too closely together on this point, he does agree that the text of Trent does not rule out the idea of a certain sufficiency of Scripture.

Council of Trent, says Geiselmann, proved Palmer to have been right.[18]

❖ ❖ ❖ ❖ ❖

A great deal of controversy was stirred by Geiselmann's interpretation of Trent. Best known of Geiselmann's critics is H. Lennerz.[19] Lennerz argues that there is no shred of evidence that Trent actually intended a *material* revision of the original report. All that Trent did was give it a stylistic improvement. He is aware that the "partly" phraseology was criticized at the council as being contrary to the sufficiency of Scripture. But he notes that the critics stood alone in their opposition and that they were themselves not above suspicion for heresy. At any rate, the council did not enter a serious discussion of their views. All we know is that on April 1, 1546, the report read "partly Scripture . . . partly tradition," while on April 8 of the same year, it read "Scripture and tradition." The Acts provide no clue as to why the change was made. The only plausible conclusion is that it was changed for stylistic reasons only. Lennerz reminds us that Trent wanted badly to come out against the Reformation doctrine of *sola Scriptura* and that the change from "partly" to "and" in the Scripture-tradition scheme did not matter as long as the council spoke against the "Scripture only" of the Reformation. Trent demanded a respect for tradition equal to that of Scripture, which is all that really counts. Certainly, says Lennerz, it is ridiculous to speak of a victory for Nacchianti and Bonuccio. Trent anathematized the sufficiency of Scripture.

A clear-cut decision for one side or other in this argument is impossible. On one hand, the silence of the Acts as to why the change was made in the report along with the common use of the "partly" phraseology directly after Trent leads support to Lennerz' thesis.[20] On the other hand, the fact of the change itself and that it came after the protest against the "partly" language gives credence to

[18] Geiselmann in *Christianity Divided*, p. 45.

[19] H. Lennerz, "Scriptura sola?" *Gregorianum*, 40, 1959, an article reprinted in *Schrift und Tradition. Deutsche Arbeitsgemeinschaft für Mariologie*, 1962, pp. 39ff.

[20] Cf. H. A. Oberman, *Quo Vadis, Petre? The History of Tradition from Irenaeus to Humani Generis*, 1962, pp. 17ff., and *The Harvest of Medieval Thought. Gabriel Biel and Late Medieval Nominalism*, 1963, pp. 407ff. Oberman also recalls the statement of Cardinal Cervini on April 6, 1546, that though changes were brought in, they were not of any substance.

Geiselmann's argument.[21] Geiselmann's point has been gaining ground recently and with it a more subtle interpretation of Trent's real intention. Tavard, for example, writes that "Bonuccio's point was accepted at the last minute" and however little support he received on the floor, his criticism of the report and his remarks about the sufficiency of Scripture were at least "not contradicted by the final decision of the council."[22] Jedin says that, in spite of the "excitement" evoked by Bonuccio's protest, it had a "surprising effect," for the change in the report meant "a decisive position" in favor of the minority viewpoint.[23]

More important for our purposes than the fact of the change and the motivations behind it is the fact that this question has suddenly begun to play an enormous role in present-day Catholic theology and that Catholic theology inspired the Second Vatican Council to inspect the report on "the sources of revelation" with utmost care. That so many have now accepted the Geiselmann thesis and see in it the real Catholic teaching about the Scripture's unique significance is nothing less than amazing. A comparable view of Catholic teaching would have been out of the question had the "partly" phraseology been maintained by Trent. It is possible only because Trent allows at least the possibility of putting an accent on the sufficiency of Scripture.

The importance of tradition is not minimized. If it were, Trent would have to be totally ignored. What is important is that Trent said nothing that would put tradition on a par with Scripture in the sense that it complements Scripture.[24] Trent did not say, to be

[21] Bakhuizen van den Brink, prior to Geiselmann's publications, wrote that the council decided to make the change after the protests were heard, and that the revision meant "a reduction of both, (Scripture and tradition) to the single tradition of Christ and the apostles on which the church rests." Cf. Meuleman's remark that the change constituted "a reduction of both to a single source of revelation" (*op. cit.*, pp. 80f.).

[22] G. H. Tavard, *Holy Writ or Holy Church*, 1959, p. 207.

[23] H. Jedin, *Geschichte des Konzils von Trient*, II, 1957, p. 72, Cf. E. Stakemeier, who says, "the offensive parallelism of two complementary and separate sources of revelation was thus dissolved" ("Das Konzil von Trient über die Tradition," *Catholica*, 1960, p. 47).

[24] Understandably, Trent has generally been and is still interpreted in the light of traditional Roman theology. Bavinck, for instance, says that Trent teaches that Scripture must be completed by tradition since Scripture contains only a part of truth, while tradition stands independent of Scripture. Cf. H. Bavinck, *Gereformeerde Dogmatiek*, I, 454ff. Cf. also A. Harnack, *Lehrbuch der Dogmengeschichte*, III, 698. Cf. Berkouwer, *De Strijd om het Rooms-Katholiek Dogma*, 1940, Chapter IV, and K. Barth, *Kirchliche Dogmatik*, I/2, p. 609.

sure, that all the truth concerning salvation is revealed in Scripture. But since Trent did not make a pronouncement on this matter and was content to contradict the Reformation with an expression of great respect for tradition, the relationship between Scripture and tradition is a completely open matter. Indeed, the matter is so open that it is now argued that the text of Trent's decree is not in conflict with the notion that tradition is not a source of revelation on the same level with Scripture, but is only an *interpretative source*.[25] Trent, it is argued, leaves Catholics free to identify themselves with the very ancient tradition of the Church according to which *all the truth of salvation is contained in Scripture*.[26] This also opens the door to criticism of the view that, after Trent, became a traditional one, namely that tradition and Scripture are on a par as sources of revelation. Karl Rahner speaks of an uncritical theology that teaches two sources of revelation each with distinct contents."[27] In contrast to this uncritical notion, it is possible to speak clearly again of the unique significance of Scripture as being the "immediate Word of God" and the heart of all theology, our primary and unfathomable source of revelation.[28]

The new accent on Scripture, which is said to be in harmony with the ancient Church as well as with the medieval Church, coincides with the liveliness of present-day Catholic biblical scholarship. All kinds of questions rise out of the new situation, foremost of which in our minds is whether a new outlook is now possible in regard to the Reformation doctrine of *sola Scriptura* which, until now, has always been considered, along with *sola fide, sola gratia* and *solo Christo*, an exclusive Reformation credo.

[25] This has to do with the *text* of Trent. It does not exclude what H. Jedin writes: "There can be no doubt but that the majority of the attending theologians while not in favor of the expression "partly Scripture — partly tradition" did approve of the sense, namely that the dogmatic tradition contains a source of revelation which complements Scripture" (*Geschichte des Konzils von Trient,* I, p. 61).

[26] Cf. P. Lengsfeld, *Ueberlieferung. Tradition und Schrift in der evangelischen und katholischen Theologie der Gegenwart,* 1960, p. 120. The "and" is less partial than the partly-partly, he contends. The "and" signifies a great respect for tradition, but does not indicate a decision in regard to whether tradition contains truths that do not appear in Scripture (p. 126). Cf. also Y. Congar, *La tradition et les traditions. Essai historique,* I, 1960, pp. 214ff.

[27] K. Rahner, "Schrift und Tradition," *Das Vatik. Konzeil,* 1963, p. 85. Cf. also his *Ueber die Schriftinspiration,* 1958, pp. 8ff, and 80, and more especially, his article "Virginitas in partu," *Schriften zur Theologie,* IV, 1960, pp. 184ff. The article is about Mariology, but it brings the matter of the sufficiency of Scripture to bear on the question.

[28] H. Küng, *Rechtfertigung,* pp. 117ff., 123.

If the popular image of two equally valuable sources of revelation is *not the Catholic* doctrine, it would seem that perhaps the controversy between Rome and Protestantism on this score has been defined by the Counter-Reformation's misreading of Trent.[29] Is there a Roman Catholic version of *sola Scriptura?* Rahner considers it *absurd* to suppose that God's revelation "in broad outline" is contained in the Scriptures while there are other elements of revelation so different from the content of Scripture that they are derived from *another* source.[30] This division is unthinkable in view of the very nature of revelation; moreover, the "unity of the object of faith, the inner harmony of the divinely revealed truth render it at least "insufficient" to speak of two materially distinct sources of revelation.[31] Rahner expresses the hope that the Second Vatican Council will leave the question open and, by refusing to make a decision, let the matter stand where Trent left it. One may wonder why Rahner did not wish for more from the council in view of his severe criticism of the "popular" double-source theory, and especially in view of his own awareness that the threat of heresy is always present in indecisiveness. The answer is that Rahner does not expect the Church "to choose for our side" at *this time,* in view of the present indefinite state of the Church's consciousness. But he does hope that the current divergence of opinion will be tolerated until the situation is ripe for a definite decision which will do complete justice to the single source of revelation, the Holy Scriptures.[32]

We ought now to ask whether any improvement in the controversy between Rome and the Reformation is discernible in the changed attitude toward Scripture and tradition with Catholicism. If the disagreement no longer can be centered on the question of a single or a plural source of revelation, where does the disagreement lie? Geiselmann, in accepting the new interpretation of Trent, points to an ecumenical aspect that he discerns in Protestant quarters as well as his own. He mentions in particular the "rehabilitation" of tradition among Reformed writers. And on both sides, then, a new approach to the problem is being made. "The turning of Catholic theology to Scripture and the return of evangelical theology to tradition offers us the hope for a fruitful dialogue on Scripture and tradition."[33]

[29] Geiselmann insists that this is the case (*op. cit,* pp. 88ff.).
[30] Karl Rahner, *op. cit.,* p. 87.
[31] *Ibid.,* p. 90.
[32] Cf. Rahner, "Was ist Häresie?", *Schriften zur Theologie,* V, 1962, pp. 560ff.
[33] Geiselmann, *Die Heilige Schrift und die Tradition,* 1963, p. 90.

Geiselmann is correct in his remark about a new disposition in Protestant theologians toward tradition. Time was when the word tradition alone was enough to evoke negative responses. For, within the polemical situation, it was the word tradition that overshadowed the gospel. At present, theologians are able to think about tradition without the negative emotional accompaniments and as a result are rethinking the matter of Scripture and tradition themselves. Oscar Cullman is ready to say that the Roman Catholic and the Protestant viewpoints on Scripture and tradition "have drawn astonishingly close together," a judgment which antedates even Geiselmann's revision of the popular interpretation of Trent. Cullman calls for a discussion "without polemical motives," and his plea is even more relevant in the light of recent events. On one hand there is the *sola Scriptura* emphasis in Rahner and Küng. On the other hand there is the awareness among Protestant thinkers that no contradiction exists between Scripture and tradition, that the faith of the Church is not a product of an existential vertical between man and God without extension in history, but a product in which the "handing down" of truth, or tradition, in the Church plays an important and even essential role.[34]

This is not merely to say that the Church is influenced, whether consciously or unconsciously, by traditions of various sorts, a fact which itself has far-reaching implications. What is meant is that tradition has been of crucial significance for the spread of the gospel through the generations and to the ends of the world ever since *the time of Jesus Christ.* If the Protestant is able to free himself from the adverse connotations that a long controversy has given to the word tradition, he is able to recognize the significance of tradition in the handing down of the apostolic witness, a tradition which the apostle himself demands be accepted and preserved.[35] Tradition is not followed because the past is more precious than the present, but because a specific part of the past has been qualified by the unique acts of God in Jesus Christ. The eyewitnesses of these acts are direct witnesses to the salvation meaning of that which occurred once and for all and of its consequent

---

[34] O. Cullmann, *Die Tradition,* 1954, p. 55. Cf. the several articles on Scripture and Tradition in *Vox Theologica,* 1963. Cf. further, A. Szekeres, "Schrift en Traditie," *Kerk en theologie,* 1963, pp. 250ff., and *Traditie en Schrift in Kerk en Theologie,* 1964, pp. 19ff.; also E. Schlink, "Zum Problem der Tradition," *Der kommende Christus,* 1961, pp. 196ff.

[35] Cf. E. Schlink, "Themen des zweiten Vatikanischen Konzils in evangelischer Sicht," *Kerugma und Dogma,* 1963, pp. 178ff., and L. Goppelt, "Tradition nach Paulus," *Kerugma und Dogma,* 1959, pp. 213ff.

importance for all time. The function of tradition is implicit in the fact that the Church is built on the foundation of the apostles and prophets with Jesus Christ Himself as the chief cornerstone.[36]

The biblical condemnation of all kinds of human traditions is directed against traditions in which a pure understanding of what is *really* handed down is lost. Jesus faces the habit that certain Jews had of piling law on law and precept on precept, and of creating a tradition of *their* laws and precepts that darkened the very Word of God (Matthew 15:1-9). According to the Pharisees Jesus' disciples transgressed against the traditions, but Jesus responded by saying that the Pharisees transgressed the law of God by means of *their* tradition (Matthew 15:3). There are traditions in which formal allegiance to the past actually robs the past of its glory. The important traditions can be exchanged for pointless human traditions whenever the source of the tradition is a private person's convictions. The New Testament points to this possibility when it warns against vain philosophies which "agree with the traditions of men" (Colossians 2:8). The question that is decisive here is to which "past" a given tradition binds one. One can be bound to a tradition which steals away the key of knowledge (Luke 11:52); one can be bound to the tradition of Balaam of the Nicolaitans (Revelation 2:14, 15).[37]

A critical distinction must always be made when one binds himself with a given past. This is of special meaning for the right view of tradition within the Church. Here commitment to a tradition can only mean a commitment to the salvation which appeared and was preached at a given time in the past. And even here the question that counts is how the Lord of the Church, the Lord of this tradition, leads His people through the past into the present. When the Reformation declared itself for *sola Scriptura,* it wanted to keep alive the question of one's commitment to the Lord and to the gospel. The Reformers were not preoccupied with a formal problem of sources. The polemics waged at the Reformation were not academic discussions about the number of sources of revelation. If this were so, the motto *sola Scriptura* would rule out every kind of tradition.

But a closer look at the Reformation shows us that this is not the intent of the doctrine of *sola Scriptura.* All one need do is recall the

---

[36] Cf. I Corinthians 11:2; Philippians 2,6; I Timothy 3:20; II Thessalonians 2:15; 3:6; Ephesians 2:20.

[37] In this verse the word *krateô* is used; it is used also as holding firm to "the confession" (Hebrews 4:14) and to "hope" (Heb. 6:18).

fact that the Reformed churches committed themselves to the apostolic confession in order to see that the single source idea did not prohibit respect for other "sources." The Reformation call to *sola Scriptura* was not a call to biblicism.

There are several categories that we need to keep in mind if we are to appreciate the function and, with it, the riches of the Word of God. When the "single source" is isolated and is made an exclusive source, the tendency is to make of it a kind of depository of truths comparable to a sourcebook of Roman law. When this happens, Scripture is shrunk to the level of a thesaurus of proof-texts to be used as ammunition in theological controversies. To speak authentically of a source of revelation, one must do it in the context of the rise and the proclamation of salvation, in the joy as of one digging water from the fountains of life (Isaiah 12:3), which is to say, from *Him* who is the fountain of life (Psalm 36:10). The Scriptures call the Word of God the sword of the Spirit (Ephesians 6:17), "living and powerful and sharper than any two-edged sword" (Hebrews 4:12). This is the sword that has the power to pierce the very thoughts and intents of the human heart. We are asked here to think of the Word of God as the sword in the hand of the Spirit, to think of God coming *in* His Word as it is preached in all its critical[38] and exposing power, judging even the deepest secrets of the heart. The image of the sword guards us against intellectualizing and formalizing the Word of God by thinking of it as a "source" in a narrow sense. The biblical metaphor of the sword is more meaningful than is the figure of the "source," at least as the notion of "source" was used by those who approached the Scriptures as a source of dogmatic texts in isolation from the proclamation of the event of salvation. They spoke of the Spirit indeed, but in a way that suggested an incidental power which opened one's eyes to the "objective" Scriptures.

The Bible can be abstracted from both proclamation and the Holy Spirit in such a way that the real force of the biblical language about the life and power of the Word is lost, as is the witness of Christ to His own words as spirit and life.[39] An abstract view of *sola Scriptura*, in which the Bible is kept as a set of propositions to be consulted for proof of one's position, results from in-

---

[38] *Kritikos*, Hebrews 4:12. Cf. Revelation 1:16 and the two-edged sword in the mouth of the ascended Lord.

[39] Cf. John 6:63; 3:34. When Calvin speaks of the Scripture as coming from heaven "as though the living voice of God was heard from there," and when Bavinck continually talks about the living speech of God coming to us through the Scriptures, both are concerned with this same reality.

sisting on the idea of a single source of revelation exclusive of all other considerations. This is the approach one takes as a rule when the authority of Scripture is touted as the "formal principle" of the Reformation while the doctrine of justification is called the "material principle."[40] *Sola Scriptura* is turned into a solution of an academic problem about sources. The perversion is complete when it is supposed that a unique theology flows once the "source" is accepted as one.

That we are not able to characterize the Reformation by means of this formal principle is the more obvious in view of its prominence even in the Middle Ages. Kropatscheck calls the medieval notion of *sola Scriptura* a "popular Catholic" belief and insists that there was not a single medieval theologian who was against it.[41] *Sola Scriptura* got its significance in the Reformation, not as a formal principle, but as a pointer to a new understanding of the Scriptures and the salvation to which they were a witness.[42] When the notion was formalized, it could and did set Scripture *(sola)* against tradition. Scripture became an exclusive "source" instead of the "sword of the Spirit" — the Spirit of Truth and of Jesus Christ. With this, the full content of the gospel and its critical and saving power took second place to the need for an exclusive *source of statements of truth*. Only as we break out of the formal notion of the *sola Scriptura* can we be freed from the easy, but rather mechanical use of the "source" as a catalogue of true propositions and set our minds on the understanding of the full witness of the Scriptures.

The Reformation tried to defend itself against the legitimacy of everyman's private interpretation of Scripture by saying that the Holy Scriptures are their own interpreter. That is, the Reformation wanted to avoid arbitrariness as much as did the Roman Catholic Church when it invested itself with the ultimate teaching authority. Vexing hermeneutical questions have been handed down by both the Reformation and Roman methods of handling the problem of arbitrariness. But the problems are surely not solved by using the notion of *sola Scriptura* as an anti-tradition principle. The Reformation itself had no idea of using the *sola Scriptura* principle in this

[40] For example in A. Ritschl, *Ueber die beiden Prinzipien des Protestantismus, Gesammelte Aufgabe*, I, 1893. H. Bavinck refers to the "so-called" formal principle of the Reformation (*op. cit.*, I, 377).

[41] F. Kropatscheck, *Das Schriftprinzip der lutherischen Kirche* I, 1904, p. 440.

[42] Cf. E. Schlink, "Zum Problem der Tradition," *Der kommende Christus*, p. 201, where he insists that the doctrine of *sola Scriptura* is something quite different from biblicistic purism.

manner. It saw in the *sola Scriptura* principle a way of keeping the Church open for the power and the normativity of the total *content* of the apostolic witness in the sense of a critical and dynamic proclamation of the gospel of the Christ who is, indeed, the Lord of tradition.

We must now observe how the Catholic Church has faced the question of the relationship between the Word of God, the Scriptures, the kerugma, the Spirit, and the Church. Or, more succinctly, we must ask about the relationship between the Scriptures and tradition. The problem of this relationship became crucial during the nineteenth century at the so-called Catholic Tübinger school, with Möhler as the most famous spokesman. Möhler saw tradition, not as a quantitative addition to the Scriptures as though tradition were *another* "source" of revelation, but as the channel through which the *original* revelation lived on in the Church by means of the Holy Spirit. The relationship between Scripture and tradition, as he saw it, was so close that tradition was really the deposit of the original revelation in the life of the Church. Tradition was to be viewed, thus, as a living reality in the Church; it was the work of the Holy Spirit, whose presence in the Church is actually nothing less than the presence of the indwelling Christ. In Möhler's way of looking at the Church, "the Catholic notion of tradition loses the wooden, objectified character usually given it and becomes instead a living, dynamic reality with a character of its own."[43] The living Church and tradition are much more intimately and vitally related than is the case when the two are thought of as distinct, each having its own content, and each separated from the actual faith of the Church. The role of the Church's faith is so vital in tradition that Möhler can say, "Tradition is the living Word alive in the hearts of believers."[44] Möhler surely does not set tradition and Scripture in tension with each other, but neither does he separate them as two distinct sources of revelation. What is significant and outstanding about Möhler's view, however, is the fact that the Church's living faith is the center and source of tradition. This has led Geiselmann to say that Möhler rejected the Counter-Reformation notion of two sources of revelation and taught instead the

[43] J. Ranft, *Der Ursprung des Katholischen Traditionsprinzips*, 1931, p. 51.
[44] Möhler, *Symbolik oder Darstellung der dogm. Gegensätze der Katholiken und Protestanten*, 1864, p. 357. Möhler insists that those who speak of a few data coming from tradition while all the other come from Scripture do not display a shred of insight into the situation. Cf. J. A. Möhler, *De Eenheid in de Kerk*, 1947, pp. 40ff. Cf. also Y. Congar, *La Tradition et les Traditions*, I, 1960, p. 247f.

dynamic view that the Holy Spirit keeps a living tradition growing in the faith of the Church.[45] But in view of Möhler's break with the quantitative distinction between Scripture and tradition, and in view of his rooting tradition in the faith of the Church, the quesiton is asked whether he sacrificed the objective normativity of the apostolic witness to the faith consciousness of the historical Church. That is, does not the mere fact that the Church believed such and such establish a given doctrine as trustworthy tradition?

Karl Barth raised this question from the point of view of a non-Catholic who put all authority in the apostolic witness,[46] and so did the Catholic G. Sohngen from a similar point of view. Sohngen too asks the crucial question about normativity; he insists that the critical importance of the apostolic situation and witness for the normativity of faith cannot be relativized by setting the authority of tradition within the faith of the Church.[47] Sohngen pus his finger on a crucial issue. What is the relationship between the indwelling of the Spirit and the Church's subjection to the normative, objective apostolic witness?[48] Once tradition has lost its isolated and *independent* significance, how is the identity of tradition with the living Spirit in the Church to be harmonized with the *abiding normativity* of tradition? If authoritative tradition is identified with the *life* of the Church, is there a real place for the critical and normative function of the gospel? Does not normativity imply that the standard is distinct and independent of the thing being measured?

[45] R. Geiselmann, *Die mündlischer Ueberlieferungen*, 1957, pp. 193ff.; *ibid.*, "Der Wandel des Kirchenbewusstseins und der Kirchlichkeit in der Theologie J. A. Möhlers," *Sentire Ecclesiam*, 1961, pp. 531-675; also *ibid.*, "Einfluss der Christologie des Konzils von Chalkedon auf die Theologie J. A. Möhlers," *Das Konzil von Chalkedon*, III, pp. 341ff. Geiselmann has also been concerned with another Tübinger theologian by the name of J. E. Kuhn who, after becoming acquainted with the "partly Scripture-partly tradition" notion, went over to a non-quantitative, organic relationship between Scripture and tradition.

[46] Cf. Barth's sharp criticism of the Tübinger theologians for their "forgetfulness of the uniqueness of Revelation and the prophetic and apostolic situations," *Kirchliche Dogmatik*, I/2, pp. 606f. and 623ff.

[47] Cf. F. W. Kantzenbach, *Zur Deutung der kontrovers-theologischen Problematik*, 1963, p. 108. The problem arose when Möhler used the idea of a "national spirit" as an analogy. Christ, he claimed, used no different law than that governing all human life. It is possible that Möhler meant the Holy Spirit by his "spirit," but even so the problem remains.

[48] H. Bavinck said that Möhler's remark about tradition being the "continuation of the believed, living Word in the hearts of believers" was far more Protestant than Catholic. Bavinck's judgment here is influenced by his assumption that the Catholic view of tradition was simply that of a complementary set of truths alongside of Scripture.

If, as theologians are saying, the Spirit is the "soul of the Church," how can the Word function normatively *over* the Church as the Sword of the Spirit? Certainly the New Testament speaks of both Christ and the Spirit living in the Church (Romans 8:9, 10; Ephesians 3:17); the congregation of Corinth was a letter written by Christ "not with ink, but with the Spirit of the living God, not written on tables of stone, but on tables of flesh in the heart" (II Corinthians 3:3). This is part of the enormous mystery of how the life of salvation is "passed down" (traditioned) in the Church, and we would never finish trying to explore it. But we know enough to realize that we will not really explain anything by saying that the Spirit and the life of salvation within the Church are "identified." For the transcendence of the Spirit is not sacrificed by His indwelling of the Church. Without transcendence, how could the Spirit really speak to the Church and how could there be fellowship *between* Church and Spirit? For this reason we ought not to speak of the Spirit as "the informing principle of the Church" or as the Church's immanent life-principle.[49] The indwelling of the Spirit must be matched by the power of the Spirit *over* the Church; the Spirit's transcendence provides the mysterious and gracious character of His indwelling. Roman Catholic emphasis on the Spirit within the Church and upon tradition as a living tradition is not intended to *identify* Spirit and Church *with* tradition; if this were so, the canonical normativity of the apostolic witness would be forfeited. The time of the Church is indeed the time of the Spirit, but Catholic theology knows that by saying this it has not escaped the problem of *how* the Spirit indwells, leads, and rules the Church.

✻　✻　✻　✻　✻

This raises the matter of the canon, and with it the abiding normativity of the apostolic witness, both of which loom large in the Roman Catholic vision of the Church. The normativity of the canon wards off all kinds of human traditions which wear the guise of authority and which have pretentions of canonicity, but which in fact are not really part of the gospel and indeed sometimes oppose the gospel. The New Testament discloses instances in which the critical, sifting power of the gospel has to oppose human traditions which threaten the light of salvation. Catholic and Protestant recognition of a closed canon suggests that both are aware of the

[49] Cf. Revelation 1:7; also cf. Per Erik Persson, "Das Amt des Geistes," *Kerugma und Dogma*, 1959, p. 115, and *Schrift und Tradition*, 1963, p. 104.

canonicity of the gospel. Rome and Protestantism disagreed on the *reasons* for accepting a given canon and on the extent of the canon (e.g., the apocryphal books), but they did not disagree on the fact that the Church had to have a canon to which it had to subject itself in faith and obedience. Both knew that the Church had to listen to its canon. In this regard it is always important to remember that, though the Church was active in recognizing the canon, it did not create it; it only acknowledged the normativity of a divinely given authority.[50]

To recognize the canon is to confess the absolute sovereignty of the Holy Scriptures for the binding together of the Church and the gift of salvation. It is in this light that we must understand why Roman Catholics deny that any Pope creates "new dogma" either out of the material of the Church's own consciousness or by way of a "new revelation." They are much more ready to insist that revelation was closed at the death of the last apostle.[51] The crucial word in connection with the infallible teaching authority of the Church is not revelation, but "assistance." With this assistance, the Church is able to keep its eyes open to the decisive "past", with the canon remaining in and for the Church a *norma normans et non normata*.[52]

❉   ❉   ❉   ❉   ❉

Indicating how crucial the normative aspect of the canon is, Oscar Cullmann maintains that, once the canon was acknowledged, tradition no longer had any standing as a criterion of truth. Acknowledgment of the canon was "an act of humility" by which the Church bound itself forever to the apostolic witness as the

---

[50] Y. Congar writes that the intervention of the Church does not mean that "the church determines the normative value of Scripture: it does not create, it can only recognize a canon" (Congar, *La Tradition et les Traditions,* II, 1963, p. 174). "Scripture," he writes, "is absolutely sovereign." Scripture is the norm for tradition, not the other way around (*ibid.,* p. 177).

[51] Denzinger, 1836. Cf. the *denial* of the thesis that "objective revelation, according to Catholic faith, was not completed with the apostles"; in *Lamentabile,* 1907.

[52] Cf. K. Rahner, *Ueber die Schriftinspiration,* 1958, p. 56, where Rahner emphasizes the decisive character of the canon as the "bridge to the future." Cf. also what Rahner says in "Was ist eine dogmatische Aussage?" (*Catholica,* 1961, pp. 161ff.) about the canonization of the Scripture as "the abiding and irreversible *norma normans, non normata* (the normative standard which has no norm above itself) for all further dogmatic propositions" and as the "pure scriptural objectification of the apostolic kerugma" (p. 182).

authoritative interpreter of the gospel.[53] A fence was erected against the encroachment of any *productive* tradition into the truth preserve of the Church. The Reformation meant this kind of normativity with its *sola Scriptura*. It did not mean to posit the Bible as a "source book" of proof-texts. It did mean to bind the Church with its confessions and its preaching to the apostolic witness. Clearly, therefore, the phrase *sola Scriptura* was not meant to suggest an opposition between Scripture and tradition; it was meant to be a sign pointing to danger zones where the sound of the gospel might not be heard.[54]

The doctrine of *sola Scriptura* does not provide a kind of hermeneutical guarantee of a right understanding of the apostolic witness. The multitude of clashing interpretations of Scripture within Protestant churches is an obvious proof of the contrary. Moreover, heresy seldom is born of a discovery of a new source of revelation; it appears among those who insist that they recognize the Bible alone as their source of truth. It has to be shown over and over again, in the concrete events of the Church's life, that the *sola Scriptura* doctrine is something more than a polemical slogan and that it in fact indicates a real listening to the apostolic witness in communion with the Lord of this tradition.

❊　❊　❊　❊　❊

On taking a long look at these problems as they have been stirring anew as a result of the newer interpretations of the Council of Trent, we also are able to see that they put their mark on the controversy between the Reformation and Rome. A change is taking place in the controversy. Within Catholicism, a new and strong accent is being placed on the unique and normative function of Holy Scripture and the notion of two independent sources of reve-

[53] O. Cullmann, *Die Tradition*, 1954, pp. 45, 47. J. Daniélou's criticism notwithstanding, Cullmann's characterization does not necessarily imply a criticism of the new theology's position on Scripture and tradition. L. Goppelt writes in the spirit of Cullmann: "The tradition of the Christ event is taken up in the canon. Every 'spiritual' or apocryphal addition to that tradition is to be rejected" (Goppelt, "Die Tradition nach Paulus," *Kerugma und Dogma*, 1958, p. 232).

[54] Cf. G. Ebeling, "Sola Scriptura und das Problem der Tradition," in Skijdsgaard-Vischer, *Schrift und Tradition*, 1963, p. 100. Ebeling interprets *sola Scriptura* as meaning that "one binds himself to this wholly original tradition, that he will not allow it to be mixed with foreign elements, and that he allows the power of this biblical tradition to function."

lation is in growing disrepute. The problem of sources of revelation is gradually giving way to the problem of the Church and its exposition of the Scriptures. With the two-sources theory, tradition was seen as a complementary source rather than a declarative and interpretative aid. The older idea of tradition as a complement to Scripture was used as a weapon against the Reformation argument that many Catholic doctrines could not be found in the Bible. Hence, the Counter-Reformation insisted that a given number of truths, though not many, were found in tradition *rather* than in Scripture. Now, however, the new theology insists that Scripture is sufficient for *all* truth, and that tradition only interprets the truth of Scripture. Some observers have insisted that this does not make much difference, because a tradition that interprets can very subtly become a tradition that creates truth. But this remark could serve as a warning to Reformed as well as to Catholic exposition of Scripture. In any case it does not alter the fact that a shift has occurred in the methods if not the substance of the controversy.

Those who use the two-sources theory usually work with a quantitative view of the Bible. For instance, when the dogma of Mary's assumption was declared in 1950, the absence of any reference to it in Scripture was acknowledged. But, it was added, "The Catholic church teaches that there are two sources of revelation from which we can derive divine truth, the written Word of God and unwritten tradition. We know Mary's ascension into heaven through tradition." This sort of approach dooms any attempt at discussion. But now that the new Catholic theology stresses the fact that all truth is located in Scripture, we have a new meeting ground for discussion.[55]

*   *   *   *   *

The new theology sees tradition, then, as the authentic interpreter of Scripture. Tradition still is given great value in the life of the Church, but only within the Church's marriage to the apostolic witness. In keeping with Trent, the tradition of the Church stands alongside of Scripture and is given "equal honor" with it; the Holy Scriptures and the Church's translation of them are in full har-

[55] Geiselmann interestingly notes that the encyclical *Munificentissimus Deus* appeals to Scripture as the ultimate basis for the assumption of Mary. Cf. Geiselmann, *Der Heilige Schrift und die Traditionen,* 1962, p. 272.

mony.[56] This is also of a piece with what Trent says about the exposition of Scripture. The Bible may not be expounded in one's own wisdom nor in a way that contradicts the Church's teaching, for the Church is given the task of judging the true sense of Scripture.[57] The new approach to Trent invests this statement with high significance. Given the sufficiency of Scripture, the problem of tradition now centers on the right *understanding* of Scripture.[58] The exposition of the Bible must not be handed over to anybody's arbitrary ideas of what it teaches. Trent said this too, and cited words from II Peter to the effect that there are unqualified and irresponsible men who distort the Scriptures to their own destruction whereas in fact "no prophecy of Scripture is subject to individual interpretation" (II Peter 1:21).

Rome then posits the Church as the institution with the task of interpreting Scripture in defense against the individual interpretation that Peter speaks about. The objection to the Reformation is no longer so much that it accented too forcibly the sufficiency of Scripture, but that it was never clear on how the exposition of Scripture could be preserved against individualistic and arbitrary interpretations. There must be a unity between the Spirit of the Scriptures and the Spirit of their exposition. The *guarantee* of preserving that unity was given to the Church, according to Catholi-

[56] A great deal of discussion was aroused by this "equal reverence" *(pari pietatis affectu et reverentia)*. During the Council of Trent it was suggested that "similar reverence" be substituted for "equal reverence." Trent's maintenance of "equal" is used by critics of Geiselmann as a proof that Trent really meant to teach two distinct sources of revelation. Cf. A. Spindeler, *Pari pietatis affectu. Schrift und Tradition*, 1962, pp. 78ff. Geiselmann rejoins by saying that "equal" was temporarily changed to "similar" (after Nacchianti had referred to the word *pari* as impious). The new interpretation of Trent sees no implications here for two sources of revelation, but only the assertion of an authoritative interpretation.

[57] "Furthermore . . . the council decrees that no one should dare to rely on *his own judgment* in matters of faith and morals affecting the structure of Christian doctrine and to distort Sacred Scripture to fit meanings of his own that are contrary to the meaning that holy mother Church has held and now holds; for it is her office to judge about the true sense and interpretation of Sacred Scripture" (Denzinger, 786).

[58] We encounter this problem in St. Vincent of Lerins (d. 450) who talked of both the canon and tradition, "not as though the canon were not sufficient by itself in all things, but in view of the fact that the divine Word is subject to so many arbitrary interpretations and to such a variety of erroneous opinions, the one church has been given a heavenly intelligence to control the interpretation of the canon of Scripture." See *Commonitorium*, ed. A. Jülicher, 1925, p. 26.

cism. Now the rejection of the two-sources idea has brought about a shift in the way the guarantee afforded by Spirit works. (The word "guarantee," we must point out, is a word used by Catholic theologians.) In reference to the unfolding of truth in the Church it is said that "the final guarantee that the development of dogma will remain on the foundation of the Scriptures is only the assistance of the Holy Spirit which is promised to the Church and via the Church to its teaching office."[59] Rome does not, then, posit a creative authority which ignores the responsibility of the Church to keep listening (to be the *ecclesia audiens*): it believes that it has a *sure* help in its listening and its believing. The controversy as to Scripture and tradition centers increasingly on this *a priori* guarantee. Trent established tradition alongside Scripture, not as a second and independent source of revelation, but as a way of saying that the Church is constantly led to a right understanding of the Scriptures. With this, the Roman Catholic asks the Protestant whether it is or is not true that the Church has been promised the presence of Christ and the guidance of the Holy Spirit for its journey through the ages (Matthew 28:20; John 16:13).

We have now met one of the most profound issues of the controversy, the ecclesiastical-pneumatological issue. We would miss the point were we to suppose that Rome's emphasis on the guaranteed teaching authority of the Church means that an understanding of the truth comes without genuine human effort. These days especially Roman Catholics are feverishly engaged in the study of the Scriptures, and this study is not simply aimed at getting ammunition to defend the Church's established dogmas. Catholic biblical scholarship is presently taking all sorts of new paths and raising all sorts of new questions, including the question of the role of biblical scholarship within the official authority of the Church to judge the sense of Scripture. For instance, in view of the hard labors demanded by scriptural research as over against the Church's *a priori guarantee* of the correct understanding of Scripture, the question rises as to *how the charisma of infallibility really functions in the Church.*

This question bears a relation to many that fairly buzzed around the council at the Vatican. When the two-sources theory was upheld in the first report turned in to the council on this subject, the debate that followed was obviously not a mere difference of opinion between two established schools of thought. A completely *new in-*

---

[59] K. Rahner and H. Vorgrimler, *Kleines theologisches Wörterbuch*, 1961. See the article on "Tradition."

sight into the question of tradition accompanied the growing acknowledgment of the unique significance and the material sufficiency of the Scriptures as the source of revelation. Though the Roman Church was surely not about to enter a period of relativism and common denominator ecumenicity, new vistas were being opened for the old controversy about *sola Scriptura*. But the moment that a new approach was opened, the discussion introduced a new aspect of the *central* question. This is the question of the assitance given to the Church in its understanding of the Word of God. Of intense interest is the fact that so many questions which became genuinely relevant to the course of the council — to say nothing of the future course of the Catholic Church, and also to say nothing of the fact that the same questions touch Reformed theology very sensitively — center on the right understanding of the Scriptures. We shall, then, turn next to the relationship between Scripture Exegesis and Teaching Authority.

Exegesis and Doctrinal Authority

5 THE COUNCIL OF TRENT CONFESSED THAT GOD IS THE Author of the Old and New Testaments and that His authorship stretches through all the books in all their parts.[1] The First Vatican Council took over this doctrine of Scripture, and it is the teaching of the Roman Catholic Church today. The holy books were written by men inspired of the Holy Spirit and were given to the Church as the pure and canonical Word of God.[2] The Second Vatican Council has expressed no doubt or hesitation in this view of the Bible. The inspiration of Scripture, thus, seems to provide a settled thesis, untouchable and unproblematic, forming a tensionless doctrine of Scriptural normativity in the background of the Church's life.

A closer look however, reveals, that for some time a host of knotty questions have hovered around this confession. The confession itself is not being questioned, but the concrete significance and the implications of the confession are subjects of intense dispute. The astounding quantity and the increasing intensity of biblical studies carried on in the Roman Church have led to inescapable problems, especially as the Scriptures have been approached with

[1] Cf. Denzinger, 783, 784.
[2] Ibid., 1787, 1788.

112

the help of scientific methods, and as scholars have become increasingly convinced that the use of scientific aids to research into the biblical literature need not involve a less profound reverence for the Bible. The Church has not been neutral in the face of these studies, but has in fact encouraged them. Three very famous encyclicals demonstrate the Church's involvement in biblical studies; *viz.* Leo XIII's *Providentissimus Deus* of 1893, Benedictus XV's *Spiritus Paraclitus* of 1920, and Pius XII's *Divino Afflante Spiritu* of 1943. The first two of these encyclicals are apologetic; the "true art of critical discipline" is contrasted to higher criticism.[3] Benedict XV uses Jerome as an example of the scholar who finds refuge in Scripture in the face of any intellectual dilemma.[4] The apologetic of the encyclicals is aimed primarily at such modern errors as the limitation of inspiration to the religious side of Scripture. The *purpose* of Scriptural study, we are told, is the garnering of arguments to "defend, illuminate and maintain the dogmas of the faith."[5] And in their work, biblical scholars are above all expected to hold firmly to and defend the Catholic teaching about the inspiration of the Bible.[6]

Pius XII's *Divino Afflante Spiritu* carries a hint of new directions. Though Pius praises Leo XIII for defending the complete authority of Scripture against critical attacks, he nonetheless manifests another tendency. He is not content to assert the Scriptural authority but introduces the question of the *nature* of that authority in view of the Church's confrontation with problems unknown to Leo.[7] The image of Scripture as a well-stocked arsenal for use against all heresy makes way for a recognized need of bringing the traditional view of Scripture into relevant encounter with "new and not inconsiderable difficulties" and for making use of every scientific aid available for this purpose. The emphasis given to this point causes many to see in this encyclical a turning point in Roman Catholic biblical studies. For in it the Pope waved scholars on into a new

---

[3] *Providentissimus Deus.*

[4] *Spiritus Paraclitus.*

[5] *Ibid.*

[6] *Ibid.*

[7] I do not mean to isolate this encyclical from the enormous work that had been done before 1943 and on which much of the 1943 encyclical was based. Lagrange (d. 1938) used the historico-literary method, and for his work received "singular tokens of unusual favor by Pope Leo XIII" (E. J. Byrne, "Catholic Tradition and Biblical Criticism," *Mémorial Lagrange*, 1940, p. 234). See as well the chapter in the same collection by J. M. T. Barton, "Recent Catholic Exegesis in English-speaking Lands."

path and told them to walk there in freedom. The fact is the more striking in view of the circumstances of the writing: the encyclical was published just after an effort was made to get the Pope to warn soundly against the dangers of biblical research. Dain Cohenel (pseudonym for Dolindo Ruotolo) directed a brochure to the Pope in which he warned the pontiff against the use of higher critical methods by Catholic scholars, accusing some of these scholars of creeping modernism. The Biblical Commission, with Tisserant as chairman, defended scientific methods in biblical study against Cohenel's attack.[8] And the encyclical was probably born of the commission's defense. In any case, a new approach was manifestly afoot.

The encyclical emphasized the necessity of interpreting the Bible according to its own intent and purpose. Pius exhorted scholars to study the inspired writer's times, their source materials and their individual styles. All these are of great importance for a proper understanding of the Bible, he argued, especially since ancient Eastern writers did not ordinarily speak in such literal terms as Western writers use. We must know how the ancient Easterners made use of poetry, how they wrote history, and how they set down laws in writing. In effect, Pius was asking scholars to remember that the Word of God is written in the language of men, of particular men of a particular time. Inspiration is not brought into question. Indeed, the Pope contended, the doctrine of inspiration, if we take it seriously, forces us to recognize that inspired writers make use of their own powers and talents, a fact which if neglected can only sterilize our ability to understand what they wrote.[9]

Pius' writing is unblemished by fear or provincialism in the face of modern-day problems; far from supporting that all new problems find their solution in past answers, it is filled with courage for the future.[10] It had the effect of stimulating biblical scholars to greater

---

[8] Cf. J. Levie, *La bible parole humaine et message de Dieu*, 1958, pp. 157ff. and H. von Soden, "Papst Pius XII über die Förderung biblischer Studien," *Urchristentum und Geschichte*, II, 1956, p. 185. The statement of the Biblical Commission, found in Denzinger-Schönmetzer, 3792-3793, is directed against the tract called: *Un gravissimo pericole per la Chiesa e per le anime*. The commission opposes the "suspicions of exegetical science" betrayed in the tract.

[9] *Divino Afflante Spiritu*.

[10] "Gone completely is the negative tone of warnings and threat. In their place we find a fresh wind of freedom and confidence through the papal writings, which reveal no trace of fear and suspicion" (H. Van Soden, *op. cit.*, p. 184).

freedom in biblical scholarship.[11] The differences that Pius introduced into biblical studies can be seen by recalling how the Biblical
Commission established by Leo XIII in 1902 operated. This commission was extremely negative; it devoted itself mostly to warnings against higher criticism and exhortations to caution. Between
1902 and 1905, the questions the commission faced were mainly
canonical and exegetical: the authorship of the Pentateuch,[12] the
authorship and historical trustworthiness of John's Gospel,[13]
deutero-Isaiah,[14] the first three chapters of Genesis,[15] the authorship and dates of the Psalms,[16] the synoptic problem,[17] the accuracy
of Acts,[18] the authorship of several Pauline epistles[19] and of
Hebrews.[20]

Now the question of the significance and pertinence of these encyclicals had to be faced. When certain exegetes ignored a warning
by Pius X that historical books of the Bible were to be literally
interpreted, the Pope insisted that they were conscience-bound to

---

[11] Of interest also has been the attention given the original text and the call
for a fresh translation. The decree of Trent on the Vulgate had to be dealt
with in this regard. For the "authenticity" of the Vulgate was established by
its consistent use through the centuries, according to the encyclical of 1943.
But the "authenticity" meant that the Vulgate was free from errors "in matters
of faith and morals." This left open the question of its critical and its juridical
authenticity. The problems implied in this were actually alluded to earlier. For
example, N. Peters said in 1905 that according to the Vulgate, Job 19:24f.
implies the resurrection of the flesh while this is in fact dubious. But the text
remains a "proof text for the dogma of the resurrection of the flesh because
the authority of the church covers it" (N. Peters, *Die Grundsätzliche Stellung
der Kath. Kirche zur Bibelforschung*, 1905, p. 21). Later, all this would
change. R. Schnackenburg recalls the "not insignificant error" the Vulgate
makes in translating I Corinthians 15:51. The Vulgate reads "we shall all be
raised, but shall *not* all be changed" *(omnes quidem resurgemus, sed non
omnes immutabimur)* which is at odds with the Greek text. Schnackenburg
then asks whether we ought to speculate further about the authenticity of the
Vulgate text (*Exegese und Dogmatik*, 1962, pp. 126f.).

[12] Denzinger, 1997.

[13] *Ibid.*, 2110 (1907).

[14] *Ibid.*, 2115 (1908).

[15] *Ibid.*, 2121 (1909).

[16] *Ibid.*, 2129f. (1910).

[17] *Ibid.*, 2148-2165 (1912).

[18] *Ibid.*, 2166-2171 (1913).

[19] *Ibid.*, 2172 (1913).

[20] *Ibid.*, 2176-2178 (1914).

follow the instructions of the Biblical Commission[21] and that failure to do so made one guilty of insubordination and disbedience. An interesting illustration of the change that has occurred since Pius X is the acceptance of deutero-Isaiah by the translation "La Sainte Bible" under the direction of the Dominican school of biblical studies in Jerusalem in spite of the fact that the notion of deutero-Isaiah was emphatically condemned in 1908. The conservatism of the Biblical Commission of that time was doubtless a reaction against modernism. Though at that time problematics of a later day were beginning to show through, the official line was that of exceeding caution.

Time went on, and it appeared that the Church's answer to modernism had not answered a single question raised by modern biblical studies. What A. Kuyper recognized as the "Promethean labors" of the higher critics of his day, labors not barren of good fruit,[22] were not lost on the Roman Catholic Church. Time and again, the Biblical Commission had to give up standpoints taken earlier, and in doing so to call attention to the relative authority of its own positions. By the time the first smoke of the commission's attack on modernism had evaporated, the commission had to give room to a more positive, less reactionary and defensive approach.[23] Later it was recognized that the panic created by modernism was premature, and that the trails blazed by modernism could not be followed in a legitimate and responsible manner without fear and inhibitions.

❊   ❊   ❊   ❊   ❊

The shifts that have gradually taken place in Catholic biblical studies do not lend themselves to neat description. There is surely an unavoidable relationship between an increased concentration on the witness of Scripture and several changes in point of view which

[21] Cf. Denzinger, 2113. The Biblical Commission, while it did not forbid further research, did set itself as a standard of the carefulness that ought to mark exegetes. The Biblical Commission is also said to "have had a suspicion of Catholic exegetes."

[22] A. Kuyper, *De hedendaagse Schriftkritiek in haar bedenkeljike strekking voor de gemeente des levenden Gods,* 1881, p. 29.

[23] Cf. H. Hermelink, *Die Kathol. Kirche unter den Pius-päpsten des 20. Jahrhunderts,* 1949, pp. 106-113. We may recall the way things went from the time the discussion of the textual-critical problem of I John 5:7 (or 8, depending on the version) received a negative response in 1897 until the statement of the Holy Office in 1927 which left room for textual-critical questions. It was then (1927) said that the negative criticism of 1897 was directed, not so much against the science of textual criticism as against the "boldness of individual teachers."

have gradually won a consensus, and in which there is hardly any vestige of the attitude that prevailed at the beginning of the century.[24] The encyclical of 1943 played a part in the change, as is evident in the well-known letter that the Biblical Commission wrote to Cardinal Suhard in 1948. In response to questions which Suhard had sent to Pius XII, the Pope ordered the Biblical Commission to study the matter of the authorship of the Pentateuch and the question of the historicity of the first eleven chapters of Genesis. The results of the commission's inquiry, approved by the Pope in an audience given to its secretary, one Jacob M. Voste, gave to scholars a new freedom within "the limits of the teachings handed down by the church." The commission's letter appeals to the 1943 encyclical in suggesting that biblical scholars give due attention to the literary genre of the Scriptures, in which the writers accommodated themselves, by use of simple and metaphorical language, to the limited knowledge of an intellectually primitive people.[25]

The commission recalled that the first part of Genesis raises problems that were not apparent at the turn of the century. At the time of earlier Church pronouncements, Genesis 1-3 was assumed to be history, and such biblical narratives as the creation of the world and of man, the single origin of the human race, and the creation of woman from the body of man were not subjects of differing interpretations. Suhard's letter reflected the changes that had taken place since then; it raised the question of how such matters as the literary, scientific, and historico-cultural backgrounds to these chapters should be brought to bear on their interpretation. Thus, in 1955, the commission made it clear that it approved of the application of these factors to the interpretation of Genesis. And in doing so, it stamped previous statements of the Biblical Commission as being unhelpful for biblical scholarship of today. Old pronouncements reflected the tensions of their day and could not give direction to Catholic biblical scholarship of the present time. But, though this was significant, it also gave greater urgency to the deeper question of how a free biblical exegesis could

[24] This is parallel to the privilege of private Bible reading which was furthered by the appearance of many new Catholic translations. We may compare the present encouragement given to Bible reading by all believers to the papal bull (*Unigenitus Dei Filius*) of 1713 which condemned the proposition that "the reading of the Holy Scriptures is for all."

[25] Cf. Denzinger-Schönmetzer, 3862. The letter is found in the addendum to the encyclical *Divino Afflante Spiritu.*

function while biblical scholars were subject still to the teaching authority of the church.[26]

The shifts in biblical interpretation are most obvious in the case of Old Testament studies. The Genesis stories were beginning to be studied in terms of their religious *intent*. The creation stories were openly said to be not journalistic accounts of the creation, accounts dictated by supernatural revelation, but as witnesses to the reality, the meaning, and the purpose of creation, witnesses clothed in the garb of history. No Catholic scholar has denied the inspiration of the accounts. But inspiration was understood as a work of the Spirit which fully respected the human character of the writers, and put that human element into the service of divine revelation without in any sense destroying the human servant.

The change in viewpoint is demonstrated at several specific points. Karl Rahner writes, for example, that an increasing number of theologians see in the creation of Eve from Adam's rib only the important truth that man and woman are of the same essence. Rahner accepts this interpretation himself, without any sense of restraint from the pronouncements of the Biblical Commission. Rahner insists that such views as this are not born of a critical rejection of the literal reading of the story. Rather, they are born of an effort to give the *original sense* of the material its due, to allow the literal reading to speak according to its own peculiar literary genre. In this way, the literal text is not the less, but the more respected.[27] Generally, the dangers of *missing* the divine sense of

[26] For an insight into the biblical questions alive at the time of the Biblical Commission one can well consult the two encyclicals directed against modernism in 1907: *Lamentabili* and *Pascendi dominici gregis*. The severity of these encyclicals has suggested a strong contrast between Leo XIII and Pius X. Cf. Kübel, *Geschichte des Katholischen Modernismus*, 1909, pp. 151ff. Others contend that the severity was simply the result of the Pope's keen awareness of the dangers implicit in modernism. Cf. N. Peters, *Papst Pius X und das Bibelstudium*, 1906. *Humani Generis* (1950) has been called a set-back for progressive Catholic theology as compared with the 1943 encyclical. So, for example, in H. Grass, *Die Kath. Lehre von der Heiligen Schrift und von der Tradition*, 1954, p. 62. Notable is the fact that, on the other hand, the appeal to Cardinal Suhard's letter has been criticized as being an erroneous interpretation of the encyclical.

[27] Overhage-Rahner, *Das Problem der Hominisation*, 1961, pp. 34ff. Cf. P. Schoonenberg, who interprets the decretal of 1909 in the light of the encyclical of 1943. Schoonenberg, *Het Geloof van ons Doopsel*, I, 1955, p. 145. Cf. J. Feiner, "Ursprung, Urstand, und Urgeschichte der Menscheit," *Fragen der Theologie heute*, p. 246. Both Schoonenberg and Feiner interpret the story of Eve's creation as a dramatic expression of the theological truth of the essential sameness of woman with man.

Scripture in this approach are recognized. But the awareness of dangers is coupled with a realization that simplistic historical interpretations of former exegesis can no longer be maintained if scholars are to honor the principles laid down in the encyclical *Divino Afflante Spiritu.*[28]

The shifts that have taken place in response to the question of evolution are as notable as those about the text of Genesis. The Roman Catholic Church in the past has unambiguously ruled out every form of evolution. The theory of evolution was seen only as a threat to faith. But this has changed now that the development of science has gone hand in hand with an altered understanding of Scripture. The change is discernible in the encyclical *Humani Generis* which otherwise is full of the severest attacks against many new streams of thought. This encyclical states that the Church "leaves the doctrine of evolution an open question as long as it confines its speculations to the development, from other living matter, of the human body. That souls are immediately created by God is a view which the Catholic faith imposes on us." This remarkable statement was issued at the same time that the Pope was saying that Catholic faith could possibly accept the notion of modern physics that the earth is at least five million years old. Clearly, Pius XII wanted to come to terms with specific conclusions of science in the conviction that no scientific fact could ever endanger faith, and his conviction on this point was expressed in his statement about evolution.[29] If the period just before 1940 could be called the time of silent indulgence of "evolution enamored" publications, the present time could be called the time of "theology's emancipation of the theory of evolution" from suspicion of unbelief. More and more Catholic scholars are convinced of the "harmony between biological evolution and the teaching of the Church."[30] The limits set up by the Church's authority are not being destroyed or even confused.

[28] Cf. H. Urs von Balthasar as to what he calls "the journey between the Scylla of radical biblical criticism and the Charybdis of sheer traditionalistic theology" (*Der geistige Sinn der Schrift,* 1952, Foreword).

[29] Pius XII frequently addressed himself to scientific problems. For example, cf. his address: "The proofs for God's existence in the light of modern science," of 1951, his address to the World Congress for Astronomy, and one to a convention of geneticists. In the latter he reiterated his distinction between the *problem of* the origin of the body and the *dogma* of the creation of the soul. W. Luypen criticized Pius' paper on the proofs for God's existence on the ground that an exposition of natural science was not expected from the Pope, but from the physicists themselves (W. Luypen, *Fenominologie en Atheisme,* 1963, pp. 106ff.)

[30] Overhage-Rahner, *op. cit.,* p. 29.

When Pius XII said that the only limits to scientific research were those set by proven hypotheses, he was speaking from a faith that divine revelation and the conclusions of genuine science would be in harmony.

But *Humani Generis* set clear limits to any accommodation to science when he spoke about polygenism. In answer to the question of whether the human race stemmed from more than one original pair, it says that "it does not appear how such views can be reconciled with the doctrine of original sin, as this is guaranteed to us by Scripture and tradition and proposed to us by the Church. Original sin is the result of a sin committed, in actual historical fact, by an individual named Adam, and it is a quality native to all of us, only because it has been handed down by descent from him." This problem need serve us here only as an illustration of the complications that exist in the relationship between modern problems and churchly authority. Since it was issued in 1950, the question has been whether *Humani Generis* must be received as a definitive and irretrievable decision of the Church on the question of polygenism. Some Catholics insist that the *Humani Generis* must not be considered a final decision, and that monogenism is not a theory to which Catholics are bound. This particular matter is very illustrative of the broader problem since the Church never really confronted it in the past; it was summarily dismissed by the citing of a few Scripture passages. Now, however, it is asked whether Paul, in Romans 5, uses "Adam" to suit his own purposes, merely accommodating himself to an Old Testament image, or whether Paul is actually teaching that Adam was a single living individual, whose historicity is necessary to support the doctrine of original sin. Renckens says that "the exegetical side of the monogenism question has hardly been touched as yet." And so, the relation between the doctrine of original sin and the scientific theory of polygenism remains an open question, *Humani Generis* notwithstanding.[31]

Such questions as these cluster around the conclusions of natural science, the fixing of doctrinal statements in the past, the teaching authority of the Church as exercised today. And all these center around the exegesis of Scripture. In the schema introduced at the Second Vatican Council, polygenism was condemned even more outrightly than it was by Pius XII. Here polygenism was not only

[31] H. Renckens, *Israels Visie op het Verleden*, 1956, p. 195. Renckens is clear in his judgment of how closely all this is related to his notion of the nature of Genesis and its literary genre. Cf. his statement, "The thesis that Genesis is an historical book is too narrow a basis for exegetical research" (*Ibid.*, p. 192).

said to be out of harmony with, but that it contradicted the Catholic faith and was condemnable. For support, the schema quoted Romans 5, and Acts 17:26 as well, obviously with the purpose of showing that the New Testament did not simply take over an Old Testament figure of speech, but that it expressly taught that all men stemmed from a single individual, Adam.[32] Though this schema was never discussed at the council, it illustrates the seriousness with which free exegesis is limited by the context of the Church's teaching authority.

Nowhere is it clearer than here how deep the problems within Catholicism since 1943 are. Trent, in fixing the doctrine of original sin, had no inkling of the role that the literary genre peculiar to Scripture would play in future exegesis. The theologians at the council of Trent simply built on Augustinian premises and used the Vulgate which has since been pretty well abandoned as an adequate translation. How then must the exegesis of Scripture and the teaching authority of the Church be rhymed as times change and totally new problems arise?[33] The question would be pointless had the Church rejected all the new methods of biblical research as a threat to its dogma. But since the Church not only refused to reject, but actually stimulated the new methods of biblical study with its implicaions for the meaning of doctrinal authority, it placed itself in the midst of a drove of problems. What must the Church now do about freedom of exegesis in the light of Trent's insistence that the meaning of Scripture is subject to the determination of the Church? As may have been anticipated, the Second Vatican issued no statement on the several concrete exegetical questions that are still in the air, which only means the Church still faces the basic issue of how it must exercise its teaching authority in the face of the changed exegetical insights into the real meaning of Scripture. It is not merely an interesting theological question for Rome; it touches the very character of the Church. Obviously, it no longer will do for the Church merely to recall statements on doctrine made in the past (infallibly?). The Church has to say something about all this, and it clearly is not of a mind to disavow the new developments as unbelief. It could not do so; it has reached

[32] A statement of the Biblical Commission in 1909 held that the "unity of the human race" was essential to the "literal historical sense" of the Genesis account.

[33] Though Rahner holds to monogenism, he does not mean to give up the approach to Genesis by way of its literary genre. He limits severely the "scope of Genesis 1-3 in its implications for monogenism" (Rahner, "Theologisches zum Monogenismus," *Schriften zur Theologie*, I, pp. 253ff.).

a point of no return. How, then, must the Church, as Rome sees its calling, be both "Mother and Teacher," not only on social questions,[34] but on the problems of natural and biblical sciences? Catholicism faces no more crucial problem than this. Ruffini has asked a pertinent question in this regard: "How can the exegetes suppose that the Church, our Mother and Teacher to whom the mandate has been given to judge the true meaning of Scripture, has held out this book to her children for nineteen centuries in ignorance that its literary genre is the key to its correct explanation?"[35] The question has been taken by most as meaning to suggest that exegetes run the danger of throwing complications into the meaning of Scripture that will not be understood by the great majority of people in the Church. The caveat is answered by pointing to the fact that appeals to the "simple meaning" of Scripture have often seriously misled people in the Church. Sectarians, too, insist that we respect the simple and literal meaning of Scripture without their having reckoned with the literary genre of the apocalyptic books. In the face of history, the Roman Catholic Church is not prepared to leap back to pre-1943 days, not only because this is impossible, but also because the conviction is growing that the new approach to Scripture does not adversely affect its authority and its message, but that it reveals the true nature of Scripture more wonderfully.

In view of the unchangeability and infallibility of the doctrine delivered at Trent, the temptation is real to read the newer insights of our day into the formulations of the past. Catholic scholars are generally alert to this temptation. Rather than saying that Trent really meant to say what the contemporaries are now saying, they point to the historically limited horizons within which the earlier councils had to speak. For this reason, they say, it is pointless to try to retroject modern insights into past statements. Hence comes the present tendency to look for the preservation of room *within* the doctrinal definitions for later nuances, room that must exist because the councils did not intend and, of course, could not have intended to answer questions that did not exist in their day.[36]

---

[34] Cf. John XXIII's encyclical *Mater et Magistra.*

[35] From *L'Osservatore Romano,* August 24, 1961.

[36] It seems clear to me that the problem of room within various official pronouncements for nuances of opinion creates some basic problems for the Church and its theology. This appears, for instance, in what Rahner says about the eschatology of medieval times. Cf. Rahner, "Theol. Prinzipien der Hermeneutik eschatologischer Aussagen," *Schriften zur Theologie* IV., 1960, pp. 421f. Cf. also Berkouwer, *De Wederkomst van Christus,* II, 1963, pp. 206f.

The situation at this time is this, on one hand the way has been opened for further inquiry by natural science and biblical science, while on the other hand the limitations which the Church sets on the sciences is also kept in sight. However, it is not always clear even for Rome precisely where the limits must be drawn and how far beyond the previous limits set by official, even though not infallible, statements scientists may go.[37] The problem of churchly limits to scientific work is usually very complex. The case of Teilhard de Chardin and his concept of evolution reflects the tensions within Catholicism on this question. On one hand his views are gaining a steady influence among Catholics, on the other hand the Holy Office emphatically warned against dangerous tendencies and errors in his work.[37a] Teilhard confronted the Church anew with the same problem that has faced it many times, a problem that, once let in, brings countless more with it, none of which are unrelated to the dogmas of the Church. All of these problems were present at the council, and they form the background against which the council was called. And with this, they form the background to the life of the Roman Catholic Church today, a Church which therefore is forced to ask itself anew what it means to claim for itself the prerogative to determine the meaning of Scripture.

The problems we have mentioned have had special bearing on the Old Testament, and in particular on the early chapters of Genesis. But New Testament problems have also intensified the question of the relationship between scientific exegesis and the teaching authority of the Church. Here, too, a remarkable change has taken place. The Church has dealt in the past with specific textual, canonical, and exegetical questions of a more or less incidental character. Now, it is faced with a central problem that touches the character of the Gospels, the problem of form-criticism and its methodology. The Roman Catholic Church has a peculiar interest in form-criticism because the Roman Church insists that it alone is in direct line with the apostolic proclamation; its founda-

[37] The limit set in *Humani Generis* regarding evolution of the body and the creation of the soul has been much discussed. Cf. A. Hulsbosch, *De Schepping Gods*, 1963, pp. 34, 42, 45; Hulsbosch says that *Humani Generis* posits a dichotomy between the two parts of man, and portrays God as making a left-handed intervention in an otherwise dynamic evolutionary process, a notion that is at home only in a very static view of creation. B. Delfgauw finds the term "immediate creation" to be unfortunate (B. Delfgauw, *Geschiedenis en Vooruitgang*, III, 1964, pp. 184f.).

[37a] The reaction of the Church to Teilhard is complicated by the difficulty in arriving at a unanimous interpretation of his views. Cf. the much discussed *Monitum* issued by the holy office on June 30, 1962.

tion is the primacy and the infallibility of Peter and his successors. Do the results of modern studes in the Gospels rhyme with the traditional approach to them on which the apostolic origin of the Roman Church has rested? This question has made New Testament exegesis a very existential matter to Catholic biblical studies.

The Catholic encounter with modernism involved the question of the historical reliability of the New Testament. The encyclical *Lamentabili* (1907) defended the historical accuracy of Paul's report of the institution of the eucharist, of the New Testament teaching of the sacrament of penance, of Jesus' messianic consciousness, of the establishment of the Church, and of the primacy of Peter, and of the reliability of the Gospels.[38] The Pope rejected the possibility that additions and corrections were made to the evangelists prior to the canon's formation,[39] as well as the theory that John's Gospel was really a meditation on the mysteries of salvation and not an historical report.[40] Though everything condemned in that day has not revived within Catholicism today, it is true that many of the questions that agitated earlier scholars are openly being discussed in Catholic circles today. The exact form of the questions may not be the same, but they are problems that stem from an awareness that the formation of the Gospels is a far more complicated matter than was supposed by the Pope in 1907, and that form-criticism was at least an effort to make sense of the complex historical growth of the Gospels. Today, Catholic scholars move within this area in considerable freedom.[41] This is possible only because the conviction has grown that such scholarly latitude in no way conflicts with the teaching of the Church on the authority of the Scriptures. And this conviction is based on the realization that believing scholars see no need for a contradiction between apostolic *kerugma* and gospel *history*.

An *oral* gospel precedes the writing down of the apostolic preaching, it is generally assumed by modern Catholics, as it is

---

[38] Denzinger, 2045-2055.

[39] *Ibid.*, 2015.

[40] *Ibid.*, 2015, 2016. Cf. *ibid.*, p. 2017, against the idea that John exaggerates Jesus' miracles in order to display more obviously the glory of the incarnate Word.

[41] The form-critical methods have interested Catholic scholars for some time. Cf. E. J. Byrne, in *Memorial Lagrange*, 1940. Byrne said that the theory of form-criticism makes us realize all the better the Church's witness of the Gospels as primitive and fundamental. It was Lagrange who introduced the historico-critical method into Roman Catholic biblical studies. For his work and the tensions within his thinking, cf. V. Baroni, *La Contre-Réforme devant la Bible*, 1943, pp. 501ff.

that the written Gospels present us with a proclamation history and not merely a journalistic history.[42] We meet the historical Jesus only by this route. Kerugma and history are *interwoven* "mysteriously and inextricably." The events of gospel history are recorded *in the light of faith,* not of objective, academic disinterestedness. Between the historical Jesus and us lies an interpretation of His history, and the writer insists the historical Jesus must be seen through this interpretation if He is to be seen truly.[43] The Gospels are "edited collections" of apostolic sermons. The methods used in transforming oral proclamation into the edited form of "Gospel" must be an essential element in our interpreting of the message. On the other hand, a reversal of form also takes place in the case of John's Gospel. John is writing of the historical Jesus; but he interprets His life and work and in this way witnesses to and proclaims the Jesus that John's own faith has come to know. And in this way, not as a journalistic record of the life and work of Jesus, but as a preaching tract, the Gospel of John was taken into the canon. To get behind this preached history — this interpreted history — of Jesus to the "Jesus of history" in the objective, matter-of-fact sense of modern history, and thus come to know *exactly* what happened in Galilee, is impossible. The reader of the Bible cannot get around the interpretative account of the believing, preaching Gospel tractarian. The Gospels, then, are writings that rose from a situation, they are tracts for a very specific purpose. They are witnesses of those who saw, not with the eyes of an objective journalist, but with the wide eyes and open heart of faith. This is how they came into the canon, and why they are given canonical authority.[44]

What makes the views we have just been describing interesting is not that they are brand new, but that they are typical of views held by many Catholic Bible scholars. That they are not new is

[42] R. Schnackenburg, "Zur dogmatischen Auswertung des N.T.," *Exegese und Dogmatik,* 1962, p. 18; F. Muszner, *Der historische Jesus und der Christus des Glaubens,* p. 153.

[43] Muszner, *op. cit.,* p. 173.

[44] *Ibid.,* p. 176. Cf. Schnackenburg, *Neutestamentliche Theologie. Der Stand der Forschung,* 1963, "The early church did not list the simple words of Jesus without reflecting its own faith-understanding of them and in the same way it did not simply report the acts of Jesus without setting them down in the light of its faith in Him as the Christ" (*Ibid.,* p. 14).

clear from Kahler's work before the turn of the century.[45] However, though most Catholic scholars will never go back to the notion that the Gospels are biographies, lives of Jesus in a specifically historical sense, there is a marked difference as to the degree of critical liberties that are allowed in interpreting the Gospels as kerugmatization of actual history. Catholics are almost unanimous in their criticism of Bultmann's notion of the relationship between kerugma and history. They agree with Bultmann's assertion that the so-called historical Jesus is not available to us, but in line with the "post-Bultmann phase" of New Testament criticism generally, Catholics are eager to maintain the truth and credibility of the New Testament kerugma of the incarnation, the cross, resurrection, and ascension of Jesus. The crucial content of the gospel history must, in their mind, not be watered down. This explains the intense interest in the problem of salvation history manifest in the Catholic symposium *Kerugma und Mythos*, which on every page insists that while history is kergumatic history, the actual history has not been shorn of its meaning as history by the kerugma.[46]

With this, Catholic scholars are holding out for a biblical kerugma that is tied to history, a kerugma that is not created out of an illusory faith. A point of contact is made here with former pronouncements by the Biblical Commission on the *historica veritas* (true history) of the biblical record. But the way in which the subject is approached by today's Catholics is markedly different from the method used by the commission. The commission spoke of the Gospels as being accurate biographical accounts of the life of Jesus, with little notice given to their kerugmatic character and less to the process involved in the creation of the Gospels. The kerugmatic character of the Gospels is the element

---

[45] M. Kähler, *Der sogenannte historische Jesus und der geschichtliche, biblische Christus*, 1892. Kähler, who in this work insisted that the Gospels were not mere biographies of Jesus but were proclamations of the crucified Messiah, did not exercise much influence on Catholic theologians until the twentieth century. Dahl speaks of the demise of the *Leben Jesu* theology in the rise of kerugmatic theology (N. A. Dahl, "Der historische Jesus als geschichtswissenschaftliches und theologisches Problem," *Kerugma und Dogma*, 1955, p. 112).

[46] *Kerugma und Mythos*, Vol. V, "Die Diskussion innerhalb der Katholische Theologie," 1955. Bultmann's deepest motivations are extensively analyzed here, but opinions are divided on it among Catholics. Cf. also A. Hulsbosch, "Het reformatorisch Karakter van de Entmythologisierung," *Tijdschrift voor Theologie*, 1964, pp. 1-34. According to Hulsbosch demythologizing is "a wholly logical consequence of the basic principles of the Reformation" (p. 22). He gives an extended criticism of G. Hasenhütl's work *Eine Begegnung mit R. Bultmann aus Kath. Glaubensverständnis*.

which is now being underscored by Catholics, a fact which brings them into a remarkable consensus with many Protestant scholars.

H. N. Ridderbos, the conservative Reformed scholar, shows a genuine admiration for the methods of form-criticism and shares with it a keen interest in getting at the original circumstances in which the raw data took the form of Gospel writings and in the original form that the writing took. He is critical of the criteria that many scholars use to determine these original situations, criteria which are frequently born of biased skepticism concerning the credibility of the writings.[47] Along with Catholic exegetes, Ridderbos is convinced that the kerugma stands or falls with the factuality of the saving events recorded in the Gospels. But this does not prevent him from acknowledging the peculiar nature of the Gospels as tracts with little interest in giving a formally exact reproduction of what was said and done by Jesus.[48] For example, he insists that John's account of Jesus' words is "heavily influenced by the fact that his witness is directed to the production of faith" in his readers. "The content and the power of his witness is created by the assurance that faith can rest in what is said and written about the events; they do not depend on the completeness and objective concern for detail in the writing of the history."[49] This is how the evangelists function "as infallible witnesses of Jesus Christ." Ridderbos' views have their parallel in much Catholic scholarship, and it is this sort of approach that has led to tension within the Catholic world.

[47] Cf. H. N. Ridderbos, *Christliche Encyclopedie,* VI, under "synoptic question."

[48] Cf. Ridderbos, *Matthaeus, Korte Verklaring,* I, p. 14. Ridderbos refers to "the remarkable literary genre of what we call gospel stories." Ridderbos says that the gospels are written "with an obvious kerugmatic purpose" and not as histories in the "ordinary sense of the term." They are "not historical records of the words and works of Jesus, but a description of Jesus as the Christ" (*ibid.,* p. 17).

[49] Cf. Ridderbos, *Heilsgeschiedenis en Heilige Schrift,* p. 131. John gives "another slant to the words of Jesus than do his fellow evangelists" and adds "purposeful changes which are explained by the kerugmatic purpose of his witness" (*ibid.,* pp. 129f.). Cf. the words that Bavinck quotes from Kuyper: "If words appear in the four gospels which, though reported as uttered on the same occasion, are not reported verbally the same, we need not contend that Jesus used the various forms at the same time. The Holy Ghost purposed only to give the church *an impression* of what Jesus said which does not contradict the original words of Jesus" (H. Bavinck, *Gereformeerde Dogmatiek,* I, p. 415).

Understandably, the question must be raised whether the Catholic sympathy for the methods of form-criticism and for the attempt to understand the literary genre of the Gospels touches on the very foundation of certain essential elements in Roman Catholic doctrine. Does kerugmatized history leave intact the objective historical facts on which parts of Catholic doctrine is based? Catholic scholars have not avoided this issue; Schnackenburg, for instance, talks of a "certain problematic" involved in the Catholic acceptance of the kerugmatic character of the Gospels.[50] The revelation of God comes through human voices. The Spirit permeates humanity and through it and not in spite of it, brings about revelation. We must face the "mystery of the divine-human character of the Holy Scriptures," he writes. Roman Catholics share with Protestants a problem that is "a long way from a clear and satisfactory solution."[51] Still, there is no doubt about the way ahead. The question is not whether the Gospels are trustworthy or not. The question is how their trustworthiness can best be demonstrated in the relationship between kerugma and history.

The question can be illustrated by reference to the Great Commission and its trinitarian baptismal formula (Matthew 28:19). Most scholars, including Roman Catholics, think that the Commission was not the beginning of the Church's preaching of the trinity, but rather the "climax, the finale of the primitive Church's wrestling with an understandable way of stating the mystery of the trinity."[52] This opinion would have been scotched by the Biblical Commission not long ago as an attack on the authority of the Bible. It is taught now with no suspicion that either the Scripture or the significance of baptism is devalued by it.

The case of the establishment of the primacy and the infallibility of the Pope in Christ's word to Peter in Matthew 16 is of very special interest. The First Vatican Council based the teaching of the Church on the "witness of the gospel" and in doing so underscored Matthew 16.[53] Now, however, Matthew 16 has been subject

[50] Schnackenburg, *op. cit.*, p. 15.

[51] *Ibid.*, p. 16.

[52] *Exegese und Dogmatik*, p. 56. Schnackenburg prefers not to use the term "Church theology" because the Protestant-critical school understands the post-Easter Church by this phrase (*op. cit.*). Cf. Karl Rahner's chapter in the same work, in which he speaks of a "re-arrangement resulting from oral tradition" and of a "clarification made because of a specific theological interest" (*ibid.*, p. 43). Rahner insists that this does not undermine the authority of the accounts, since "they themselves by virtue of their own character call for such questions" (*ibid.*).

[53] *Juxta evangelii testimonia*, Denzinger, 1822.

to a searching analysis in view of the fact that while all three synoptic Gospels include Peter's confession, only *Matthew* includes Christ's promise to Peter along with it. Oscar Cullmann has raised the question whether the promise to Peter could not be an addition to the text made by a later generation of the Church.[54] Cullmann himself supposes that the words cited by Matthew did not originate in the Caesarea Philippi setting of Peter's confession, but that they are of pre-Easter origin and that Matthew simply set them conveniently in the context of the Caesarea Philippi incident. The Catholic scholar, Vögtle, who happens to disagree with Cullmann's conclusion, does agree that the question can and ought to be studied objectively and that, should study reveal that Jesus did not give His promise to Peter at Caesarea Philippi (as Matthew has it), the genuineness of the promise of primacy would not be affected. These words would then be seen to "share the destiny of most of Jesus' words as handed down, concerning whose original kerugmatic situation and exact original context we can afford to be indifferent, since they are neither significant for the kerugma nor inexpendable for doctrine."[55] Vögtle himself thinks the connection Matthew makes between the confession by Peter and the promise to Peter is unhistorical. If it were historical, we would not be able to explain the shorter account of Mark. Moreover, he rejects the notion that Matthew himself knew the tradition of Jesus' promise to Peter and set it in the context it now occupies. In his judgment we are not able to discover the time and place that the promise was made, and there is a possibility that Jesus first said the words after the resurrection.[56]

The traditional image of the founding of the papacy has surely been altered in this position. Whereas formerly the beginning of the papacy was simply assumed to have been made by Jesus during His life on earth,[57] the new approach to Scripture makes the traditional assumption at least debatable. Problems like this do not arise without causing unrest, for the whole traditional assumption seems uncertain now. Schnackenburg talks about a suspicion

54 O. Cullmann, *Petrus*, p. 201.

55 A. Vögtle, "Messiasbekenntnis und Petrusverheissung. Zur Komposition Mt. 16:13-23," *Biblischer Zeitschrift*, 1957, p. 253.

56 *Ibid.*, *Biblischer Zeitschrift*, 1958, p. 101, 103.

57 An extensive discussion of all these questions may be found in F. Obrist, *Echtheitsfragen und Deutung der Primatstelle Mt. 16:18 in der deutschen Protestantischen Theologie der letzten dreissig Jahren*, 1961, pp. 27-77. Cf. J. Schmid, "Petrus, 'der Fels' und die Petrusgestalt der Urgemeinde," *Begegnung der Christen*, 1959, p. 347.

sown by the new Gospel studies. Much modern Catholic biblical work is seen as "a fruitlessly technical debate, a dangerous, yes a destructive enterprise, that rather hurts than helps faith, and that breaks up the unity of Scripture, relativizes the truth of revelation, and undermines the certainty of dogma."[58] The new kind of "historical trustworthiness" ascribed to the Gospels does not offer the traditional sort of certainty, the kind that points to the errorless journalism of the Bible, and with the absence of that certainty unrest has set in.

The restlessness aroused by the new scholarship cannot be attributed to reactionary conservativism. Even Karl Rahner speaks sympathetically of those who have a "sense of being victims of an historical swindle" and are disturbed at hearing that the Gospels do not give a stenographic record, or a tape-recorded account of the precise words and works of Jesus.[59] People feel a threat to their assurance, and wonder about the further implications of a "kerugmatized history" which seems so unlike ordinary factual recording of events as they happened. If Grossouw speaks of "kerugmatized history" as a superior form of history and if Ridderbos calls it a unique presentation of history, others wonder whether it must not logically lead to skepticism about the history of Jesus Christ. But even though such fears may not be a form of frightened conservatism, we may and ought to ask whether they rise from a self-imposed requirement of a specific kind of certainty that is presumed to be obtained only in the traditional view of the Gospels. Moreover, and more materially, there is the question of how best to account honestly and responsibly for the striking dissimilarities between the Gospel accounts individually and between the three synoptics and John. The acceptance of kerugmatized history, by conservative New Testament scholars as much as by any other, is to be explained by the nature of the Gospel records themselves, not by a temptation to undermine the authority of Scripture.

[58] R. Schnackenburg, "Der Weg der Katholischen Exegese," *Biblischer Zeitschrift,* 1958, p. 161. Cf. S. Schulz, "Die römisch-katholischer Exegese zwischen historischer-kritischer Methode und lehrambtlichen Machtspruch," *Evangelische Theologie,* 1962, p. 152.

[59] Rahner, *Exegese und Dogmatik,* p. 33, 42, 44. The feeling of dizziness bothers Grollenberg as he asks: "Where does all this leave us?" And he says: "He who has accepted the Old Testament against this background will eventually feel no trouble when he loses all his former certainty about many details in Jesus' life." He asks about the balance between the gains made by a "better understanding" of the intent of the stories and the loss of certainty about their accuracy (*ibid.,* pp. 50ff.).

Pastoral concern for those who identify the precision of journalistic reporting with the trustworthiness of the Gospel records obliges us to emphasize the motives of the new scholarship. Only as it is made clear that the scholars are only seeking the New Testament's own interpretation of the reality of Christ's saving work can the suspicions and fears of people be allayed. At the same time, the criteria with which scholars work in the terrain of New Testament research must be constantly examined.[60]

An example of the suspicions that Rahner talks about is the extremely bitter criticism that Romeo directed at the new ideas which, he suspects, are concentrated in the papal Biblical Institute in Rome. Romeo contends that the new directions in exegesis run contrary to the encyclical of 1943 and sees in them only a deadly danger for the Roman Church.[61] His attack, about which there has already been much ado, did not go unanswered. The Biblical Institute responded to it and to others that originated at the Lateran University, and particularly addressed itself to Spadafora, who accused the Institute of surrender to rationalistic criticism of the Bible as well as of teaching the evolutionistic theory of the Old Testament and accepting destructive form-criticism methods for the study of the New Testament. Spadafora felt that everything the Church held precious was at stake in form-criticism. He was particularly fearful of the new approach to the founding of the papacy in Matthew 16. According to Spadafora, the new exegesis considered the founding of the papacy a creation of the primitive Church's imagination, or at least of its *a posteriori* interpretation. The Biblical Commission's answer to all of this on March 8, 1961, did little or nothing to ease the tensions. The names of Zerwick and Lyonnet are introduced at this point. Zerwick was accused of denying the historicity of the Lord's promise of the papacy to Peter. Lyonnet

---

[60] The problem of faith and the pastorate in connection with research into the Gospel stories is examined illuminatingly by H. Cunliffe-Jones in his chapter on "The Fourfold Gospel as a Theological and Pastoral Problem for Today," *The Gospels Reconsidered*, 1960, pp. 46ff. Cunliffe-Jones seeks in the face of critical tendencies to dissociate the witnesses of the four Gospels to keep them in view as a whole "so that we may still, with complete integrity, think together their witness in a way that is fruitful for theology, preaching, and private devotion." He says this by way of response to C. H. Dodd's remark that "the Jesus of Mark and the Jesus of John are quite different persons."

[61] Romeo, "L'enciclica *Divino Afflante Spiritu* e le 'opiniones novae,'" *Divinitas*, III, 1960. The article was later published separately, but was soon unobtainable in Rome. Cf. Rahner on Romeo, in *Exegese und Dogmatik*, p. 26, where he speaks of Romeo's "unworthy suspicions."

was accused of denying the annunciation stories in the Gospel of Luke. The Biblical Commission threw up its hands, saying that discussion under the conditions created by such "wild assumptions, monstrous slanders, and conscious threats" was impossible.[62] But the contest was on, and the "innovators" were accused of stealing away the clear historical truth and sense of Scripture, even of the very words and acts of Christ.

The conflict had a final outburst when, just before the Second Vatican Council met, a number of anonymous warnings were written against the new theology. Once again the matter of form-criticism was brought up, and the case of Heinrich Schlier was mentioned as a frightening example of new theology ideas. In these anonymous publications, concern was expressed, not simply for some of the conclusions, but for the whole approach that views the Gospels as written preachments, or kerugma. Schlier was signaled out for attack because he, like Vögtle and others, taught that Jesus could not be known except through the proclamation of Him as Jesus the Christ, a proclamation defined by the "Easter-faith" of the preachers. Moreover, Schlier saw in the New Testament "an accumulation of fixed traditions of faith and formulations of faith."[63]

The attack against Schlier is the more striking since he had been converted to Catholicism as late as 1953 *by means of his New Testament studies*. It was his view of the New Testament as a body of faith-traditions put in writing that led him to Rome[64] where he became an apologete for Catholicism over against the Reformation which he came to see as the way of spiritualism and enthusiasm not unlike that which Paul warned the Corinthian Church against.[65] But Schlier's Catholic critics could not be deterred by Schlier's anti-Reformation apologetic. For this could not compensate for the dangers he created for Catholicism by his New Testament views. These undermined the certainty, the historical truth of the Bible, and so undermined the foundation of the Church as well.

---

[62] *Ein neuer Angriff gegen die katholische Exegese und das päpstliche Bibelinstitut*, 1962.

[63] H. Schlier, "Ueber Sinn und Aufgabe einer Theologie des Neuen Testament," *Biblische Zeitschrift*, 1957, p. 13f.

[64] Cf. Schlier's "Nachwort," *Die Zeit der Kirche*, 1956, pp. 308-314; and S. Schulz, "Katholisierende Tendenzen in Schlier's Galater-Kommentar," *Kerugma und Dogma*, 1959, p. 24.

[65] Cf. H. Schlier, "Das Hauptanliegen des ersten Korintherbriefes," *Die Zeit der Kirche*, p. 147f. Cf. W. Furst, *Kirche oder Gnosis. H. Schlier's Absage an den Protestantismus*, 1961, pp. 8ff.

That Schlier, the convert to Catholicism, should be the object of attack shows that the struggle transcends personalities. The kerugmatic approach to the Bible is, in the view of its critics, irreconcilable with the historical truth of Scripture. Moreover, the critics feel that the kerugmatic approach was implicitly condemned by the Church in the papal bull *Lamentabili* in 1907. In this bull the notion that the Christ of history is less than the Christ who is the object of faith was rejected.[66] Form-criticism proceeds, the anonymous writers said, from false premises: it denies the supernatural order, it has a false view of miracles, it mythologizes Scriptural accounts, and it practically leads to the notion that the resurrection itself is a myth. In brief, this method follows the Reimarus-Lessing line that Christ and the apostles were deceivers. So when the new theology shows sympathy for the same method used by these radicals, it forfeits all right to a Catholic hearing.

* * * * *

The recent Catholic criticism of the new theology misses the whole point of its New Testament views. There is a tendency in the attack to brand the new theology with the kind of skepticism that was true of biblical critics of the past, but which the new theology in fact opposes. For instance, the charge that the new approach to the Bible sees the Gospels as "creations" of the primitive Church[67] or that it mythologizes miracles betrays a failure to understand the new theology. The reference to the papal bull *Lamentabili* exposes this failure, for the kerugmatic approach does not even hint that the historical Jesus is less than the Christ of faith. It is interested in the kind of proclamation that is done by the evangelists, and places the heaviest possible accent on the bond between the kerugma and gospel history. Schnackenburg refers to the "historical value" of the evangelists' witness, even while he insists with Ridderbos that the intention of the evangelists was not to furnish a "historical report" or to provide a biography of Jesus. The message of the gospel is not in any way relativized; indeed, the apostolic witness is normative. The interpretative "interjections"

---

[66] Condemned is the error that: "It may be conceded that the Christ who appears in the light of history is far inferior to the Christ who is the object of faith." (*Concedere licet, Christum quem exhibet historia, multo inferiorem esse Christo, qui est objectum fidei* – Denzinger, 2029).

[67] In a schema submitted to the Vatican Council, there appears a paragraph which rejects the notion that the Gospels are subjective projections of the writers or of the primitive Church, a paragraph that contributed nothing to the problems that face New Testament scholars.

that have been included in the process by which the written Gospels took their present form have served only to enrich our knowledge of the historical event of salvation.

A pastoral concern can sometimes be felt in the bitter attacks, a concern reflected also in the warning issued by the Biblical Commission in 1961 that pastors should exercise prudence and reverence lest the consciences of the faithful be confused.[68] No one is likely to misunderstand or ignore this pastoral concern. On the other hand, it must be said that the critics of the new theology have contributed practically nothing to a resolution of the very real problems that the new theology has tried to face, problems that concern Roman Catholic as well as Reformation theology in a most urgently real way. To see in the newer approach to the New Testament little more than an unbelieving humanizing of the Bible is terribly short-sighted.

The anonymous tracts challenged the Second Vatican Council to defend the Church of Christ with vigor against the "gravest dangers" now threatening her. They suggest how intimately the problems discussed by New Testament theology are involved within the life of the Church. As I see it, the Roman Catholic Church is going to have to make a decision in this crisis. I do not mean that a new encyclical, or a pronouncement on this and that exegetic question will have to be issued. But the Catholic Church will have to make its leadership clear on the manner in which the profound search for the meaning of the Scriptures may legitimately be carried on. Since the encyclical of 1943, Catholic scholars have been pursuing a course that, though packed with dangers, is one on which they are searching out the truth of the Word of God, listening there for the *vox dei* in the *vox humani* of the Scriptures. Without hazarding a prediction, one can say with confidence that the Catholic Church will never again retreat behind *Divino Afflante Spiritu*.

*   *   *   *   *

The role of the teaching authority of the Church takes on a special urgency in all these problems. How can the Church's teaching authority provide effective leadership in the changing times with their new kinds of problems? How must the Church point the way through all the complexities? The question is important because of its pastoral involvement; the pastors and the faithful are expected to look to the Church for direction. One answer seems

[68] Opinions that "cause anxiety to both pastors and Christian believers" are mentioned. Cf. S. Schulz, *op. cit.*, p. 155.

simple and clear: the infallible authority of the Church will *necessarily* show the way. Confidence that this is the final and sure answer to the present confusion shows through many discussions of the matter. For instance, Muszner writes that "the undeniable fact of the matter, which can cause no one unrest, is that the norm for faith is the living voice of the Church."[69] This, he says, is the difference between the Roman Catholic and Protestant situation. "The tragedy of the Protestant discussion concerning the historical Jesus is forced upon it by the fact that Protestant theology, with its weak concept of the Church, has no sure route to the truth status of the apostolic 'interjections' found in the gospels."[70] The synthesis between kerugma and history and, therewith, the trustworthiness of Scripture can be found only in the Church's teaching authority, an authority which alone can provide escape from the tensions of scientific exegetical work. "The guarantee of sound exegesis lies with the Church, thanks to its apostolic charisma."[71] The Church offers the only sure way to avoid falling into the trap of arbitrary individualistic exposition of Scripture.

The Church's teaching authority does not imply that it alone exegetes Scripture. A large area is left for free exegetical work. Pius XII said in his 1943 encyclical *Divino Afflante* that the Church defines only a few instances of exegetical conclusions, leaving many questions on which scholars are given full freedom of research.[72] The Church has expounded the scriptural record of the events of salvation at certain specific points, and in so doing has exercised the power that provides the guarantee for the Church's continuity. The Church, according to its own conviction, never lapses into creative or arbitrary exegesis, never sets itself above Scripture, but only discovers and defines the true meaning of Scripture. For this reason no one is permitted to expound the Scriptures in a sense contrary to that which the Church has established and maintains as the right one; to do this would be to attack the foundations of certainty. The Church's interpretation always gives the true sense and right interpretation of Holy Scripture.[73]

But how does the Church manage always to discover the true sense of Scripture? In *Humani Generis* of 1943, we are told that

---

[69] *Exegese und Dogmatik*, p. 187.

[70] *Ibid.*

[71] E. Schillebeeckx, *Exegese und Dogmatik*, p. 97.

[72] *Divino Afflante Spiritu.* As examples, we may mention the exposition of Romans 5 (Denzinger, 791), the institution of the eucharist (*ibid.*, 874), and the institution of the papacy (*ibid.*, 1822).

[73] Denzinger, 786.

churchly interpreters exercise the greatest care to discern the *literal meaning* of the words of the Bible. It assumes that the literal sense is always discernible, and, for that matter, the spiritual sense as well. They are there to be discerned for the simple reason that God put them there. The holy books have their own special sense and it is God's intention that it be apparent in and with the words. So the Church's authority in digging out and translating the sense of Scripture is based on God's own intention with the Scripture. The spiritual, more hidden and profound sense,[74] is never a mysterious projection of human thoughts into the Scripture. The spiritual meaning is uncovered and taught by the evangelists themselves. Hence, there is no real problem as to how the Church can be sure of its own interpretation. The Church *listens* for the right meaning. And, with the charismatic help of the Spirit, it hears the meaning that is objectively and clearly there, just as it is put there by God.[75]

*   *   *   *   *

One is hard put to find in the above explanation a clear hint as to *how* the Church goes about discovering the true sense of Scripture. We find a warning against individualistic expositions, against mystical interpretations which are not based on the historical sense and against superficiality of all sorts. Presumably, all this has relevance to the Church's official interpretation as well as to anyone's interpretation, particularly at a time when exegetical questions are exploding on all sides as they have been since 1943. But what *is* the relevance of biblical study to the Church's *unique* prerogative of establishing the true meaning of the Bible? Is the Church dependent on research? Or does it have resources at its disposal which are not available to the biblical sciences? How, in short, does the charisma operate in concrete instances? Does Kuss's statement that the true sense of Scripture is "established only on the hard road of philological and historical exegesis" apply to the Church?[76] The way that churchmen sometimes use the word "charisma" does leave the impression that the Church works at the truth of Scripture within a framework wholly other than that used by ordinary biblical scholars.

Much of today's Catholic theology, as we have seen, does not

---

[74] Cf. also the "interior sense" and the "deeper sense" as well as the "typological sense," in *Spiritus Paraclitus*.

[75] Cf. R. E. Brown, *The Sensus Plenior of Sacred Scripture*, 1955, pp. 123ff.

[76] O. Kuss, "Exegese als theologische Aufgabe," *Biblischer Zeitschrift*, 1961, pp. 175ff.

concede to the Church a supernatural insight which guarantees the Church's authoritative interpretation of the Bible. It is denied that the charisma provides a "special kind of clear-sightedness" that can serve as a source of understanding and provide the Church with a sure hand for setting limits to biblical studies.[77] But this very denial of special perspicacity throws several problems into view. If the charisma meant that a supernatural miracle took place in the Church's thinking, the distinction between teaching authority and ordinary biblical research would be clearly defined. The Church would receive its understanding from beyond the arena in which the problematics faced by scholarship exist. But if the charisma does not work in this miraculous manner, what is the relation between ordinary exegesis and charismatic insight? Does the historical conditionedness that qualifies so much of the Church's speech apply to the Church's "discovery" of the meaning of Scripture during times when exegetical horizons are limited? We have already noted that the doctrine of original sin was formulated on the basis of a questionable text of the Vulgate. And many other statements are available that show how shifts of teaching occur, if not in substance then in modes of expression. In respect to statements issued by the Biblical Commission, these shifts are generally acknowledged. And undeniable problems exist even in regard to encyclicals. Now the charisma of the official teaching authority is said to occur on a human level, though with the aid of the Holy Spirit. The complexity of the question is underscored by Schnackenburg when he says that the exegete cannot work with the "fuller meaning" (*sensus plenio*) of Scripture; this is the priority of the Church.[78] He adds that while the exegete must indeed make use of the authoritative exposition of the Church, he cannot employ it as part of his methodology; here he can use only the tools of science, otherwise his method is unsound. But if the Church does not receive supernatural revelation in its charisma, and since the Church never adds anything to but only discovers the meaning in Scripture, can it really exegete the sense differently from the way any scholar does? The dogma of infallibility cannot mean a flight from responsible scholarship with all its tensions and all its problems of interpretation. So, again, if the teaching authority affords no escape from exegetical labor, how does it acquire such certain

---

[77] "The infallibility of the Church and its teaching office should not be understood as a miraculous effect of a special perspicuity granted by God" (Rahner-Vorgrimler, *Kleines theol. Wörterbuch*, 1961, p. 370).

[78] Schnackenburg, *Biblischer Zeitschrift*, 1958, p. 61.

understanding that it provides a guarantee for the whole Church that a given interpretation of Scripture is the only correct and the truly complete one? The infallibility of the teaching office has sometimes been portrayed as a door suddenly opening to a refugee from tensions and uncertainty. We have the distinct impression that this image has been forsaken by many Catholic scholars. It has all become more human. And the discussions about the charisma have tended to center on the assistance given by the Holy Spirit in the completely human experience of charismatic gifts. But the central problem remains.

✿   ✿   ✿   ✿   ✿

There was a time when the Church's authority was used as a refuge from the tensions of uncertainty. When late-medieval nominalism appeared to undo the synthesis between reason and revelation, it could have introduced a period of "ecclesiastical positivism."[79] The loss of faith's "reasonableness" did not, however, issue in a criticism of the Church's teachings. Rather, the Church's authority loomed as a bow stretched above the dubiousness and tensions of human thought, and if it could not resolve the tensions, it could transcend them. This was possible then because at that time Church authority was thought to be elevated above historical factors. In this kind of situation Church authority functions as a compensation for the uncertainties that plague men on the historical niveau.[80]

There are those who think the new theology is unwittingly reintroducing this nominalistic notion of compensation. Those who say this do not mean the same thing that was said in the anonymous publications issued just before the Vatican Council. There the new theology was accused of nominalism only in the sense that it was critical of scholastic theology and, in particular, of Thomism: it did not mean nominalism in the sense of a flight into an autocratic view of the Church's teaching authority. We refer here to Ebeling's notion that Catholic theologians are able to make concessions to modern biblical science because they know that the

---

[79] The term is from R. Seeberg, *Lehrbuch der Dogmengeschichte*, III. The term "positivism . . . is a rather vague term easily confused or identified with blind faith" (H. A. Obermann, *The Harvest of Medieval Thought*, p. 69). It is clear, however, what Seeberg is getting at.

[80] Cf. Obermann's way of putting it: "The intellect, it is alleged, must to some extent be sacrificed and replaced by a self-effacing confidence in the reliability of data which escape the critical test of experience and abstraction" (*op. cit.*, p. 69).

Church will in the end assure right conclusions. The concessions to modern methods are made "under the insignia that removes before-hand the critical seriousness of the hermeneutical problem."[81] Ebeling touches on a real possibility, for the assurance of transcendent protection can give one a sense of freedom; he can use dangerous methods without being involved in the real danger of the situation. Ebeling quotes Muszner to the effect that a man need fear nothing if he believes in the teaching authority of the Church. Still, Ebeling's critique fails to recognize important nuances and does not take seriously enough the genuine mobility in Catholic biblical studies. He sees the Roman Catholic Church as so certain of its position and of the strength of its tradition that it need feel no serious threat in the form-critical method of getting at Scripture. But as a matter of fact the new theology, with its new approach to biblical studies, has aroused a storm of criticism within the Church precisely because it is seen by some as a very real threat. Moreover, the new developments in Catholic theology have not come about because scholars have lusted for a taste of scientific freedom without the risks of that freedom; they have risen because scholars have been inescapably confronted with very vital problems.

Nominalism and its corollary, ecclesiastical positivism, has a dualism about it. Teaching authority and intellectual tensions exist side by side without really touching each other. This kind of dualism would be unbearable in today's situation because Catholic scholars are demanding that the Church be inwardly and outwardly honest. The guidance given by the Church's teaching authority is not in doubt, but it is not expected to solve all problems with sudden interventions of transcendently guaranteed truth statements. The very urgency of some of the problems makes such interventions impossible. But more than that, the assistance that the Holy Spirit gives to the Church is no longer accepted as a charisma foreign to the tedious task of biblical study. In short, today's situation is very different from the one suggested in Ebeling's treatment. Perhaps this fact helps explain the bitterness and the emotion of the fight waged in some Catholic quarters against the new theology and the contemporary biblical studies which the new theology endorses.

Obviously, then, the current charge that the new theology is nominalistic does not have in mind a neo-nominalism of the posi-

81 G. Ebeling, *Wort und Glaube*, 1960, p. 43. Based on this is also his statement that the encyclical *Humani Generis* produced no advance toward an exegetically based understanding of the confessions.

tivistic type that expects all the dangers of new thought to be removed by the assurance of Church pronouncements. The attacks against the new theology are not set at rest by the thought that a neo-nominalistic positivism may prevail in it and allow Church authority to settle all disputes and preserve it from all intellectual dangers. Critics are not put at ease by the possibility that considerations of the human and historical character of Scripture, the admission of literary genre and form-criticism into exegesis will be innocent pastimes and will not endanger traditional positions because, after all, the new theologians' willingness to subject themselves to Church authority will keep everything safe. The very severity of the criticism betrays a fundamental fear that a new crisis and a revived skepticism may undermine the foundations of the Church in spite of the new theology's acceptance of the teaching authority of the Church.

✸   ✸   ✸   ✸   ✸

Not many Catholics really want the Church to speak definitively on the question of Scripture. They believe that only continued serious study of Scripture will shed helpful light on the multitude of questions that have risen since 1943. But warnings reminiscent of Dolindo Ruotolo's outburst against biblical scholarship in 1941 are being heard again. They are not expected to call forth a new encyclical defending the freedom of biblical science. No one expects that Catholic scholarship is now going to forfeit its freedom. Catholic scholars will work under the shadow of the Church's *monitum* to prudence and reverence. But since prudence and reverence can be exercised only in confrontation with specific issues, the Catholic scholars can only be aware of their duty to exercise academic freedom in responsibility at each concrete point of study. If the reactionary theology represented by Romeo and Spadafora should win the day, responsible Catholic scholarship would be impossible. For, as pastorally concerned as the reactionaries may be, they are able only to fall back on traditional doctrinal strongholds that are impervious to fresh appeals from the Word of God.

The critics of the new theology lament that, while formerly the Scripture was simply called the Word of God, these days scholars speak of the Bible as a human book which must be investigated in its human and historical setting. This complaint is somewhat typical of the false antitheses set up by the critics, antitheses which offer no help in understanding the problem. Certainly the concern lest the mystery of the Word of God be swallowed up in human words is a genuine concern. But the Bible cannot be dis-

sected into the "divine" and the "human" aspects. To try to dissect
the divine from the human is to dissolve, not solve, the mystery of
the Scriptures. As long as we speak of two sides or aspects of the
Word of God, we open ourselves to the danger of excluding or
minimizing one or the other side. The Scriptures face us with the
divine witness *in* human words. As long as this is kept in mind,
we can concentrate full attention to the human words of the Bible
without fear of depreciating the divine Word that comes in them.
Resistance to the Word of God as the Sword of the Spirit is always
violent and strong; it manifests itself in criticism of the Scripture,
but it manifests itself as surely in instances where formal recognition is given to the Bible as divine but actual subjection to its
authoritative content is refused.[82] For this reason, full attention given
to the human character of the Scripture does not create a danger.
The danger is created when anyone refuses to bind himself to
the authority of Scripture in his *life and thought*.

In the midst of these dangers, Rome underscores the guidance
given by the Church through its infallible charisma. Catholic
theology of our generation has thrown into the open new and
radical problems, of which one of the most radical is that of the
relationship between the infallible teaching authority of the
Church and the work of biblical scholarship. No one would contend that the new theology has solved this problem. But its willingness to face the problems involved in the humanity and historicity
of the Church is not a token of revolt; it is proof of its demand for
integrity. In its desire for latitude, the new theology is not expressing latent or incipient heresy. It is trying to honor the unique and
authoritative character of the Word of God. The new theology
trusts that the Word opens its own meaning to the Church as long
as the Church will be content to be receptive rather than *creative*,
but still be very active in understanding what the Word has to say
to the Church which receives it.

✼   ✼   ✼   ✼   ✼

We must acknowledge that we are not able to look on the
tensions within the Roman Catholic Church on this point from a
restful Reformed eminence, as though Reformation theology is

---

[82] Opposition to the Scripture "does not arise in the first place and perhaps
not at all from the criticism to which it is subjected in our day. The Bible as
the Word of God encounters resistance and unbelief in every natural man. In
the days of dead orthodoxy unbelief in regard to the Scripture was as powerful
as it is in our historically and critically minded century" (H. Bavinck,
Gereformeerde Dogmatiek, I, p. 411).

untouched by similar problems. One could maintain such an illusion only by supposing that exegesis is an individual and not a Church concern and that exegesis is secured against error by the motto, *sola Scriptura*. Actually, the question of Scriptural authority is a most pressing one within Reformed churches. Ever since they abandoned a mechanical view of Scripture's inspiration and came to terms with an "organic" view, they have been faced, wittingly or not, with problems parallel to Catholicism's problem of the Church's teaching authority and free exegesis of Scripture. Pius XII wrote in his encyclical, *Divino Afflante Spiritu,* of the writers of Scripture as "organs" and "living, rationally gifted instruments" of the Spirit. He emphasized the authority of Scripture, but his acknowledgement of the human writers as "organs" opened the question of *how* the organs functioned in the service of revelation and how their dynamic function affects the character of Scripture's authority. Evangelical theology faces the same question. The witness of Scripture itself along with the "biblical studies of our time" faces evangelical churches with problems that only a docetic view of Scripture can ignore. Hence, in view of the similarity of the problems that each faces, we must ask whether the controversy between Rome and Protestantism is still adequately delineated by saying that Rome pretends to have charismatic guarantee for correct exposition of the Scriptures while Protestantism wrestles with the uncertainties of an uncontrolled individualistic exegesis. As long as the difference between us is characterized in this way, real discussion will be frustrated at the start. Catholics point to the danger of arbitrary interpretation of Scripture, and Protestants accuse the Catholics of a vain pretension of having a supernatural "perspicuity" at their disposal. Today the controversy takes on a more complex nature because Catholics reject the pretension of a supernatural "perspicuity" and accept the responsibility for studying the Scriptures with the use of all scholarly tools. The Church is not stimulating biblical study as a concession to eager young scholars, but in awareness that biblical scholarship is of crucial importance to the Church itself. While Reformed students are more aware than ever of the dangers of arbitrary exegesis, Roman Catholics are impressed as they have rarely been by the necessity of honest and conscientious biblical study.

In view of their conviction that an understanding of the Scriptures is gained only by asking the right questions of Scripture, and cannot be gained by a creative act of the Church, Roman Catholic scholars are facing the problem of hermeneutics as they have never faced it before. The Church's obligation to teach the truth of Scripture, it is realized, cannot be isolated from the hard job of getting at what the Scriptures say. Rahner insists, for instance, that the Roman view of the Church's teaching authority does not vitiate the Scriptures as the only revelation of God. Should the Church intend to put Scripture in second place to its own teaching authority, as though the Church could determine what the Scripture actually says and may say, says Rahner, it would be guilty of self-deification.[83] But when the Scripture is truly admitted as the authoritative Word of God, a complex relationship is created between responsible exegesis of the Word and the Church's authority to teach it. And, says Rahner, since this is the case, free and unhampered biblical scholarship, far from being a threat to the Church's teaching authority, can only be of indispensable service to it.

A common complaint is heard among both Protestants and Catholics that scientific biblical study makes the understanding of the Bible so complex a matter that the Church's task is made inordinately hard. This complaint overlooks the fact that the Church is obligated to respect the Scriptures as they are, not as the Church would like them to be. And, as Bavinck says, the real Scripture is subject to the same conditions as are all other writings.[84] The manifold hermeneutical questions that face us are very real to those who seek to read Scripture afresh, unbound by traditions that could, if we accepted them uncritically, keep us from listening with undivided attention to the Bible itself. The Reformation dared, it is said, to "gamble" with the thesis that "Scripture is its own interpreter." Of course, this self-interpretatiton does not happen miraculously, outside of man's control. The Scripture interprets itself only through responsible effort on the part of those who study it, and who study it as it is, not as they may "idealize" it.

Roman Catholic theologians have been much aware that exegesis of Scripture affects the life of the Church. And, impressed as they are with the developments and changes that have taken place in biblical studies, they are not going to be satisfied to have the Church speak out on all sorts of specific details of Scripture. And in fact, the Catholic Church is not now of a mind to settle questions of exegesis by means of pronouncements on matters of

---

83 K. Rahner, *Ueber die Schriftinspiration,* 1958, p. 39.
84 H. Bavinck, *op. cit.,* p. 405.

detail. But it is concerned about maintaining trust in the guidance that the Church has given by means of its teaching authority through the centuries. This is the real background to the Catholic insistence on the teaching authority of the Church. But it also explains its sympathy for the revitalized Scripture study going on within the Church. It bespeaks a faith on its part in the harmony that exists between the normative Word and the life of the Church, a harmony guaranteed by the Spirit who was promised to the Church forever.

When Pius XII pointed to the limited extent of official expositions of the Scripture, and implied that freedom of exegesis is correspondingly broad, he did not have mere matters of exegetical detail in mind. He was expressing his faith in the trustworthiness of the Church's authority. As we shall see, the conviction that the Church shall always be preserved as the people of God overshadows the latitude given to Catholic scholars. In view of the strides that biblical studies, especially in the question of hermeneutics, are making, the Church is not likely to be in a hurry about formulating new statements as to the meaning of Scripture. It is inconceivable that the Church would ignore the very studies to which it has given so much encouragement. The Catholic Church is alert to the fact that it has no automatic supernatural perspicuity at its disposal; it knows it must wait on the responsible labor of exegesis. At the same time, the Church and its theologians are studying the decisions the Church has made in the past. In the present Catholic situation, both in its theologizing and at its Council, the question of how these former decisions must be understood is most acute. And in interpreting the past, Catholics today are intensely preoccupied with the Word of God on one hand while on the other they are profoundly convinced of a real continuity in the life of the Church.

An *actualization* of the past appears, it seems, to be taking place in the Vatican Council and in Catholic theology: the Church, holding on to the past, is listening anew to the gospel according to the Scriptures. This bond between current listening for the gospel and an unbreakable tie with the past unavoidably creates a great many new problems for the Church. These problems are accepted and put on the agenda for discussion. That they are *openly* accepted is reflected both in the unrest within the Church and in an enthusiastic acceptance of the hard road of biblical study. Relativism and vague irenicism are not part of the picture. For in the immediate background of all the vigorous activity stands the common conviction of the mystery of the Church living under the power of the Holy Spirit, of Him who was promised *in* the Scriptures. It is not surprising, then, that the question of the Church, ecclesiology, looms as the issue at which all points of the controversy converge.

The Pope and the Bishops

6THE THESIS THAT MOST POINTS OF CONTROVERSY BETWEEN Rome and the Reformation converge on the doctrine of the Church is supported by the fact that this doctrine became the center of debate at the Second Vatican Council. When Pope John appointed his mixed commission to revise the report on the sources of revelation,[1] everyone assumed that this subject would be first on the agenda when the council re-opened in September of 1963. In spite of the fact that the commission had a report, *On Divine Revelation*, prepared and lying on the table, the second session replaced it with the ecclesiastical question. That it did was due to the importance that the new Pope, Paul VI, obviously saw in the doctrine of the Church, its essence, and its status and function in the modern world. In his opening address, Paul went into this doctrine extensively, recalling, for example, the various images that the Bible used for the Church: the house of God, the temple, the people of God, the flock, the bride of Christ. He also called to mind Pius XII's encyclical *Mystici Corporis* of 1943, saying he thought the time.

[1] Cf. Chapter IV.

had come for further examination of what the Church thinks about itself.[2]

The Council of Trent did not formulate a doctrine of the Church, but an obvious conviction as to its nature formed the very basis for everything else the council said. The First Vatican Council concentrated on the Church and its structure sufficiently to provide a tentative answer to what Paul VI asked.[3] This applies even more to Pius XII's encyclical on the mystical body, for in it the Church was the main concern. Still, it is understandable why Paul VI called for a new self-examination by the Church. He did not mean to ask the council for a new theoretical definition. He wanted a self-examination that had to do with a deepened practical knowledge of faith, an examination that would lead to renewal of the Church in life rather than a revised definition in theory. What he was after was the testing and calling that a self-examination implies, so that the Church would be able to show its face to the world and say: "He who sees me, sees Christ." The Church, then, was called by Paul VI to reconsider what it is and what it was meant to be, what its essence and task, its structure and mandate were for this day.[4]

✻　✻　✻　✻　✻

There is one question in particular that Paul VI himself considered of utmost importance and which came quickly to the foreground in discussion. In his address at the reconvening of the council on September 29, 1963, he asked the council to consider the function of the bishops in the Church. Of all the questions involved in the doctrine of the Church, that of the place of the bishops took top rank in importance. And Paul VI called for a deeper study of it than had yet been given, a study which would provide the criterion for the Pope to use in the fulfilling of his own

---

[2] *Salvete.*

[3] On the unity of the Church, see the encyclical *Satis Cognitum* ("On Church Unity" — 1896). Denzinger, 1954-1962.

[4] Paul VI speaks in *Salvete* about "the true, definitive, and complete notion of the Church as founded by Christ" still lacking "more precise definition." "This truth," he said, "must be subjected to a more intensive examination and formulated — not perhaps, as a solemn dogmatic pronouncement — but certainly in declarations expressing in a clearer and more authoritative form the Church's teaching about herself. . . . It must be a definition that will give a deeper understanding of the Church's actual, fundamental constitution, and show more clearly her diversified, salvific mission."

office.[5] We have reason, then, to begin with a study of what Paul VI had in mind.

The new consideration of the office of bishop, said Paul, had to be addressed to the questions that were left open by the First Vatican Council. At the First Vatican Council a strong statement was made about the primacy and infallibility of the vicar of Christ, the bishop of Rome. With this statement the books were closed on a long and agitated controversy within Catholicism. But it was concentrated on the Pope in particular, and left many questions about the structure of the Church unresolved. The calling of the Second Vatican Council aroused the hope that this council would address itself to another and no less important question touching the structure of the Church: the place, authority, and function of the episcopate. The day after the First Vatican Council declared the Pope to be infallible, it was suddenly forced to adjourn in view of the outbreak of the French and German war. This abortive closing of the council has left the impression that it never finished its work on the Church, and that, ending where it did, the central place of the Pope was left one-sided.

One-sidedness does not make the decision of 1870 a false one, but it does have the marks of incompletion, of needing the complement of other facets of the episcopacy. So, further light was desired from the Second Vatican Council so that what was begun in 1870 could now be completed. Hans Küng thought that it was John XXIII's original intention to give special weight to the importance of the bishop's office[6] and others shared Küng's opinion that this would be expected of the council. The relationship between the bishops and the Pope would have to be clarified. And Paul VI provided an obvious stimulus for this expectation. The First Vatican left many questions open; that they were given top priority at the Second Vatican underscores their importance.

What was said about the Church at the First Vatican? A schema was introduced first which did not particularly stress the infallibility of the Pope. The Church was discussed in several aspects: the Church as the mystical body, the visible unity and the necessity of the Church for salvation, its indestructibility and infallibility, and finally its plenitude of power. But the infallibility of

[5] "The first among the many different questions to be dealt with by the Council is one which pertains directly to you as bishops of the Church. . . . The doctrine to which we are referring is that of the episcopate, its functions and its relation to Peter" (*Salvete*).

[6] H. Küng, *Konzil und Wiedervereinigung*, 1960, p. 197.

the Pope was not expressly mentioned. This subject was introduced on January 21, 1870, in an *addendum* to the schema on the Church. This *addendum* completed the original schema by adding a discussion of papal primacy.[7] And it was this addition that became decisive. It became the content of the famous constitution, *Eternal Pastor*. And the endorsement of this constitution was the final act of the council. Historical emergencies kept the council from further defining the relationship of the Primate to the other bishops. The question then rose at the time John XXIII called the Second Vatican Council whether the broken thread would be taken up again and lead to a fuller and clearer understanding of the structure of the Church.[8]

No one suggested that the First Vatican Council intended to minimize the office of bishop. We read in the decrees of 1870 that episcopal jurisdiction is in no sense excluded by the authority given to the Pope; the bishops, it reads, were established in that office by the Holy Spirit and, as successors to the apostles, they are the true shepherds of the flock.[9] The First Vatican, then, left a point of contact for a later completion of the sentence begun in 1870. After 1870, the feeling was at times expressed that no real authority was left for the bishops and that their office, its apostolic origin notwithstanding, was in many crucial senses absorbed into the universal jurisdiction of the Pope. Bismarck said in 1872 that he would deal with the bishops from then on as men under orders, as the Pope's clerks, without any authority and without their own distinctive function in the Church. The German bishops vehemently protested Bismarck's position. They denied absolutely that the authority of the episcopate was swallowed up in papal dominion. The bishops, they argued, did not owe their authority to the Pope; they received it immediately from Christ, as succes-

---

[7] On this sequence of events, see J. P. Torrell, *La Théologie de l'Episcopat au Premier Concile du Vatican*, 1961, pp. 21ff.; H. Rondet, *Vatican I*, 1962, pp. 117ff.; R. Aubert, "L'ecclésiologie au concile du Vatican," *Le Concile et les Conciles*, 1960, p. 254; C. Butler, *Das I. Vatik. Konzil*, 1961, Chapters VII and X; G. Thils, *Primauté pontificals et Prérogatives épiscopals*, n. d.

[8] H. Küng, *op. cit.*, p. 200. R. Aubert talks of the need for a more balanced theology which will reconcile the powers of the episcopate with those of the Pope. He would not hazard a guess as to whether the Second Vatican would do this, but we at least know how intensely this question of structure occupied the council.

[9] Cf. Denzinger, 1828: "This power of the Supreme Pontiff is far from standing in the way of the power of ordinary and immediate episcopal jurisdiction . . ." (Tantum autem abest haec Summi Pontificis officiat ordinariae ac immediatae illi episcopalis jurisdictionis potestati . . .).

sors to the apostles. What is important here is that the bishops' stand was given the emphatic and laudatory approval of Pius X who recognized it as valid statement of the intent of the First Vatican Council.

There are, then, sufficient grounds for assuming that 1870 did not mean that the Pope had a monopoly on churchly authority. But this does not remove the fact that the concrete relationship between the power of the bishops and the power of the Pope needed a great deal of specific clarification.

※ ※ ※ ※ ※

The relationship between Pope and bishops has not been clarified by practice during the time since 1870. Leo XIII published his encyclical *On the Unity of the Church* in 1896. Here he returned to the question, but without offering much new light. He expressed the need for a close scrutiny of the relationship, but strangely enough he simply concentrated again on the utmost importance of the one visible Head of the Church. He incidentally ascribed a kind of authority to the bishops as successors of the apostles, but underscored only their unity with the Pope who alone is Head of the Church and alone has the keys to bind and unbind. Their unity with the Pope implied the bishops' subjection and obedience to him, a subjection which applied not only to the bishops individually but to all of them in the assembled episcopate. Even if the Popes themselves defend the authority belonging to the bishops, the practical significance of their office lay in its subjection to the papacy.[10] In view of this disappointing encyclical, the hope that the Second Vatican Council would issue a strong statement on the peculiar authority of the bishops and its integral part of the structure of the Church is more than understandable.

※ ※ ※ ※ ※

The First Vatican decree on papal supremacy must be seen in the light of a strong sentiment within Catholicism at that time against the steadily increased concentration of power in the papacy. The decree called a halt to all anti-papalist tendencies and in particular to *conciliarism,* the conviction that the councils, representing the entire Church, stand above the Pope. Since 1870, conciliarism has had no legitimate place in the Church. Yet, here and there, writers have pointed to elements of truth in the conciliar

[10] *Satis Cognitum.* The power of the Pope is of the highest sort, which sets the power of the bishops within specific limits and renders them partly dependent.

movement. The motive behind conciliarism gains respect even where the movement is rejcted as a solution to the question of authority. Conciliarism's penchant for a democratic political structure drove it out of touch with a Church that was concentrating more and more of its authority in the papal chair. But it did carry an element of the essential *communion* of the Church, an element which is the real *spiritual* brake on papal power. The fixing of papal authority in 1870 left the function of those who represented the communion of the Church unclear. And though conciliarism was condemned, the question it raised was left unanswered: what are the limits to papal authority?[11]

What was wanted from the Second Vatican Council was not simply another decree to balance the decree on papal infallibility. The question was one of the relationship of bishops to the Pope, so that when the episcopate was considered a new and further consideration of the papacy would also be implied. After all, as soon as the bishops are granted their own exclusive authority, the Church will have pointed away from extreme papalism. Hence, it was not a matter of bishop *or* Pope or of bishop *and* Pope, but of both in their reciprocal relationships. And this is what conciliarism was all about.

Conciliarism was never simply a theory about sovereignty of the people. Marsilius of Padua (d. 1342) supported conciliarism on this basis, but the movement was always more than that. Jedin has pointed out that it rests on the corporate nature of the Church — the Church as head and members, each with its own rights and duties, working in organic harmony.[12] Popes have often seen the conciliar movement as little more than a refusal to give the obedience demanded of believers. They frequently failed to recognize the true motive of its anti-papalism, which was a fear of concentrated, autocratic power in the hands of the papacy. And since this fear was not given reason to be quieted, impulses that stirred the conciliar movement were never really laid to rest. This has become clear in our day once more, even though conciliarism as a movement has no support. The *corporate* image of the Church is again accented. Plans are made for a more sensitive relationship between Pope and bishops. It has been said that 1870 created a

---

[11] Hans Küng has given a profound treatment of the whole problem of the structures of the Church in his book, *Strukturen der Kirche*, 1962. He deals with the significance of the Council of Constance at which on one hand there was a strong conciliar inclination and on the other led to the end of the papal schism and thus to the strengthening of the papacy.

[12] H. Jedin, *Kleine Konziliengeschichte*, 1959, pp. 61ff.

strong new papistic movement exploiting the half-finished decree of the First Vatican Council and robbing the episcopate of some of its inalienable functions and authority.[13] Hans Küng is probably right when he says that conciliarism would never have recognized the office of Peter, but that "if we build our ecclesiology exclusively on the decrees of the First Vatican Council, we will never see the Church as the great council of all believers, those led by the Spirit (Rom. 8) and made a royal priesthood."[14]

A simplistic, one-sided approach was certain to be unacceptable in this situation. Not one point of departure, but two, had to be understood, the two poles which Matthew pointed to when he reported the words spoken to Peter and to *all the apostles* (Matthew 16:18 and 18:18). Congar thinks that the Western development of the one pole, the primacy of Peter, has developed as a reaction against those who stressed the idea of the Church as a communion.[15] This development finally became a "settled position." Evidence for the development is seen in the fact that, while the term "vicar" used to be used for bishops, priests, even kings and emperors to indicate the divinely ordained office they held, the term gradually was reserved for the Pope.[16] The time has now come, it is felt, for the Church to rid itself of one-sidedness, and to acknowledge the full authority of the bishops, not merely to settle an ecclesiastical-juridical question, but to live into the full structure of the mystery of the Church.

Since the Second Vatican Council, whatever else it could have done, could not contradict the decrees of 1870, we must glance at those decisions. The most crucial decree stated that the infallible definitions of "the Roman Pontiff are therefore irreformable because of their nature, but not because of the agreement of the

---

[13] At a meeting held in Rome during the council, J. Ratzinger voiced the opinions of the German bishops on the papacy and the episcopate and, more particularly, on the ancient Christian notion of the Church as a communion. He suggested that the council ought to honor this *communion in the college of bishops.* "That the Vatican condemned extreme papalism as well as episcopalism is a fact that must be imprinted on the public consciousness of Christendom far more clearly than has until now been done" (J. Ratzinger, *Primat, Episkopat, und Successio Apostolica Catholica,* 1959, p. 269).

[14] Küng, *Strukturen,* p. 284.

[15] Y. Congar, *Begegnung der Christen,* 1959, p. 414.

[16] *Ibid.,* p. 415. In regard to reactionary moments and the dangers accompanying them, see J. Ratzinger, "Der Einfluss des Bettelordenstreites auf die Entwicklung der Lehre vom päpstlichen Universalprimat unter besonderem Berücksichtigung des heiligen Bonaventura", *Theologie in Geschichte und Gegenwart,* 1957, esp. pp. 721ff.

Church."[17] In this statement, the Pope appears to be set off by himself, sharply prescribing the influence that the Church as a whole might have on dogma; his infallible teaching authority seems independent of Church consensus. What is the deepest intent of the phrase "because of their own nature?" Is this what the Eastern Churches have accused Rome of, the isolating of the Pope to within a circle of independent power quite separate from the Church, giving him power to make decisions independent of the faithful? Is this the intent of the other decree of 1870, that the Pope possess the "full and supreme power of jurisdiction authority over the entire Church"?[18] Does this suggest that the Pope in fact stands above and outside of the college of bishops?

Hans Küng contends that the First Vatican never intended to make the teaching authority of the Pope and unlimited and independent one.[19] The Pope is infallible only in association with and as directed toward the whole Church. That papal statements are authoritative "because of their own nature" does not mean an *individualistic* authority. What was meant was that the judicial basis, the binding authority, rests in the *office*, but it did not mean that the Pope could define truth by himself without a prior consensus having been obtained throughout the Church.[20] Rahner too underscores this point, insisting that there can never be a dichotomy between the Pope and the Church (represented by the bishops and the councils) in the matter of teaching authority. The Pope cannot be isolated from the Church if only because the college of bishops shares in the promise of the immediate assistance of the Holy Spirit. The bishops cannot be limited to a mere approbation of the Pope's decisions, because their approbation must be implicit in the decision. Even when the Pope acts "alone," he acts as head of the college of bishops.[21]

According to this view, which has much support, the First Vatican did not support a kind of papal independence that might find support in a papalist view of the Church. Its decree must be seen against the background of the *organic* harmony between the papacy and the episcopacy. Of course, the problem of this relationship did play a role at the First Vatican. A certain Cardinal Guidi of Bologna gave a speech directed against any tendency to give

[17] Denzinger, 1839.
[18] *Plenum et supremum potestatem iurisdictione in universam ecclesiam* (Denzinger, 1831).
[19] Küng, *Strukturen*, p. 330.
[20] *Ibid.*, p. 335.
[21] K. Rahner — J. Ratzinger, *Episkopat und Primat,* 1961, pp. 87ff.

the Pope an independent position of infallibility, insisting that the Pope had to speak only in association with the bishops, who were witnesses of the faith of the Church. It was on the same evening of the day Guidi gave his speech that the Pope, in a personal interview, said to Guidi, "I am tradition." Butler called this a "painful hour" for Guidi, and it became a rather sensational event. But it would be untrue to the situation if the Vatican decree were to be interpreted in the light of the Pope's celebrated *faux pas.* Aubert maintained that the Pope was badly informed, supposing that Guidi was speaking for conciliarism, and that his pretentious statement was an ill-timed reaction to a misunderstanding.[22] All that can be said is that the phrases "because of their own nature" and not because "of the agreement of the Church" were the council's final blow at conciliar notions, and that, given the historical context, they need not support the total independence and isolation of the Pope in his teaching authority. They do not support a lonely papacy.

❋ ❋ ❋ ❋ ❋

In the third chapter of the "First Dogmatic Constitution on the Church of Christ" the Vatican Council of 1870 declared that the Pope has "the primacy over the whole world" and that he has been given "the full and supreme power of jurisdiction" for the governing of the whole Church.[23] All shepherds and believers of whatever rank owe obedience to him, and it is only in unity with *this* bishop that the Church is one flock under one shepherd.[24] The Pope is the "supreme judge of the faithful" and his judgment is "not subject to review by anyone" nor may anyone "appeal from the decisions of the Roman Pontiff to an ecumenical council, as to an authority superior to the Roman Pontiff."[25] In view of the "full and supreme power" ascribed to the Pope, can the peculiar rights and authority of the episcopate, as expressed in councils,

[22] R. Aubert, *Le Pontificat de Pie IX*, 1962, p. 354. Aubert speaks of a "regrettable scene." Harnack sees in this remark the end of the development of the post-Trent conception of tradition (*op. cit.*, III, p. 731).

[23] The council reaffirmed the definition given at the ecumenical council of Florence. Florence said: "We define that the holy Apostolic See and the Roman Pontiff have the primacy over the whole world, and that the same Roman Pontiff . . . was given by our Lord Jesus Christ the full power of feeding, ruling, and governing the whole Church" (Denzinger, 694).

[24] The council said that the Pope has the "plena et suprema potestas" not only in matters "that pertain to faith and morals, but also in matters that pertain to the discipline and government of the church throughout the whole world" (Denzinger, 1831).

[25] Denzinger, 1830.

really be respected?[26] At any rate, the function of the bishops was not defined in 1870. There were printed materials available at the Vatican Council that spoke on the subject. For instance, Kleutgen wrote a report for the council that laid heavy stress on the episcopate. He contended that the power to bind and unbind was given to all the apostles, not only to Peter. Kleutgen tried on this basis to support a twofold seat of authority: the college of bishops united with the Pope and the Pope individually.[27] But Kleutgen's paper was never even passed out to the council members and, of course, was never discussed by the council. Perhaps the time was not ripe in 1870. Aubert ascribes it to providential arrangement that Kleutgen's ideas were not accepted.[28] For now after new biblical and patristic research, the subject can be approached with greater insight than was possible in 1870.

✷   ✷   ✷   ✷   ✷

The first schema introduced at the Second Vatican Council discussed most of the issues left hanging by the First Vatican, but without adding any wisdom to them. This schema, citing the First Vatican, repeated that the Pope spoke infallibly "by himself and not at the agreement of the Church," to which was added, "nor of the other bishops."[29] At the same time, it said that the Pope did not speak as a private person, but as shepherd of the entire Church and as head of the college of bishops. The chapter on the unity of the Church spoke of the infallible magisterium of the Church in terms of the Pope by himself *or* in conjunction with the college of bishops without offering a hint as to their relationship. It reflected the old problem, but failed to suggest a solution to the dilemma between the Pope as having single authority and the idea of a *double seat* of authority — "the Pope alone *and* the Pope along with the college of bishops." Some saw in the schema an attempt to avoid the problem in order to keep a concentration of power in the papacy: if it had succeeded it would have removed the bottom from all expectations of new approaches by the council. Later, the much briefer schema on the Church again taught the "complete and universal power" of the papacy, but rejected the idea of a double seat of power. It was a springboard for a very

26 Seeberg mentions objections to the First Vatican that came down to the charge that the "new teaching would debase the episcopacy and emasculate the councils" (*Dogmengeschichte*, IV, B, p. 913).

27 Aubert, *Le Concilie et les Conciles*, p. 257; cf. J. P. Torrell, *La Théologie de l'Episcopat au Premier Concile du Vatican*, 1961, p. 260.

28 Aubert, *op. cit.*, p. 261.

29 Reference was made to Denzinger, 1838.

relevant discussion on the relationships between the papacy and the episcopacy. It began at the first session when the schema on the doctrine of the Church was criticized as being too juridical and too negative in respect to the episcopate and the college of bishops. At that time Cardinal Bea sought to put the papal primacy into the broader context of the infallibility of the Church, and he recalled the purposes that John XXIII had expressed for the council in terms of the bishops.[30] But it was in the second session that the discussions achieved their high point.

An unwillingness to stand pat with the verbal recognition of a sphere of authority for the bishops became increasingly evident. The episcopal authority had to be defined so that all misunderstanding and all one-sidedness could be avoided. Moreover, it had to be acknowledged in a way that episcopal authority could truly function in the *life* of the Church. The bishops were described as having a "plenitude of power" as the "true vicars of Christ."[31] Appeals were made for the council to restore a balance that would avoid all dangers of papalism. Again and again, the *twelve* were underscored, the apostles and Peter, the bishops and the Pope. In this connection, a plea was made for giving new significance to bishops' conferences, especially in mission areas, so that the conferences would not be mere gatherings for mutual advice, but real Church assemblies with "law-making powers."[32] In all this, the task of completing the First Vatican appeared to be much more than one of adding formal Church laws. It soon involved a revised view of the Church in all its functions. Decentralization of the Church was promoted as a movement that would actually serve rather than break down the unity of the Church.[33]

[30] Cf. R. Kaiser, *Inside the Council,* 1963, pp. 205ff.; A. Wenger, *Vatican II, Premiére Session,* 1963, pp. 152ff. Cf. the plea that Maximus IV, patriarch of Antioch, made to the council "to clarify and elaborate" the decrees of the First Vatican Council in "the light of the divine ordination of the episcopate." See Y. Congar, H. Küng, D. O'hanlon, *Konzilsreden,* 1964, p. 55.

[31] Thus, Ignace Ziadé, Maronite archbishop of Beirut, *Konzilsreden,* p. 85.

[32] By Eugene d'Souza and Elias Zoghby. Cf. *Ibid.,* pp. 92, 95.

[33] Cf. the remark by E. d'Souza: "Are we bishops of the twentieth century so dangerous?" (*ibid.,* p. 98). The question of the reform of the Roman curia got involved in the question of decentralization. D'Souza said that it "must be completely reformed." Many points of contact were evident here with the Eastern churches, with their theory of the councils and of the whole Church as communion. In the so-called Sobernost idea we find a remarkable likeness to the communion character of the Church which was accented at the Second Vatican council. Cf. N. Afanassief, *La Primauté de Pierre dans l'Eglise Orthodoxe,* 1960, and *ibid.,* "L'infaillibilité de l'Eglise dué point de vue d'un théologie orthodoxe," *L'Infaillibilité de l'Eglise.* Cf. also J. G. Remmers, *Oecumene,* 1962.

Toward the end of this discussion, a question was put to the council fathers in an effort to get a tentative sampling of opinion. *"Is the corps or college of bishops the successor of the college of apostles and does it have the office of spreading the gospel, of sanctifying the world, and ruling the faithful, and does this corps, together with the Pope, its head, and never without him, since he has complete and universal supremacy over all pastors and believers, does this corps thus have complete and sufficient power over the entire church?"* To this complex question, more than three-fourths of the council fathers gave an affirmative answer — by a vote of 1808 to 336. Any effort to brand the vote as revived conciliarism was extinguished by the acknowledgement of the Pope's position as head of the college of bishops. But what is important is that it conceded to the college of bishops the complete and sufficient power over the whole Church. The statement echoed the frequently expressed hope that the council would remove the lacunae of 1870 and would remove all appearance that the Church's power was in fact concentrated in the famous "full and supreme power" of the Pope.

The authority of the bishops was formulated so positively in this question that papalistic theories were almost impossible in view of it. What we see here is not a hierarchical structure of the Church in which the papal power is fully secured and, thereupon, some power is conceded to the bishops. The authority of the bishops came in as an *essential* element within the structure of the Church. Their relationship to the Pope as their head was not ignored, but their own function could never again be exhaustively described in terms of obedience and subjection to the Pope. Now a tension or, rather, a polarity of seats of authority is crucial. The bishops, it is urged, must take their place and exercise their powers in the Church *with* the Pope. The council itself gained new significance through this vote. It saw itself as functioning with its own authority; and the question of infallibility was taken out of its confinement within the authority of the Pope and set in the context of the entire *Church*.[34] The vote was only a sampling of

[34] Cf. Y. Congar, "Konzil als Versammlung und gründsätzliche Konziliartät der Kirche," *Gott in Welt. Festgabe für Karl Rahner*, 1964, II, pp. 136ff. Though a council is something more than the kind of assembled expression of opinion via letter of the type carried on by Pius XII prior to his proclamation of the assumption of Mary in 1950, this kind of questioning of the bishops is more than a Pope seeking information or advice. It would have been possible to have fixed that dogma "in the name of the college of cardinals," according to Congar.

opinion; but it cannot be undone, and its effect on the whole Church will be great.

The primacy and infallibility of the Pope was established in 1870 at the initiative of the bishops; but at the Second Vatican the initiative for establishing the authority of the *bishops* was given by Pope Paul VI. At least he created the psychological atmosphere for an overwhelming majority vote in favor of the principle of collegiate authority by making it clear that a vote for it was not a vote against the authority of the Pope.

The significance of the vote was also reflected in the resistance to it that came afterward. Opponents clearly saw in it more than a repetition of things said by the First Vatican. They were afraid that it would open the door to a dangerous independence among the world-wide episcopate and to a weakening of the papacy. Did not the terminology, according to which "full and complete" power formerly reserved for the Pope was now ascribed to the college of bishops, pose a real threat? The resistance to the "decision" was really a fear of any power in the Church competing with that of the Pope.[35]

It is clear from the council's discussions, and not least from the emotions that pervaded them, that the relationship between papacy and episcopacy is not a formal, ecclesiastical-juridical problem that can be isolated from the other questions that faced the council. There were new aspects of the papacy question as it took shape at the council, new because the papacy was being looked at from the viewpoint of the Church as a *communion* and as a *mystery*. This was what made this discussion different from that of the First Vatican Council. Rejecting the trends toward democracy and aristocracy, the fathers did nonetheless want to keep the perspective clear on the Church as a communion. They turned their backs on a competitive struggle between two powers and two jurisdictions and chose to consider only the mystery of the genuinely *ministering* office. The idea of a *serving* office is obscured whenever the matter is phrased in terms of power or mastery.[36] The offices of the Church are not positions of privilege or power which ele-

---

[35] Cardinal Ottaviani brought the test of opinion to the floor later when he claimed that the divine right of the episcopate implied devaluation of the primacy of Peter. He thought that the theological commission should not be bound by the vote (cf. Laurentin, *op. cit.*, p. 131). Ottaviani provoked strong reactions with this. E. d'Souza complained that, in the light of the 85 percent majority, Ottaviani was "scorning the council."

[36] Küng thinks that the First Vatican's decrees spoke more "juridically than biblically," about the position of the Pope (*Strukturen*, p. 209).

vate their holders above the Church, but are special positions of service *within* the body of Christ. The offices of the papacy and of the episcopate have to be liberated from a complex of competitive claims of power over the Church. This idea is not being pushed because of a devaluation of the papal office, but to give this and other offices their true evangelical character and to protect them from power-conscious perversion. The office, every office, was underscored in the light of what Paul wrote to the congregation at Corinth: "Not that we lord it over your faith; we work with you for your joy"[37] (II Corinthians 1:24).

Church office with its implied authority does ask for obedience, but only on the basis of the blessing and the joy of this special authority and this particular kind of service, an authority and service which is always "a humble vocation" and is pursued in humble service to Jesus Christ the universal Lord.[38] This is the kind of approach to the question of power that is accented in the new theology and the renewed discussion of the papacy-episcopate relationship. It is not simply a matter of getting the juridical question cleared up and given a new formulation;[39] it is a desire to have the whole problem enlightened by the gospel and in this light to denude it of any hint of a power struggle. The point is very simple: one can be "first" only if he is willing to be "last," the slave of everyone else (Mark 10:44). Mark it well, the new theology does not deny the juridical character of the Pope's authority. It does try to put that authority in the light of gospel authority, a kind of authority that does not involve any competition with other authorities, but only service *within* the corporate body of the entire Church as the whole people of God.[40]

[37] Note that Paul is a minister according to the *ad*ministry entrusted to him *(diakonos-oikonomia)*. Cf. also I Peter 5:3, and Colossians 1:25.

[38] Cf. Luke 22:27: "in your midst as one who serves."

[39] Cf. J. N. Bakhuizen van den Brink, "De Paus en het Concilie," *Nederlandse Theologische Tijdschrift*, 1963, pp. 141ff. He points to the hard time the Church has in illuminating the unity and the duality of Pope and council by means of canonical formulations. This is especially true if one rejects the theory of the double seat of authority. There was, for example, something dialectical in the question put to the council for an opinion sampling. The *harmony* between council and Pope must not be disturbed; and the route that formulations must take to avoid disturbing the harmony is sometimes tortuous.

[40] To gauge the scope of the new accent on office as service, see the following: H. Küng, *Strukturen*, p. 226; K. H. Schelke, *Jungerschaft und Apostelamt*, 1961, pp. 31ff.; R. Schnackenburg, *Die Kirche im Neuen Testament*, 1961, pp. 21ff.

We are forced at this point to make another qualification of the new theology's outlook. By putting the relationship between the papacy and the bishopric within the notion of the Church as an all-embracing communion and within the notion of holy office as call to service, the new theology has no inclination to let the concept of office be surrendered to every man's idea of how he can find his own effective way to serve the body of Christ. There are well-defined frameworks within which service must be performed frameworks established according to the Lord's will in the Church's tradition. The notion of an office is formed within ecclesiastical order; but this order must be *in*formed by the religious character of its service. Among Catholics strong conviction prevails that these frameworks are clearly revealed in the New Testament and that these are in fact honored within the structure of the Roman Catholic Church.

Schlier says that he found his way to Rome *via* a truly Protestant way, for the way was pointed out to him by the New Testament. Free, unbound historical exposition of the Bible brought him irresistibly to his discussion.[41] For him the question of office was first of all a question of the exegesis of Scripture. The Protestant scholar E. Käsemann has made some exegetical judgments on the basis of which Roman Catholic scholars have reinforced their claim that unbiased exegesis *must* lead to the Catholic Church structure. Käsemann believes that the Church first arrived at offices in self-defense against outbursts of fanaticism. In the primitive Christian view, every Christian received the Spirit at baptism, according to Käsemann, but circumstances gradually pushed this original vision to the background.[42] In order to meet the new situation, frameworks were created in which the continuity and order in the life of the Church were protected through established offices and in which the giving of the Spirit was increasingly bound up with ordination to those offices. Offices were stipulated in the face of a growing spiritualism. The result was an inevitable difference between clergy and laity. To combat undisciplined enthusiasm, the life of the Church was entrusted increasingly to fixed offices. Käsemann discerns in this process a steady movement toward what he calls "primitive catholicism," a situation in which Paul's charis-

---

[41] Cf. H. Schlier, "Die Zeit der Kirche," *Nachwort*, pp. 308f.; H. Küng, *op. cit.*, pp. 149.

[42] E. Käsemann, "Amt und Gemeinde im Neuen Testament," *Exeget. Versuche und Bemühungen*, I, 1960, p. 128.

matic thinking was neither followed nor understood, or more likely not dared.[43]

The notion of "primitive catholicism" within the New Testament became a point of ecumenical discussion almost at once. Both Protestants and Catholics took a keen interest in the idea, since it involved an issue of broad significance for both. Protestants took it up as evidence that catholicism grew up in the Church in opposition to the New Testament itself. Catholics saw it as evidence that the Catholic idea of office, far from being at odds with New Testament Christianity, was implied in it from the beginning. Käsemann claimed that the trend toward catholicism was present in the works of Luke and the Pastoral Letters of Paul. Catholics were quick to recall that they had always laid heavy stress on Paul's *Pastoral* Epistles. Hans Küng, understandably, brought the matter into the discussion by pitting Käsemann against the Protestant scholar Diem, who had insisted that catholicism came about *after* the time of Paul. Küng employed Käsemann's work by letting the Protestant Käsemann point out that the offices, ordination, apostolic succession, and even the monarchical episcopate are evident within the New Testament itself.[44] Käsemann, to be sure, sees this New Testament trend as a serious swinging away from the gospel, while Küng sees it as a support for the Roman Catholic notion that the sacred office is integral to the very structure of the Church.[45] But Käsemann's criticism of "primitive catholicism," Küng is quick to say, is really a criticism of New Testament Christianity. And thus, in Küng's view, the way is now open for more meaningful ecumenical dialogue. Now we can talk about more than a few crucial texts; we can talk about the entire phenomenon of New Testament Christianity.

❋ ❋ ❋ ❋ ❋

We contend that Käsemann's characterization of the idea of office, contrasted to the Spirit and His charismatic gifts, as primitive catholicism is a misleading approach to the controversy between Rome and the Reformation. The Reformation of the sixteenth

---

[43] *Ibid.*, p. 133. See also Käsemann's "Paulus und der Früh-Katholizismus," *Zeitschrift für Theologie und Kirche*, 1963, p. 84.

[44] Küng, "Der Frühkatholizismus im N. T. as kontroverstheologisches Problem," *Tübinger Theologisches Quartalschrift*, 142, 1962. This article was reprinted in *Kirche im Konzil*, 1963.

[45] Käsemann refers to Küng when he talks about "the satisfaction Catholic theologians find in the rediscovery of primitive catholicism in the New Testament" (Käsemann, *op. cit.*, p. 88).

century and later Reformed theology never suggested a contradiction between office and Spirit. The Reformation was deeply influenced by the Pauline letters, but not the letters of the Paul that Käsemann portrays. Käsemann insists that all officials and institutional factors in the Church were a departure from simple evangelicalism and from Pauline ecclesiology; he uses the phrase "primitive catholicism" to show his condemnation of the "un-Pauline" trends. But now a further question arises which Käsemann must clear up. Why, after the Church had made its switch from simple spiritual Christianity to institutionalized catholicism, did it adopt the Spirit-dominated letters of Paul into its canon? This was possible, says Käsemann, only because the early Church superimposed its own "image of Paul the Saint over Paul's real life."[46] The image of Paul as "the outstretched arm of the Original Apostles" gradually prevailed over the real Paul of the letters. And, since the real Paul was lost in the cloud of the popular image, his letters were adopted into the canon even though they in fact contradicted the trends the Church was taking. Once in the canon, however, they created a continuous crisis within the Church.

Is Käsemann right in branding as "primitive catholicism" the rise of offices in the New Testament Church? He has met criticism from such scholars as the German Von Campenhausen, who says we should not be intimidated by the presence of "Church constitutional" traces in the New Testament. He thinks that the phrase "primitive catholicism" betrays an over-simplification, and chooses instead to speak of the element of *order* in New Testament Christianity. In short, he rejects the basic thrust of Käsemann's thesis that there is a contradiction between the charismatic Christianity of the early Pauline Christianity and the official Christianity of the Church of later New Testament days. Von Campenhausen thinks that the rise of official positions, offices, in the New Testament is the fruit of the Spirit's work in the Church. There is, then, no real difference between Luke (Acts) and the Pastoral Letters of Paul on one hand and the essential Paul of the earlier letters on the other. And since the issue is not one of order versus charisma, offices versus Spirit, the controversy between Rome and the Reformation cannot be set up as though Rome sides with order and offices in the Church while the Reformation takes the part of charisma and the Spirit. The discussion should not, then, be con-

[46] Käsemann, *op. cit.*, p. 87.

fused by Käsemann's construction of New Testament Christianity.[47]

The Reformation did not protest against the presence of sacred offices as part of the Church's structure. It protested against what it thought had become a perverted view and *use* of the sacred offices. Indeed, the Reformation meant to defend the dignity and the authority of the Church offices. It gives no hint of turning its back on the official and institutional form of the Church: it betrays no suggestion of trying to revive a kind of spiritual and charismatic substitute for order in the Church. Anyone who reads the Reformers knows how they reserved some of their harshest invectives for the "spirituals" who wanted to shed the Church of its ordained offices.[48] The Reformation was no more of a mind to dismiss the official character of the Church to replace it with a spiritualistic-charismatic Church life than is the present-day Catholic ready to reject the order and offices of the Church just because he also discovers a spiritual and charismatic element in the Church of the New Testament.[49] Once everyone understands that Käsemann's Paul is not the real Paul, and that the real Paul is the Paul of both the early and late letters, the discussion between the churches on the subject of the Church offices can be a very meaningful one.

✿ ✿ ✿ ✿ ✿

The Reformation churches were much concerned with the role of offices in the Church and they had no feeling at all for an

---

[47] Von Campenhausen, "Das Problem der Ordnung im Urchristentum und in der Alten Kirche," *Tradition und Leben*, 1960, p. 162.

[48] Cf. Calvin, *Institutes* IV, iii, 1. Calvin speaks of the human work of the ministry as "a sort of delegated work." He says that ministers speak "in the name of God." He also speaks of ministers as "called to represent his person." The Lord, says Calvin, "entrusted to men the teaching of salvation and everlasting life in order that through their hands it might be communicated to the rest." Cf. also IV, iii, 3, where Calvin speaks of the "dignity" of the office of the ministry as something "to be held among us in highest honor and esteem" and as of "singular benefit."

[49] Cardinal Suenens gave a speech at the council on the "vital importance of the charismata for the building up of mystical body" (*Konzilsreden*, 1964, p. 24). In it he spoke of the church as a *spiritual* reality built on the foundation of the *prophets* as well as apostles. He objected to the schema on the Church because it did not seriously reckon with the spiritual character of the Church. He insisted he was not minimizing the office, since the office is called to honor the charisma so as not to quench the Spirit. Cf. also K. Rahner, *Das Dynamische in der Kirche*, 1958, pp. 45ff.

amorphous Church.[50] The Belgic Confession, reflecting Calvin, acknowledged three kinds of offices: pastors, elders, and deacons. These offices were not incidental or peripheral; the offices were part of the Church by divine ordination. The Church was not left to individualistic and arbitrary forms. There could be no contradiction between the Spirit in the Church and established offices in the Church. The question that enters the ecumenical dialogue at this point is not whether the Church should honor and take seriously its offices. The question is whether the New Testament gives a clear indication of *how* the offices should function in the Church. Von Campenhausen thinks it is not possible to read a clear "mandate as to the official organization of the Church" in Scripture. It is simply not possible to range the leading figures of the New Testament Church "in a scale, one above or beneath the other in defined order." He adds that the Protestant idea does not come off better than does the Catholic because Protestantism too proceeds from the disproven proposition that the Bible provides us with "a definite, though embryonic, Church order."[51] E. Schweizer, in the same vein, denies that the organization of the New Testament Church establishes a rule for us always to follow.[52] We are, in fact, reminded by scholars on all sides that the New Testament portrayal of the government of the Church is far too complex to be used as a model on which later generations of the Church must forever be patterned. The historical development of the Church determines various aspects of its organization at different times; it is futile to try to "preserve a reproduction of the New Testament Church."[53]

In spite of the divine direction given the Church in the New Testament, there is no implication that it forever hardens the framework in which the offices are arranged, as though this arrangement may never be affected by the changing circumstances of the Church in history. Even in the New Testament, Church offices function in many different ways. Consider, for example, the many kinds of "ministries" the New Testament mentions: apostles,

---

[50] Cf. Küng, *Strukturen,* pp. 195ff. Consider how clearly Calvin expresses his concern for the political structure of the Church in his commentary on I Corinthians 14:40.

[51] H. F. von Campenhausen, *Kirchliches Amt und Geistliche Vollmacht in den ersten Jahrhunderten,* 1953, p. 30.

[52] E. Schweizer, *Gemeinde und Gemeinde-Ordnung,* p. 7.

[53] *Ibid.,* p. 12.

prophets,[54] elders,[55] overseers,[56] deacons,[57] and others not clearly delineated, but leading figures.[58] These are all bound together in service to the gospel, but they do not lend themselves to clear-cut definition. The "presbyters" could be considered a division of the single office of apostle. The service of the deacons in the New Testament reflects a historical situation (Acts 6). Hans Küng puts the exegetical question regarding Church organization this way: "The office in the Church is doubtless divinely ordained. But how far does the divine ordination spell out the distribution of the offices?"[59] He adds that this question must be part of the current dialogue. It has a bearing on the broader question of whether the contours of the Church's whole structure are clearly drawn and whether they are fixed, specific, and universally valid norms for the Church of all ages. The answer to Küng's question has radical significance for the important discussions now going on about the various offices — in particular, the papacy and the episcopacy — of the Church.[60]

The issue, then, is not the offices as such, but the manner in which they are carried out. In the discussions at the council, the exegetical matters hardly were broached and Küng's question seemed to be unnecessary because an affirmative answer was assumed. The New Testament data were discussed, of course, but only to demonstrate Peter's oneness with the other apostles and to show that the Pope may not be isolated from the episcopate nor the episcopate minimized in relationship to the Pope. The appeal to the New Testament was based on an *a priori* certainty that both the papacy and the episcopacy belong to the unchangeable structure of the Church. There is no hesitation within the Catholic Church on these constitutive elements of the Church's structure.

[54] I Corinthians 12:28. The apostles were also distinguished as being apostles in either the narrower or broader sense. Acts 14:14 and Romans 16:7. Cf. H. N. Ridderbos, *De apostolische Kerk,* 1954, pp. 43f.

[55] Acts 14:23; 11:30 and in the Pastoral Letters.

[56] Philippians 1:1; Acts 20:28.

[57] I Timothy 3:8-13; Acts 6:1ff.; Philippians 1:1.

[58] Cf. I Corinthians 12:28.

[59] Küng, *Strukturen,* p. 191. Cf. *ibid.,* p. 155. There must be "no harmonization and levelling down of the different ecclesiological viewpoints of the New Testament." On the other hand, there must be no "hypercriticism" of the kind that no longer searches for the deepest unity between them. Cf. also Schlink, *Der kommende Christus,* p. 192ff.

[60] Schnackenburg points to the great variety in the organization of the first Christian congregations, a variety that is "very hard to get into a single picture." He speaks of the historical records of early Christianity as "full of variations and never of one piece" (Schnackenburg, *Die Kirche im N. T.,* 1961, pp. 21, 25).

These continue to define and govern the life of the Church, as is seen in the present effort to strengthen the hands of the bishops. The appeal that was made for the council to grant a more effective and powerful position to the episcopate was based on the assumption that the bishops are successors to the apostles.[61] Both Trent and the First Vatican Council said that the bishops ruled the Church as the apostles' successors by virtue of their ordination by the Holy Spirit.[62] Apostolic succession is a crucial point in today's discussions because it is intimately involved with the way the Church has been led by the Spirit through the centuries.

Reformed thought contends rather unanimously that the doctrine of apostolic succession rests on a misunderstanding of the special function of the apostles, a function which was defined by the situation within the history of salvation in which they were ordained, a situation which renders their peculiar office untransferable and unrepeatable. Oscar Cullmann has performed a noteworthy service in showing that the *once-for-allness* of the "salvation time" that broke into the world with Christ gives to the apostles, as eye-witnesses of that time, a unique position.[63] The Reformed consensus insists that though offices were properly established to govern the Church as time went on, these offices were not *apostolic* offices. They were means by which the apostolic *proclamation* would be continuously recalled, so that Christ's high priestly prayer would be fulfilled in the Church. For He prayed for those who "would believe in Me through their (the apostles') word" (John 17:20).

61 "The holy Synod [Trent] declares that besides the other ecclesiastical grades, the bishops *who have succeeded the Apostles,* belong in a special way to this hierarchical order . . ." (Denzinger, 960).

62 "This power of the supreme Pontiff is so far from interfering with that power of ordinary and episcopal jurisdiction by which the bishops, who, 'placed by the Holy Spirit' (Cf. Acts 20:28), *have succeeded to the places of the apostles"* (Denzinger, 1826). In his address opening the second session of the council, Paul VI addressed the bishops as: "And you too are apostles, drawing your origin from the college of apostles whose true heirs you are" (*Salvete,* in *The Pope Speaks,* Vol. 9, No. 2, 1964, p. 126). The phrase "and you too are apostles" is very telling, coming as it did from the Pope himself.

63 O. Cullmann, *Petrus,* p. 246. (E. T., *Peter, Disciple, Apostle, Martyr,* 1953, p. 222). Illustrative is the fact that Matthias was selected to take Judas' place from among "the men who have accompanied us during all the time that the Lord Jesus went in and out among us" so that he, with the others, could be "witnesses" of the Christ's resurrection (Acts 1:21; also II Peter 1:16). Cf. E. Schweizer, *op. cit.,* p. 194, on the never-to-be-repeated character of the "historically unique witness" and the "unique importance of the past event." And E. Schlink, *op. cit.,* who says, "Their office is and remains wholly once-for-all." Cf. also J. K. S. Reid, *The Biblical Doctrine of the Ministry,* 1955, pp. 42ff.; H. N. Ridderbos, *De apostolische Kerk,* pp. 54ff. and 65ff.

A remarkable facet of contemporary Catholicism is the emphatic emphasis laid by Catholic theologians on the unique character of salvation time and the normativity and canonicity of the apostolic witness.[64] Karl Rahner, for example, writes that the continuity of the Church is not exactly a matter of succession, since, according to Catholic teaching, revelation was closed with the death of the last apostle. Hence, revelation reaches the Church, according to Trent, "wholly and exclusively as mediated through the apostles."[65] Thus there appears to be unanimity at least in the attention given to the unique salvation time in which the apostles were called to give their specific and unique witness. The uniqueness of the time of salvation does not imply a break with later times; it remains the norm and continues to define the later development of the Church by virtue of its uniqueness. This leaves room for the decisive significance of a "succession of the Word" and a "succession of proclamation." But along with these, we also hear of a "legitimate unfolding of the apostolic office" in *those* functions of the apostolate that are required for the continued existence of the Church. Within this confined aspect, we are told, it is possible to speak in a true sense of popes and bishops as true successors of the apostles in an unbroken line until the present day.[66] At this point, it is clear, the unanimity of concentration on the uniqueness of salvation time and of the apostles within it is broken off and the parties go in different directions. The Roman Catholics whose thought we have been representing do not intend to detract from the decisive uniqueness of the salvation time, but they see in the apostolic succession a guarantee that the Church will continue to live on the foundation of that unique time and its events.

We encounter a similar situation when we turn to the question of Peter and his successors. Cullmann contends that there is no real hint of a line of succession beginning at Peter. Peter left Jerusalem to be succeeded there by James. James received his authority, not

---

[64] Cf. H. Küng, *Strukturen*, p. 165: "Their office *as a whole* is in view of its nature unrepeatable."

[65] Cf. Denzinger, 783: "transmitted as it were from hand to hand." Cf. Denzinger, 2021. One of the errors condemned by Pius X in *Lamentabili* was this: "Revelation, constituting the object of Catholic faith, was not completed with the apostles."

[66] Jean Frisque criticizes Cullmann, contending that though the apostle is the foundation, this "uniqueness of the apostolate" does not necessarily imply that the foundation is merely temporal. If it were temporary, Frisque asks, "how could it be secure?" Frique, *Oscar Cullmann, Une Théologie de l'Histoire du Salut*, 1960, p. 148.

from Peter, but from Christ. And when Peter left Jerusalem, he ceased to be the head of the Church there and never was the head of the whole Church.[67] Opposed to this thesis is the Roman position that Peter's office is continued in the Church by episcopal succession. Obviously, behind this sharply outlined disagreement there lies a basic difference of insight into the nature of the Church's assured continuity and its relationship to the apostolic witness. The issue is not exhausted with the word "succession." No Reformed theologian wants to make a complete break between the original time of salvation and later Church history or between the apostolic office and other offices. Nor is it meant that the unrepeatable apostolic offices have no analogies in the offices of another time.[68] What Reformed theology wants to emphasize is that the offices of the Church are indissolubly bound to the *witness* given by the apostles. Reformed theologians have always felt that Rome's idea of succession lays out the offices in their formal structure in such a way as to contain the continuity of the Church automatically within the offices as such. They were convinced that Rome created a mechanical arrangement that the Church could control by means of this structuration of the offices.

Catholics recognize this danger as more than illusory in view of the actual history of the Church. Apostolic succession can be set loose from the living realities of the Church in its communion with Christ and turned into a mechanical guarantee of the Church's unity.[69] When this happens, the notion of succession is formalized into a problemless and demonstrable structure having no spiritual connection with the succession of *witness*, with no suggestion that the Church lives under the domination of the Word of the apostles and that the Church has authority only within that *submissive* status. The very idea of a guarantee is secularized and mechanized, forfeiting its bond with the deepest dimensions of saving power.

[67] Cullmann, *op. cit.*, pp. 252ff. (E. T., *Peter*, p. 230.) "In the life of Peter there is no starting point for a chain of succession in the leadership of the church at large."

[68] Schlink does not contradict his emphasis on the *not-to-be-repeated* character of the apostolic office when he writes of "the ongoing of that which the apostles accomplished" and of the "setting in motion of the service for which the apostles laid the foundation" (Schlink, *Der kommende Christus*, pp. 135 and 188).

[69] Karl Barth uses the term "mechanical" in this connection (*op. cit.*, I/1 p. 106). Cf. von Campenhausen, *op. cit.*, p. 325, where he says that the idea of a "cutting away of the spiritual authority by the church offices" is as "senseless" as it would be to imagine the official authority being handed over to all those who had the gifts of the Spirit.

Our day has seen an unprecedented Roman Catholic awakening to the danger of formalism. Catholics want to see the apostolic succession in intimate relationship to the bond of faith in which alone a true spiritual continuity can exist. This is why such a strong accent is being put these days on the succession of witness and on the power of the Spirit that has been promised and given to the Church, but to which the Church can respond only in fear and trembling in faith and obedience, and can respond truly only within its tie to the canonical form of the gospel.[70] Catholics today want to guard against a mechanical arrangement that seems to provide automatic guarantees which the Church can use to protect and preserve the true succession. Küng and Rahner want to bind continuity to the episcopate and then not in the sense of a list of bishops in physical contact with the apostles. They point to the real intention of the succession: the binding of the Church to the once-for-all event of salvation and the tying of the service of the Church to the words of the apostles.[71] Thus, they maintain that the heart of apostolic succession is indeed a succession of the Word of witness.

We are obliged to pay careful attention to this development in Catholic thought in view of the strong accent laid by the Reformation on succession of the *Word* of the apostles. Is this a point on which the dialogue can be renewed with fresh approaches by both sides? Roman Catholics are striving for a synthesis between the pneumatic and the historical character of apostolic succession. They recognize the dangers of formalism and automation in the historical succession, but they also insist that the legitimacy of ordination to witness must be guarded against arbitrariness that can threaten the bond between the *Church's* mission and the *apostolic* witness. Unquestionably, in spite of the problematics inherent in the Catholic situation, the emphasis is falling on a legitimacy of historical succession with conformity to the succession of apostolic *witness*. We discern a groping for the real meaning of apostolic succession, a meaning sought in the combination of an historical succession resting on legitimate ordination and a succession of witness, with the historical ties created by a physical laying on of

[70] Cf. H. Küng who recalls the decrees of Trent in this connection. Their language about the orders must be explained in the light of Catholic reaction against the same libertines who plagued the Reformation. The negative result of this reaction was the "terrible formalism and legalistic hardening" of the post-Trent period. Today's discussion of the question of Church office has been informed by exegetical and historical knowledge not available to Trent (Küng, *Strukturen*, pp. 187, 190).

[71] K. Rahner, *Episkopat und Primat*, p. 70; Küng, *op. cit.*, p. 173.

hand by proper bishops being given content by the spiritual tie with the apostolic word.[72]

Behind the legitimacy of Church office stands the question of the relationship between the Church with its offices and the Holy Spirit. An objectivized relationship cannot be pinpointed between ecclesiastical office and the Spirit of God; this is made clear by the fact that the Church is always in danger no matter what historical circumstances it may be in. Irenaeus' famous sentence suggests one view of the correlative connection between the Church and the Spirit: "Wherever the Church is, there the Spirit is; and wherever the Spirit is, there the Church is; and there is every grace."[73] If the first part of the sentence alone were kept, the presence of the Spirit would be guaranteed in an objective and mechanical fashion. The mere fact of the Church would be proof of the Spirit's presence. But since Irenaeus also says that wherever the Spirit is, there the Church is, he wards off the possibility of such a self-evident guarantee of the Spirit. The whole sentence contains a warning that the bond between Church and Spirit can be kept only in faith and responsibility and that it cannot be objectified by a static state of affairs.[74]

The concentration of contemporary Catholic thought on the importance of faith in the correlation of Church and Spirit of God is expressed in an intense concern about the dangers that threaten the Church. Once men begin to protest seriously against a mechanical formalizing of that relationship and against the pretension that it can be guaranteed by a formal act of the Church, they become aware of the burden of keeping alert to the many dangers that threaten the continuity of the faithful Church. The papacy has been hidden in a shroud of faithlessness and corruption at times, as is freely acknowledged by Roman Catholics.[75] Given the fundamental significance of the papacy within the Catholic hierarchy, the problem of the papacy's corruption is a sensational moment in the consideration of the dangers always facing the Church. The popular

[72] In connection with Cullmann's use of John 17:20, J. Ratzinger agrees that the apostolic succession is indeed *successio verbi*, succession of the Word; but he insists that a succession of proclamation is impossible and unthinkable without ordination and legitimate commission. Ratzinger, "Primat, Episkopat und successio apostolica," *Catholica*, 1959, p. 270. From this, Ratzinger concludes the legitimacy of the Roman Catholic "line of succession."

[73] Irenaeus, *Adversus Haereses*, III, 24, 1.

[74] The same problem is implied in the words that are found on one of the walls of the St. Peter cathedral: *Ubi Petrus, ibi ecclesia.*

[75] Cf. B. Schneider, "Bemerkungen zur Kritik an der Kirche," *Gott in Welt. Festschrift Karl Rahner*, II, 1964, pp. 246ff.

notion of the papacy and infallibility still thinks of the Catholic notion of succession as an automatic guarantee that the history of the Church will continue until the Lord's return. Reality, however, has led Catholics to a recognition of a problematic element in the papal succession.

The thesis of Hans Küng that not only bishops can be heretics, but that popes can be heretics[76] may sound strange to those who hold to the popular notion of papal infallibility. Actually, however, Küng has brought up a problem that was present in the middle ages and right up to the First Vatican Council, and that indeed has been involved in most theological and canonical studies. With it, we confront what may be the most profound problem of Catholic ecclesiology, for it involves the guarantee and the continuity of the genuine life of the Church. Hosius revealed how the problem can be over-simplified when, on being asked what would happen if the Roman Pontiff should turn into another Caiaphas, he brushed the question aside as meaningless.[77] The real possibilities of corruption are many, though the one mentioned by Küng was heresy. If heresy is a possibility, what would happen if a pope became a heretic?[78] It is a fascinating question. But what interests us is the very possibility. If this is a possibility, the popular notion of papal infallibility falls. For here there is a serious attempt to come to terms with the humanity and therefore with the danger zone that no one, not

[76] Küng, *op. cit.*, p. 172.

[77] *Quid ergo, si Romanus Pontifex fiat Caiaphas?"* Answer: *Quid si caelum ruat?* From L. Bernacki, *La doctrine de l'Eglise chez le cardinal Hosius*, 1936, p. 235.

[78] In connection with canonical law: "the highest throne is under no one's jurisdiction." Cf. Küng, *op. cit.*, p. 219. The solution must be found in the ecumenical council as representing the entire Church. In conflict with a Pope, such a council has "the choice and the duty to set itself against the Pope" (*ibid.*, p. 240). Küng insists that this is not "radical conciliarism" — suggesting a competition between council and Pope — because the council itself spoke of an "inner limit" which "inheres in the papacy as a finite-human institution established by the Lord" (*ibid.*, p. 243). The council in such a case would make a "declarative judgment"; that is, it would declare that the Pope in fact had already ceased to be Pope. The council would not remove him, therefore, and would not be setting itself above his authority in only declaring to the Church that he had removed himself (*ibid.*, p. 244). Küng is not pushing for a superior conciliar authority.

See also P. de Vooght, "Esquisse d'une enquête sur le mot 'infaillibilité' durant la période scolastique," *L'infaillibilité de l'Eglise. Journées oecumeniques de Chevetogne*, 1962, pp. 136ff. De Vooght mentions Jean de Turrecremata who says that divine guidance does not exclude the possibility of an heretical Pope and that in the event of papal heresy, the Pope in question would automatically cease to be Pope.

even the Pope, ever transcends. Küng says that when Catholics are aware that even popes are subject to spiritual danger, the popular idea that "the Church could simply be delivered into the hand of any Pope who taught or lived contrary to the gospel" would be laid to rest.[79] Reckoning with the possibility of heresy, one obviously cannot work with an *a priori* guarantee that is provided simply because a Pope is in historical succession and is properly established in his office. There is a limit to papal infallibility that goes even deeper than the limits defined by the First Vatican Council. At that council the notions of a *personal* infallibility and of infallibility as an essential attribute of the papacy were condemned. Infallibility is an incidental, endowed attribute given to the head of the Church in his *ex cathedra* statements on faith and morals. It has nothing to do with special inspiration or revelation. It has only to do with an assistance afforded by the Holy Spirit for the purpose of preserving the inheritance of faith.[80]

If Küng is right in saying that papal heresy is an ever present possibility, we must ask how this can be rhymed with the promised assistance of the Holy Spirit.[81] We must realize that Küng's view is not taken seriously by all Catholic scholars. The question of whether the Pope could ever be anti-Christ was bandied about during the middle ages and was certainly taken seriously in the Reformation, but this was usually considered an inherent impossibility because real heresy is excluded from the highest teaching authority of Church by the presence there of the Holy Spirit. But that a problematic element in this profound matter should appear is not surprising. On one hand the holy office is acknowledged to be of utmost necessity for the preservation of the Church and on the other hand the humanity of office bearers is fully appreciated. The depth of awareness that this problem really exists is reflected in Karl Rahner's talk of the "real problematic in polemic theology" in reference to the offices and the institutional Church.[82] Does the guarantee given to the Church as a fruit of Christ's work imply that

[79] *Ibid.*, p. 240. Cf. also p. 237.

[80] Denzinger, 1836: "For the Holy Spirit was not promised to the successors of Peter that by His revelation they might disclose new doctrine, but that by His help they might guard sacredly the revelation transmitted through the apostles and the deposit of faith."

[81] According to Suarez, God can see to it that an heretical Pope would do the Church no harm, but he adds that we may draw from the "gracious ways of providence" that God would never allow a Pope to be heretical.

[82] K. Rahner, "Kirche und Parusie," *Catholica*, 1963, pp. 119, 122.

the institutional Church of any given time — including its offices — enjoys that guarantee?

According to Rahner, the Church's future is guaranteed "through the power of the promise" and there is therefore no possibility of the Church as such "lifting itself up against God and the truth and the grace of Christ."[83] If there were this possibility, we would be in the same situation as the synagogue; we would not be the Church of the end-time to whom it was promised that the gates of hell could not prevail against it. It must be recognized that *men* in *office* could, in themselves, deny Christ and thus bring the Church into apostasy and turn it into the synagogue of Satan. But from God's side alone it is sure that "the offices of the Church cannot be used as weapons against God in the most real and essential sense."[84] Two aspects of the Church are brought into play here. From the side of man there is a deadly danger that surrounds the office. But from the side of God's grace such a danger will necessarily at the crucial point be averted. Rahner is not trying to cover up the sordid side of the history of the Church. Rather, he sees its history as evidence that much of the Church's official life cannot be integrated with the sanctity of its Lord. But through it all, its offices remain subject to the charismatic influence of the Spirit, and the Church demonstrates that, as a hierarchically ordered institution, it shall be guided and assisted by the prevailing Spirit to the end of the age. To be sure, he admits, the offices of the Church do not have the "same quality of eschatological indefectibility" as does the Church as a whole.[85] But still there is a kind of indefectibility in the office, for after all the office established by Christ constitutes the eschatological Church of the redeemed. Thus it is not possible that the *Church* "should ever forfeit its truth and its love by acts of the offices instituted by Christ."[86] This guarantee functions as the *divine* guarantee in the midst of dangers inherent to the humanity of the Church.

Rahner's refusal to idealize the Church, to elevate its real history above the pitfalls and snares of earthly existence, brings this central point of Catholic ecclesiology into bold relief. Guilt and error exist together in every dimension of the Church's life. The mystery of iniquity is part of the mystery of the Church. This fact is underscored by contemporary Catholics over against the churchly triumphalism that has blinded the eyes of many churchmen to the

---

[83] Rahner, *Das Dynamische in der Kirche,* 1958, pp. 38ff.

[84] *Ibid.,* p. 39.

[85] Rahner, *Kirche und Parusie,* p. 123.

[86] *Ibid.,* p. 125.

facts of life in the Church. Han Urs von Balthasar is one of the Catholic theologians who are driving home the dangers that the Church lives among. What does it mean, he asks, that Paul wept over the bad servants of the gospel and that Peter wept for himself? "Both weep for the same thing, for the failures of the institutional Church." What means the "glaring disparity between men and their office"? Von Balthasar says that it means the Lord must do His work through humbling circumstances. Peter was crucified head downward; his cross is "the ultimate symbol of the hierarchical situation." Only so, in the humiliation of the churchly office, does the hierarchy become a real "diakonia," only so is the hierarchy tolerable in the Christian sense.[87]

The nuances in the various treatments of the ecclesiological problem by modern Catholics do not indicate a real difference between them. All of them reflect the polarity between the Church offices in their possession of the eschatological guarantee and the realities of the offices as they often function in the Church's life. All of them want to say that there can be no simple identity between the guarantee promised the Church (to the end of the age) and the promise given the specific offices in their day-by-day operations. Now that the actual functions of the offices are being underscored, and warnings are being sounded of the dangers threatening all offices, including the episcopal and papal, dangers to which the holders of all the offices must be forever alert, the atmosphere of the controversy between Rome and the Reformation on *this* point, the papacy, has been significantly changed. The earnest warning that is heard within Catholicism, a warning which the Pontiff must take as seriously as any other office-holder, shows that the hard core of meaning in the apostolic succession is the succession of witness, the successsion of the Word. The apostolic succession, with its core meaning being the succession of the Word, is sustained through the Spirit who warns and comforts, and whose presence in the Church is realized only *in the way of* warning and comforting. This being emphasized in today's Catholicism, we have a new opportunity for dialogue on this specific issue.

There is only one solution to this existential possibility of official corruption. While it opens its eyes to the darksome possibility of heresy in highest places, it must keep trusting in the Spirit-given

---

[87] H. Urs von Balthasar, *Herrlichkeit*, I, 1961, p. 544f.; Cf. von Balthasar's emphasis on office and humility in contrast to the misuse of the office by yielding to a worldly goal or in fear and flight from suffering. On the same subject see, Rahner, *Das Dynamische in der Kirche*, p. 42.

guarantee that the Church living in fellowship with its Lord will indeed abide until He comes. The imperative warning that rises from the pages of Church history must not lead to the false conclusion that the Church's path through history is only a forbidding,[88] impossible route through an infinite desert of hostility. There is always a window open to the divine promise that the Church will stand. But this assurance is coupled with the essential *mystery* of the Church. And the possibility that the infallible Pope can be a false teacher leads irresistibly to the miraculous aspect of the *Church's* indefectibility.[89]

❊ ❊ ❊ ❊ ❊

How seriously is the problem of the possibility of heresy in the papal office taken by the Roman Catholic Church? When the case of Pope Honorius' monotheletic heresy was broached at the First Vatican Council, all sorts of ways were suggested of resolving his condemnation by the Council of Constantinople with papal infallibility. The answer most commonly used was that in this case the Pope was not speaking *ex cathedra*. Besides, it was said, he was not condemned for teaching heresy himself, but for supporting the heresy of others. Obviously, the problem of papal heresy was avoided rather than faced at the First Vatican Council.[90] But the problem is now taken seriously and without embarrassment in a time when the image of the papacy is such that the problem can hardly be considered a matter of immediate urgency. So the problem can now be discussed calmly and without a hint that those who raise it are rebels. The popes themselves encourage discussion of it. One of the values of the present discussion is its point of reference within the broad ecclesiological problem. That is, we are dealing here with more than the questions of whether the offices are biblically organized and whether the present offices can be traced to the New Testament Church. Of course these are important aspects of the question. But on these matters we must recall that non-Catholics have not clearly made a universally accepted case for the

---

[88] Cf. Küng, *Strukturen,* p. 237.

[89] Cf. Chapter VII.

[90] A revealing illustration of escape from the problem is provided by Hefele's work on the history of the councils. In an edition that appeared after the First Vatican Council, Hefele revised his discussion of Honorius to fit the position of the council. On the several solutions, see Granderath, *Geschichte des Vatik. Konzils,* II, 1903, pp. 298ff.; Butler-Lang, *Das I Vatik. Konzil,* 1961, pp. 397ff.; H. Küng, *op.cit.,* and along with these, W. Plannet, *Die Honoriusfrage auf dem Vatik. Konzil,* 1912, pp. 41f.

New Testament basis for Protestant Church organization. Consider the ecumenical discussions about the historical episcopate as an example of the disagreement among non-Catholics.[91] The more reason, then, for giving close attention to the issue of the *essence of all offices.*

Küng thinks that the original Reformation opposition to the office of Peter was directed not so much against the existence of that office within the institutional Church as against papal pretentions of power and actual papal corruption.[92] There is some truth in what Küng says. The Reformation was not against the papacy because it was for a more democratic Church organization. The Reformers were against the papacy because of their conviction about the gospel and its implication for the genuineness and purity of the office. The Reformers insisted that all offices in the Church, if they were to have genuinely Christian authority, had to be of service to the gospel. And if the Church were truly to be the teaching Church (*ecclesia docens*), it had first and always to be the listening Church (*ecclesia audiens*). They had no feeling at all for disqualifying ecclesiastical offices in the New Testament as "incipient catholicism." They knew the importance for the Church that offices be "held in honor."

Isaiah comforted the people in his day by saying that "your Teacher will not hide himself any more, but your eyes shall see your Teacher" (Isaiah 30:30). The "guarantee" for the Church was to be discovered along the way the Church had to walk: "And your ears shall hear a word behind you, saying, 'This is the way, walk in it,' when you turn to the right or when you turn to the left" (Isaiah 30:21). The Reformation gave witness to this kind of guarantee for the Church. It did not devaluate the meaning of Church offices. It did set them in the context of responsibility and assurance, lest the mere fact of their divine establishment be isolated and abstracted from their involvement in the true and humble service of the gospel for which they were instituted. When the office is seen *within* the circle of responsible service, the problem of the organization and arrangement of offices can be approached anew. But then this problem will be set within the profound issue of how the arrangements and categories of the offices can find their meaning and justi-

---

[91] Cf. J. K. S. Reid, *The Biblical Doctrine of the Ministry*, 1955, pp. 46ff.

[92] H. Küng, *Strukturen.* In any case it is clear that Luther was not bothered by the formal problem of the arrangement of offices. He was concerned with the office only in connection with whether the gospel is clearly preached through the office.

fication in their connection with the real life of the Church as it serves under the scepter of the gospel.

The ecumenical discussion of our time demonstrates that, given what was just said, many problems still remain about the offices of the Church.[93] That there is no contradiction between the free work of the Spirit and the established offices of the Church has been more clearly understood by all than it has been before. The question facing all parties is how the offices can best serve the Church of Christ. Accepting the burden of this question, the churches have seen a renewed exegetical effort to piece together the extremely varied pointers toward the offices within the New Testament. The task is to do full justice to the complex historical picture of the offices within the New Testament without losing the force of the basic meaning of the office itself.[94] With this, the most important issue is the *nature of the guarantee* given to the Church that it will prevail to the end of time. We have seen that this guarantee is the background to the Catholic discussion about the papacy and the episcopate, and that in this discussion the promise of the Spirit to lead the Church into all truth was constantly recalled. The appeal to the Holy Spirit adds a dimension of utmost responsibility to the entire controversy. For it recalls to us all the miracle of the Church as the pilgrim people of God walking through the history of this world. It leads us to the question of the foundation of the Church, and to its guidance by the Lord, to its assurance, and its mystery. For we are all living in the mystery of the Church against which the gates of hell shall not prevail, the Church which shall have the Lord at its side to the end of the world (Matthew 16:18; 28:20).

[93] For a discussion of all these questions, see the excellent work by E. Kinder, *Der evangelische Glaube und die Kirche*, 1960, esp. pp. 171ff. and 69ff.

[94] Cf. the views of E. Schlink, who, without systematizing the New Testament data and without avoiding the significance of the New Testament "arrangements for church order," does draw some lines that the Church may follow in the light of the New Testament witness (*Der kommende Christus*, pp. 178ff.). See also A. A. Van Ruler, *Bijzonder en algemeen ambt*, 1952, pp. 95ff., on the question of whether the New Testament offers a model for Church organization. He contends for a general presbyterial-synodical form of Church order which can take on new forms under new conditions.

The Mystery of the Church

7 THE FIRST SESSION OF THE COUNCIL RECEIVED FROM THE Theological Commission a long schema titled "On the Church."[1] Its eleven chapters dealt in sequence with such matters as: the necessity of the Church for salvation, the episcopate, the laity, the teaching authority of the Church, the preaching of the gospel, and ecumenicity. The schema provoked extended debate in which, along with some appreciation of it, a good deal of biting criticism came to light. The work showed little awareness of modern problems, it was said, and offered little more than weary repetitions of well-known utterances from the First Vatican Council. The ecumenical perspective was lacking. It was weighted on the side of Church authority and Church privileges and was very light on the duties and calling of the Church in our times. Its concern was for the juridical and clerical aspects of the Church, while it showed little feeling for the humility and servanthood of the Church. Generally, it betrayed what was called an "introverted ecclesiology."[2] It conveyed the image of a Church concerned with itself instead of di-

[1] The discussion began on December 1, 1962, after the defeat of a suggestion made by Cardinal Ottaviani to give priority to the schema on the Virgin Mary.
[2] Cf. R. Kaiser, *Inside the Council,* pp. 204ff.

178

recting its sights outward to the world and to the separated brethren.

The second session saw another report on the Church, a much briefer schema that was turned in shortly after Paul VI opened the new session with his stirring message, *Salvete, Fratres*. The new schema began with a treatment of the mystery of the Church, followed it with the hierarchy (particularly the episcopate), the people of God (especially the laity), and a call to churchly sanctification. The significance of the discussion growing out of this schema is profound. For it must be seen in part as a response to Paul VI's question: "What does the Church think about itself?" But in order to gauge the import of the discussion we shall have to stand still for a moment at the 1943 encyclical, *Mystici Corporis Christi*. For Paul's question was given a tentative answer in this letter, and the present discussion cannot be understood apart from it.[3]

In 1943, the air within Catholicism was filled with discussion about the mystical body, and Pius XII wrote his encyclical to provide leadership in that situation. At that time, concentration was set on the supernatural, invisible, and mystical quality of the Church, while interest in the Church as a visible, organized, and juridical institution was fading. The Church as a communion in fellowship with Christ through the Holy Spirit was the reality that fascinated theologians at the time. It was part of a reaction against the legalizing trends of the past and against overestimation of the juridical character of the Church. A new spirituality was alive; theologians turned squarely to Paul with his immense concern for the spiritual tie between the Church and its Lord. The most genuine and profound reality of the Church, it was thought, had to be discovered at this mystical point, though the juridical aspect of the Church was not denied.

Pius XII was quick to sense danger lurking in the new approach. Careful to say that he recognized and honored the spiritual side of the Church, he was eager to expose the "one-sidedness" of much current theology of the mystical body. He said that it tended to push the juridical side of the Church too far into the background

---

[3] Cf. K. Rahner, "Die Gliedschaft in der Kirche nach der Lehre der Enzyklik Pius XII 'Mystici Corporis Christi,'" *Schriften zur Theologie*, II, 1955, pp. 7-94. New Testament theologians have given a great deal of attention to the mystical body of Christ. See T. Soiron, *Die Kirche als Leib Christi*, 1951; A. Wikenhauser, *De Christusmystik des Apostels Paulus*, E. Schweizer, "Die Kirche als Leib Christi in den paulinischen homologumena," *Theol. Let. Zeitschrift*, 1962, pp. 161ff. and 241ff.; H. M. Matter, *De Kerk als lichaam van Christus*, 1962; P. S. Minear, *Images of the Church in the New Testament*, 1961.

in order that its mystical character could be the more obvious. Pius then tried to create a synthesis which would do justice to both the spiritual and the juridical aspects of the Church. The fundamental idea of his encyclical was that in their zeal for the blessedness of the mystical bond with the Lord, churchmen should never lose their love for the visible form: the *Ecclesia Romana*. The title words set the tone for everything that follows: "The mystical body of Christ, *which is the Church*."[4] The impression is created at the outset that the mystical body is not to be isolated from the concrete and visible institution in its authoritative and hierarchical form.

The Pope called attention to false mysticism and to the pernicious falsehood of those who dream that the Church is a fellowship born and sustained of love and who separate themselves from "the other which they deprecatingly call the governmental Church." The Pope refused to accept this kind of distinction between love and order, between the invisible presence of the Spirit and the governmental offices of pastors and teachers. His intention is clear enough. Pope Pius was eager to destroy a false antithesis between Spirit and office and to preserve a balanced perspective of the mystical aspect of the Church. When the same Pope thought it necessary in 1950 to warn anew against heretical dangers, he republished the basic lines of *Mystici Corporis* in a new encyclical, *Humani Generis*. Here he recalled again that the "mystical body and the Catholic Roman Church are one and the same."[5] The identification of the two closes off any exit from the organized Church into the invisible body. Thus no one can have Christ as Head of the Church without "faithfully following his Vicar on earth." And if one wants to do away with this visible head, and breaks the visible unity of the Church, he mangles and distorts the mystical body of the Redeemer. Pius XII had no mind to begin a new approach to ecclesiology in this encyclical. His interest is to protect the necessity of the organization and its offices as essential to Roman Catholic ecclesiology. But the situation since *Mystici Corporis* has swept the whole thesis into controversy again and with a new emphasis.

✿   ✿   ✿   ✿   ✿

We would be untrue to facts if we tried to give the impression that the discussions about the Church at the Second Vatican Council created an air of revolt against the spirit of 1943. There was no hint that the council was inclined to choose for the "Church of love"

---

[4] The greater part of *Mystici Corporis* is found in Denzinger, 2286-2291.

[5] *Humani Generis*, Denzinger, 2305-2330.

and against the "Church of organization." Nor was there a suggestion that Pius XII was wrong in saying that the authority of the
offices was essential to the Church. Still, these discussions did betray an undeniable shift of emphasis. In the first place, the reactionary and polemical element of that encyclical was missing and
in the second place the accent was shifted. Here the dangers of
mechanization and juridicalism were underscored whereas in Pius
XII's encyclical the dangers of false mysticism and spiritualism
were accented. And yet, this was done without a trace of desire to
return to the theology of the mystical body as it was expressed before 1943. This fact creates the exciting spirit of the new discussions. They do not stem from an antithesis between the "Church
or order." New forms and new characterizations are being sought,
ways in which the fullness of the Church can be expressed. And the
concept of the Church which seems to have been emerging as the
central idea of this: *the Church as the people of God.*

*   *   *   *   *

The words do not immediately convey the remarkable change
taking place. They are not merely a self-evident cliché that everyone has always used. True, the Church was called "the people of
God" in the New Testament. Peter writes (I Peter 2:9f.): "but you
are a chosen race, a royal priesthood, a holy nation, God's own
people, that you may declare the wonderful deeds of him who
called you out of darkness into his marvelous light. Once you were
no people, but now you are God's people." And in Acts we read
that it was God's intention from the beginning to "gather a *people*
for His name out of the Gentiles" (Acts 15:14).[6] In view of these
biblical references, it may seem strange that calling the Church
"the people of God" would indicate a new idea in theology. A close
look, however, shows that the words catch all sorts of new and
stimulating ideas in their net.

The first schema on the Church, introduced at the first session,
bore all the marks of Pius XII. It recalled again that it was dangerous to understate the juridical nature of the Church; it reminded
the council again that the mystical body of Christ is identical
with the Roman Church. The Church described as "the people of
God" does not oppose this thesis, but it does carry a thrust that
goes around the antithesis and avoids the suspicion of a choice for
mysticism and spiritualism and against order and government. Another door is opened for an approach from a different angle. Here

[6] Cf. Romans 9:25 f.; II Corinthians 6:16; Titus 2:14.

we are brought into the historical sphere: the people of God is the pilgrim Church on its way to the future. This is another aspect of the Church than that which concerned Pius XII in 1943.[7] It underscores the dynamic historical life of the Church, the fact of its being gathered (ecclesia) and led on the Lord's way.

The Church as the "people of God" expressed a real longing to create new relationships between the episcopate and the laity (the entire people of God) so that the life of the Church could conform to the prophetic promise that "they shall all be taught by God" (John 6:45). The people of God have come of age, it was implied, though with no hint that maturity should mean a revolt against authority. To recognize the Church's basic structure as a communion of the people, indwelt by the Spirit, on the move toward the future, is to restore an essential element to ecclesiology. And any minimizing of the role of the layman reduces the mystery of the Church. When the office of all Christians created by the anointing of the Spirit is emphasized, only clericalism and not proper official authority is being judged. The Church is a communion, a congregation of the faithful, the people of God en route as the Church militant. This is the aspect of the Church accented by many Catholic theologians today.

When the Church is defined as the mystical body, the actual and static nature of the Church is kept in view, as it is when the mystical element is combined with the juridical and hierarchical form of the Church. Only now we have the institutional Church described in its historical and dynamic character as a "pilgrim people." The Book of Hebrews comes to mind with its picture of a people seeking a future city, a people with itching feet, discontent with life in the present (Hebrews 13:24).[8] The Church's pilgrimage through history leaves us with a constant sense of "not yet" having arrived; the "people of God" concept has strong eschatological overtones. And whatever else may need to be said about the Church, insists the modern Catholic, it will not ring true unless it carries these same eschatological notes. The Church is not the triumphant

---

[7] W. Breuning contends that this encyclical brought both aspects into a harmonious sythesis. He acknowledges, however, that Pius did not mention the "people of God" aspect of the Church (Breuning, "Die Verherrlichung Christi und die Kirche," *Ekklesia. Festschrift für M. Wehr,* 1962, pp. 84f.).

[8] E. Käsemann, *Das wandernde Gottesvolk. Eine Untersuchung zum Hebräerbrief,* 1939; R. Grosche, *Pilgernde Kirche,* 1938; E. Schlink, *Der kommende Christus.*

Church nor is it the Kingdom of God on earth. And the Church will have to keep itself alert to this.[9]

✻   ✻   ✻   ✻   ✻

There are more implications in all this than at first may meet the eye. For example, the phrase "people of God" suggests an association with Israel as God's people of the old covenant. Without erasing the difference between the Old and New Testaments, the picture is drawn of a people on its way through the world, under pressure, in trouble and in danger, facing pitfalls without and weakness within. The desert march comes to mind as Psalm 95 suggests it (Hebrews 3); and then too the people who were called outside of their refuge to bear abuse for Jesus (Hebrews 13:13). Oh, the wealth of the Church is not forgotten; but its wealth may not blind us to the Church's weakness and failures, its pitfalls, defeats and guilt. We lose the wonderful character of the Church as a supernatural redemptive mystery if we lose sight of its earthly human reality. The mystery dissolves the moment we erase the portrait of the Church as the Church of the Cross and paint over it a picture of the Church of glory.[10]

Triumphalism is struck a hard blow by this approach to the Church which was so evident at the council. The term "triumphalism" is not lifted from anti-Catholic sources which can see only a triumphant self-glorification in the the Roman Church. It is a word that is born within Catholicism, used there to signal a clear and present danger. It was sounded at the council in a speech given by the Belgian Bishop de Smedt. The bishop warned against all brands of clericalism, juridicalism, and especially against triumphalism.[11] He used the word to hit hard against the notion that the history of the Church was little more than a series of brilliant victories. He used it too as a protest against a tone that churchmen some-

---

[9] Cf. K. Rahner, "Kirche und Parusie Christi," *Catholica,* 1963, pp. 113ff. Cf. Y. Congar, "Peut on définir l'Eglise?" *Sainte Eglise. Etudes et approches ecclésiologiques,* 1963, pp. 22f. Congar refers to a "discovery" of the "people of God" concept among Catholics.

[10] Cardinal Lercaro talked of the "Church of the poor" and Cardinal Gracias spoke about the "image of the Church as a servant who could not be greater than his Master who preached the gospel to the poor" (*Konzilsreden,* 1964, pp. 151ff.).

[11] Cf. R. Kaiser, *Inside the Council,* pp. 207. Stephen Laszlo, bishop of Einstadt, also spoke out against a triumphalist ecclesiology and emphasized in contrast the Church as the "Church of the Cross." He said that the unity of the Church with Christ should not let us lose sight of "the distance of the pilgrim and penitent Church *from* Christ" (*Konzilsreden,* pp. 36ff.).

times use that suggests self-sufficiency and wealth and power. The bishop's speech seemed an echo of Karl Barth's attack on the self-glorifying language the Church used of itself as, for instance, when it talked about "the century of the Church."[12]

The manifold Catholic attack against triumphalism goes hand in glove with a desire to sustain the spirituality of the Church. This is one of the essential elements of the new ecclesiological way of thinking apparent at the council. It wanted no new dogma, no new definition of the Church that would clarify everything. Rather, with the hierarchy in mind in a most existential sense, it was a summons to complete and utter humility. The Church was being told to remember that it *followed* the Lord who came not to be served but to serve (Mark 10:45).

Does the Church realize that it is great only in humble service, that it is foremost only as it becomes a slave? (Mark 10:43). Was not this the implicit message of John XXIII, and of Paul VI too when he talked of the beauty of the Christ that had to radiate from His Church? The anti-triumphalist movement seeks to approach the fact of the riches and the authority of the Church by way of the gospel call to servanthood, and it senses that this can be done only as the Church is servant in actual and loving act. Now, the Church is told, after a long history of deviation, it must become utterly clear that the Church has nothing, *absolutely* nothing, to do with a worldly power machine, with worldly pretensions and worldly self-awareness. The Church as power institute can only be a stumbling block for those who see nothing in common between the self-glorification of the Church and the self-sacrifice of the Cross. The words of Paul must reverberate through the Church: "But we have this treasure in earthen vessels, to show that the transcendent power belongs to God, and not to us" (II Corinthians 4:7). Has not God chosen the "things that are not" in order to strip those that are something of their power? (I Corinthians 1:27-29). Is not this what the Church must exemplify unmistakably in its manners and methods? The Church must never show off in pomp and circumstances, must never strut with its impressive organization; in short, the Church must never seek a glory that anyone cannot immediately trace to its servant source. Even where the Church seeks to manifest its sanctity as the communion of the saints, this must be witnessed to as "from the

12 K. Barth, "*Quo usque tandem. . . .?*" *Zwischen den Zeiten,* 1926.

depths."[13] So goes the message of the new Catholic approach to the nature of the Church.

It is clear to me that this kind of witness against triumphalism and for what is essential to the Church does not spring from hidden resentment against papal or curial power. This anti-triumphalism leaves the offices of the Church intact, though it sees them structured differently than they have been. It concentrates on the actual life of the Church, including the offices, which become actually the more important as they are "steeped in the deprivation (of Christ)."[14] The Church can be credible only as it reveals the self-emptying of the Lord.[15] Does the Church now in fact project this image, or is it more like the Laodicean Church which said: "I am rich and lack nothing?"[16] Is it recognizable first hand as the "Church of pilgrims, the weary searcher, and the frequently confused, always sinful Church of sinners?"[17]

Catholics are reminding each other that the Church is on a pilgrimage and of how different it really is from the glorious kingdom of God. They are reminding each other that the confession reads: *I believe the Church* and not I believe *in* the Church. They insist that the Church's expectation of the Lord's return is "a constitutive element of the Church as such."[18] The Church would misrepresent itself as an institution with healing in its wings if it did not recognize itself fundamentally as "the congregation of the expectant ones, the pilgrims who are still in search of their true homeland."[19] When the Church understands itself in this sense and when it shows this face to the world, the real riches of the Church will be understood rightly as the riches of the eschatological congregation, the people of God.[20]

The vision of the Church as the people of God also has consequences for the Church's attitude toward the outsiders. Anti-triumphalism has little feeling for apologetics and polemics. Once the worldly self-consciousness of the "triumphant" Church is overcome, the old categories into which the outsiders were neatly fit no

[13] Cf. H. Urs von Balthasar, "Kirchenerfahrung dieser Zeit," *Sentire Ecclesiam* 1961, p. 755, on quantity as "the enemy of quality."

[14] *Ibid.*

[15] *Ibid.*, p. 767.

[16] K. Rahner, "Dogmatischer Randbemerkungen zur Kirchenfrömmigkeit," *Sentire Ecclesiam*, p. 771.

[17] *Loc. cit.*

[18] *Ibid.*, p. 780.

[19] K. Rahner, "Kirche und Parusie," *Catholica*, 1963, p. 114.

[20] *Ibid.*

longer seem valid. There was a time when the lines were clearly drawn. The Church was on one side, and on the other were Jews, heathen, schismatics, and heretics. Now the outsiders no longer fit this black-white division. The Church is understood as it really is in its earthly existence and thus in its lack of innocence and in its guilt. Aware of its own stained self, it can no longer demand a simple, unconditional surrender of the others. The conviction has grown that the motto *ecclesia semper reformanda* applies to the essentials of the Church, as the councils have often said.

But many questions take root in this changed disposition toward the outsiders, and these were articulated at the council in various ways. Paul VI announced a new secretariat for relationships with the non-Christian religions.[21] But what was more arresting was the new attentiveness given to Israel and to the problem of religious freedom. Two chapters were given over to these matters by the Secretariat for Unity in the schema on ecumenicity. The chapter on Israel was concerned with the *religious* problem of Israel, not with the political situation in the Holy Land. It was concerned with the relationship between Israel and Christ, not with the relationship between Jewish nationals and other peoples.[22] The problem of religious freedom evoked an intense interest. A good deal of criticism was directed against the report, and the second session was adjourned without coming to a concrete decision on it. The report on Israel and that on religious freedom will be discussed again during the third session. But the failure to bring the discussion to a close does not indicate that there is no desire for a positive and unambiguous pronouncement.[23]

The changed attitude toward the outsiders does not betray a weakness for relativism or syncretism. Anti-triumphalism cannot

21 The question of the non-Christian religions has been occupying Catholic theologians a great deal in recent years. Cf. J. H. Walgrave, "De heilshistorische verhouding tussen de kerk en de niet-Christelijke godsdiensten," *Tijdschrift voor Theologie,* 1961 pp. 141ff., and especially H. R. Schlette, *Die Religionen als Thema der Theologie,* 1964.

22 The question was raised at the council whether Israel could legitimately be discussed under the theme of ecumenicity. Congar especially argued for the legitimacy of it. Cf. R. Laurentin, *Bilan de la deuxième Session,* 1964, p. 148. During the second sitting, Msgr. John Oesterreicher appeared before the German bishops gathered in Rome to make a fervent plea for a new relationship to Israel.

23 John XXIII, in his *Pacem in Terris* encyclical (1963), supported the right of everyone to worship according to his conscience. In his speech to the council, de Smedt urged that the council come to a definite decision on religious freedom during the second session.

be explained as a readiness to sacrifice its own convictions regarding the Catholic Church. It is explained instead by a renewed sense of evangelical calling to confrontation with the others. An indirect purpose in the calling of the council was to consider the relationships of the Catholic Church to non-Catholic believers. This is happening within the Catholic Church only after a long period in which the outsiders were seen only as the antithesis to Catholicism, and in which this antithesis presented no *problem* at all. One notices the change taking place in the fact that all kinds of problems that had long been considered solved are once again placed on the table as real problems calling for genuine concern.

That the problems are not theoretical, but very practical and concrete is illustrated in the new approach to the question of mixed marriages, especially as it rises against the background of Trent and the Church laws that are still in force. Several bishops pointed out that this question had immediate ecumenical import, and that a revised posture by the Catholic Church in regard to mixed marriages was in fact a test of the seriousness of its ecumenical concern. Even this question shows how complex all these matters are. For the question of mixed marriages touches on the nature of the Church as well as it does on the sacramental character of marriage. On the other hand, the fact that they are seriously confronted at the council, and are not shunted aside with quick and obvious answers, demonstrates that the Catholic concern with the mystery of the Church is not a theoretical concern irrelevant to everyday realities.[24]

❁   ❁   ❁   ❁   ❁

Having listened to this religious protest against self-exaltation, pretentiousness, and exclusiveness, we must ask how all this is to be fitted into the untouchable conviction of the Roman Church as the only Church of Christ. We would really miss the point were we to suppose that anti-triumphalism was not a most serious conviction. It cannot be suspected of being only a humble pose for practical reasons. It is too religiously saturated for this, too critical and outspoken concerning what has gone on and is now going on in the Church. Still, we must ask how the present emphasis on humility can be rhymed with the exclusiveness of the Church as we meet it throughout Rome's history and doctrine. For many non-

[24] The sharp rise in mixed marriages had become a Catholic concern long before the council. This concern led to the subject's being placed on the council's agenda. In most discussions, a revised Church law is sought on mixed marriages in keeping with a changed attitude toward non-Catholic Christians.

Catholics, talk by Catholics about humility and service is exposed as basically insincere by the pretensions that the Roman Church is the exclusive instrument of salvation. Does Romish pretension betray a certain incapacity for genuine self-criticism? Not unexpectedly, representatives of the anti-triumphalist movement were confronted by such questions. Nor can we escape the sound of the ancient dictum even at this stage: *extra ecclesiam nulla salus.*

*   *   *   *   *

We must interject here that this dictum is not the exclusive property of the Catholic Church. The phrase appears in the Reformed creeds, the Belgic Confession for example. Here the true Church is called "an assembly of those who are saved, and outside of it there is no salvation."[25] Moreover, it adds, "all men are in duty bound to join and unite themselves with it." Does this refer to a *particular* Reformed Church? Some Reformed leaders have insisted that this is what the creed does mean and that it is wrong for that reason. Others have taken a more historical point of view and insisted that the creed did not mean that a particular Reformed denomination was the only institution that mediated salvation. Granted the correctness of the latter view, it is striking that precisely these words were lifted from their long history and set within a Reformation credo. The fact that the confession does not permit us to take refuge in an invisible Church makes its use of the dictum all the more impressive. The Roman Catholic use of it raised no problems; that Church clearly intended to say that *extra ecclesiam* meant "outside of the Roman Catholic Church." There is no ambiguity or uncertainty in the Roman pretension of being the one and only ecclesia, nor is there any possibility of misunderstanding what is meant by being "outside" (extra) this Church. Or, on second thought, is there perhaps a need for a closer look at the Roman interpretation of its familiar dictum.

*   *   *   *   *

The phrase *extra ecclesiam nulla salus* goes back to Cyprian's remark that he who separates himself from the Church excludes himself from the promises of the Church and that he who does not have the Church as mother does not have God as Father. No more than it was possible to survive outside of the ark is it possible to be saved outside of the Church, said Cyprian. His use of the ark as a figure of the Church stuck in ecclesiastical jargon, and it was

25 Article 28, Belgic Confession.

frequently used in warnings about leaving the Church.[26] The Council of Florence in 1441 declared that anyone not in the Church — heathen, Jew, schismatic, or heretic — could not share in eternal life.[27] After Florence, references to those *extra ecclesiam* as being lost appear frequently, including the decrees of the First Vatican Council.[28] At the First Vatican the Roman Church was called the one flock under the one Shepherd, and anyone departing from this truth loses his salvation.

We need not recite the places in which the rule is either explicitly or implicitly repeated. Enough to say that to the present day the Church is seen as necessary to salvation. A strong warning is implied here: a decision must be made, not in the innermost soul of the individual, but at the portal of the visible Church. *Mystici Corporis* speaks of those who do not belong to the visible circle of the Catholic Church, and such as these are urged to surrender to the inward pull of divine grace and leave the state in which, outside the Church, they can never be sure of their eternal salvation. The encyclical *Humani Generis* warns against those who turn the necessity of the Church for salvation into an empty cliché. Thus, there appears to be no doubt about the seriousness of Rome as it brandishes the dictum *extra ecclesiam nulla salus.*

✳ ✳ ✳ ✳ ✳

Having said all this, we must also acknowledge that Catholicism does not maintain a clear-cut institutional criterion for salvation, as though the outsiders can be easily distinguished from the insiders by examining their papers. The *extra ecclesiam nulla salus* is used with great care and reserve. In more recent times, the

---

[26] We shall discuss at a later point in this chapter the difference between Cyprian's own understanding of *extra ecclesiam* and the Church's later interpretation of it.

[27] Denzinger, 714. The words are extremely blunt: "... those not living within the Catholic Church, not only pagans, but also Jews and heretics and schismatics cannot become participants in eternal life, but will depart 'in to everlasting fire' . . . ."

[28] Denzinger, 1827: "This is the doctrine of Catholic truth from which no one can deviate and keep his faith and salvation." In the first schema at the Second Vatican Council it was also said that no salvation could be obtained outside the Church. Cf. H. Rondet, *Vatican I*, 1962, p. 199. It also appeared in the pronouncement of 1208 against the Waldensians, in which it was said that there was no salvation outside of the Roman Church (Denzinger, 423). Again, in 1351, "no man of the wayfarers outside the faith of this Church, and outside the obedience of the Pope of Rome, can finally be saved" (Denzinger, 570b). Trent refers to "this Catholic faith, outside of which no one can be saved. . ." (Denzinger, 1000). Many more such statements could be cited.

obvious down-the-line interpretation of the phrase has been given up, and we must patiently listen to the sense given the famous and pretentious phrase by Catholics *now* in their actual encounter with non-Catholics. For some time now, Catholics have insisted that it was never their intention to claim that grace never works outside the Church. For evidence they point to the pronouncement condemning the error of Quesnel who did insist that there was no grace outside the walls of the Roman communion.[29] That the Church should have condemned Quesnel's view that no one outside the Church could be saved need raise no eyebrows, since Rome has always acknowledged the general desire of God for the salvation of *all* men.[30] The universal desire of grace does not rule out the necessity of the Church for salvation. But it does make clear that the dictum "outside the Church there is no salvation" is not meant in an *unqualifiedly* exclusive sense. But granted this to be true, it raises a peculiar problem. On one hand, nothing seems to be clearer than the Church's insistence that there is no salvation outside of the Roman Church; if a man is not in the ark, he drowns. There can hardly be ambiguity here. Yet, the history of Catholic interpretation of the Cyprian dictum shows that it is not as unequivocal as one may suppose it to be.[31]

History has clearly brought about a gradual shift in Catholic attitude on the possibility of salvation outside the Church. In an Allocution issued in 1854, Pius IX expressed himself on the problem of indifferentism by insisting that the Catholic faith holds that "outside the Roman Apostolic Church no one can be saved." For, he said, the Church is the only "ark of salvation in the great flood of divine judgment; no one outside the ark can escape the

---

[29] Condemned is the thesis that "Outside the Church no grace is granted" (Denzinger, 1379).

[30] Cf. the condemnation of the Jansenist "error" that: "Pagans, Jews, heretics, and others of this kind do not receive in any way any influence from Jesus Christ, as so you will rightly infer from this that in them is a bare and weak will without any sufficient grace" (Denzinger, 1295).

[31] On the dictum *extra ecclesiam nulla salus*, see the extensive discussion in H. de Lubac, *Catholicism. A Study of Dogma in Relation to the Corporate Destiny of Mankind*, 1952, pp. 107ff. De Lubac first delineates the universality of God's gracious will for man's salvation and then interprets the dictum within this context. He says that the texts containing the dictum "contain also the immediate qualifying statement which we should expect, excepting the case of invincible ignorance in pagans of good will" (*Ibid.*, p. 117).

destruction of his soul.[32] This appears at first glance to be an unambiguous reaffirmation of Cyprian's dictum. But he qualified the absolute statement by adding that the Lord will not hold anyone fully accountable who lives in "invincible ignorance" of the true religion.[33] Here something definitely new is added, especially since the Pope added that no man is qualified to define the exact limits within which this ignorance is a valid excuse. The Pope then went on to accent the unfathomable mercy of God. Does Pius IX lift the absolute ban on all who are outside the ark? At least he makes explicit the problem that always lay implicit within Cyprian's dictum. The problem is how the Church can reconcile the absolute exclusiveness of the *extra ecclesiam nulla salus* with its desire to leave room for the operation of divine mercy among those who are *extra ecclesiam*.

As one might have expected, Pius' Allocution has been part of an ongoing discussion about the *extra ecclesiam* dictum, especially in view of his strong attack on creeping indifferentism. Besides allowing for the possibility of invincible ignorance, he lashes out against those who teach the impiously fatal doctrine that every religion has markers pointing the way to eternal salavation.[34] But apparently he did not wish to leave an impression of unqualified absolutism, so he also allowed for nuances in the entire situation. He returned to the same theme in 1863 when, again warning against indifferentism, he reminded the Church of the familiar dogma that no one can be saved outside the Church.[35] But once more he made use of the possibility of invincible ignorance, distinguishing those who live in ignorance from those who persist in stubborn resistance to the truth.[36] Clearly, a formal repetition of the *extra ecclesiam* dictum was not sufficient grounds to exclude *everyone* outside the Church from salvation. A subjective factor came into play at this time. In contrast to the

[32] Denzinger, 1647. Prior to the reference given here, the Pope refers to "another error no less destructive" namely, that "one should have good hope of the eternal salvation of all those who have never lived in the true Church of Christ" (Denzinger, 1646).

[33] "On the other hand, it is necessary to hold for certain that they who labor in ignorance of the true religion, if this ignorance is invincible, are not stained by any guilt in this matter in the eyes of God" (Denzinger, 1647).

[34] "That impious and equally fatal opinion" (*ibid,* 1646).

[35] In the encyclical directed to the bishops of Italy, *Quanto Conficiamus Moerore.*

[36] Denzinger, 1677.

total absence of any such qualification by the Council of Florence, the psychological state of the heretic who lives outside the pale of the Roman Church was now made to figure in the possibility of his salvation.[37] Here the image of the ark begins to fall down. While the ark image continued in use, new qualifications were made that seemed to render it obsolete. And herein lies the far more complicated approach to the total problem currently being made within Catholicism.

The stubborn refusal to give up the image of the ark, in spite of the nuances that seem to disqualify it, has led to renewed pleas for the Church to get back to the simple, unambiguous Cyprian statement. While Karl Rahner was referring to the "hard inflexibility" of the dictum, a group of Americans in Boston were calling the Church back from flexibility to consistency. Father Feeney urged a rigorous interpretation of the true Catholic doctrine that all men outside the Roman Church were outside of the grace of God. But Feeney's ideas were condemned in a letter which the Holy Office wrote to Cardinal Cushing of Boston in 1949. In fact, Father Feeney was excommunicated for his persistent teaching of the strict interpretation of the *extra ecclesiam* doctrine. The Holy Office's statement said that the dictum must be understood in the sense that the Church has always interpreted it; the dictum is not open to private (Feeney's) interpretation.[38] Following the line of Pius IX, the letter goes on to explain that anyone who knew that the Church was founded by Christ and who still refused to subject himself to it was indeed lost. But this does not mean that everyone not subject to the Pope was lost. Clearly, the Church was not prepared to return to a rigorist position on the matter.

* * * * *

A clear explanation of the shift in the Church's use of the *extra ecclesiam* dictum is hard to achieve. One explanation is that Rome is merely making concessions to the unavoidable fact that there

---

[37] This does not mean that the attention given to those who err "in good faith" is a novelty. Cf. Congar, *Sainte Eglise*, 1963, pp. 422f. Congar shows that both Thomas and Abelard distinguished between persistent rejection of the truth and the error of ignorance. But the consideration of those who err in good faith has never really been part of the ecclesiological problem. Pius IX was the first to take it up in this connection.

[38] The text is found in *The Church Teaches. Documents of the Church in English Translation*, 1955, 266-280.

are innumerable Christ-confessors outside of Rome.[39] Rome, it is said, cannot go back on its dogma and it cannot ignore the facts, so it straddles the fence. Many Catholics have pointed out that the real intention of the dictum was only to underscore the fact that the message and means of salvation were given exclusively to the Church and that therefore it was stubborn refusal of people outside to hear and obey that brought upon them the exclusion from saving grace. With this, it was possible to make distinctions among those who were outside.[40] The dictum is not forsaken, for Catholics still believe that the Church is uniquely necessary to salvation and they insist that it is this belief that the dictum expressed, not a theory about the state of every last man who is ouside the Church. This may explain how the qualifying phrase "invincible ignorance" could appear in the same Allocution which warns against indifference about the dogma of *extra ecclesiam nulla salus*. Christ gave to the Church a *mandate* which makes the Church inexpendable for salvation and also endows the Church with the *means for* bestowing saving grace, thus giving the Church a double dimension of necessity — necessity of precept and of means.[41] In resistance to any indifference about these elements of necessity, the Church still brandishes the ancient terminology about *extra ecclesiam*. Meanwhile, the route from the excusability of a certain kind of ignorance as an *exception* to the rule to a less rigoristic interpretation of the dictum itself is not wholly clear. Quite likely, any further statements on it will be more qualified and expressive of the complexities involved than previous ones have been. As an example of the trend, we notice that discussions have now gone beyond Pius' general acknowledgment of the exceptional mercy of God toward those in invincible ignorance. We hear more talk these days about attitudes or dispositions in the people outside the Church which may qualify them for salvation.

This leads us to the so-called "desire for the Church," or *votum ecclesiae*. The non-rigorists are taking account of the possibility that among those outside the Church some really have a longing for what the Church could give them. This is not merely a toler-

[39] H. Bavinck explains it by saying that the facts were too strong for Rome to remain consistent with its dogma on this point (Bavinck, *Geref. Dom.* IV, 295).

[40] Cf. Congar, *Sainte Eglise*, 1963, pp. 429f.

[41] *Necessitas praecepti et medii*. Congar stresses the preceptive necessity of the Church, insisting that the dictum *extra ecclesiam nulla salus* is not meant to judge a particular person, but to establish the exclusive significance of the Catholic Church as that institution mandated by the Lord to bring the salvation of Jesus Christ to all men (*ibid.*, p. 444).

ance of non-Catholics.[42] Nor, on the other hand, is it limited to the negative exception of invincible ignorance. Something more positive is allowed for in the hearts of the outsiders. It comes to expression in the Holy Office's 1949 statement. For, in answer to the Boston rigorists, the Holy Office recalls the doctrine of baptism of desire.[42a] Proceeding from the biblical statement that regeneration is required for entrance to the Kingdom of God (John 3) to the dogma that baptism is required for salvation. Baptism, in the sense of *water* baptism, however, is not absolutely necessary for salvation. Where circumstances prevent actual baptism, the *desire* for baptism suffices. And the desire can then be a substitute means of saving grace. Usually, the circumstances preventing baptism are objective and circumstantial. For instance, the martyrdom of an unbaptized person substitutes for water baptism; the baptism of fire effects what baptism of water would have effected in normal circumstances.[43] In such cases there is obviously no inner, spiritual obstacle to the reception of baptism. A catechumen, anticipating baptism, may be martyred before his baptismal preparation is completed and in his martyrdom receive the generating grace that would otherwise have been his at baptism.

The question now before us is what connection this traditional allowance for baptism of desire has with the "desire for the Church," particularly among those thousands who feel no *conscious* desire. At this point a distinction is made between an *implicit* desire and an *explicit* desire, between the *votum implicitum* and *votum explicitum*. The catechumen obviously has an *explicit* desire for the Church. But an *implicit* desire is present in those whose soul longs for conformity with the will of God.[44] Where this desire is present, there is an unconscious desire for the Church. It can exist in a person who is totally ignorant of baptism, but does

---

[42] In the matter of tolerance, we have to do with a respect for, and a patience with the opinions of others. Tolerance has no implications for the relationship to the Church and its faith of those whose "errors" are tolerated. The *votum ecclesiae* has direct implications for the relationship to the Church of the person "desiring the Church." Cf. W. Brugger, "Was ist Toleranz?" *Festgabe K. Rahner*, II, 1964, pp. 592ff.

[42a] *Votum Baptismi*, Denzinger, 796. The *votum* also comes into play in connection with the sacrament of penance (Denzinger, 807).

[43] *Baptismus flaminis*. Cf. Denzinger, 388, 413.

[44] Thus also in the letter addressed to Cardinal Cushing by the Holy Office. "When a man is invincibly ignorant, God also accepts an implicit desire, so called because it is contained in the good disposition of soul by which a man wants his will to be conformed to God's will" (*The Church Teaches*, 275).

wish to do the will of God.[45] Back in 1863 mention was made of people who zealously pursue the natural law of God that is written on the hearts of all men.[46] And since then much more has been made of the desire, either implicit or explicit, in those outside the Church to do what the Church commands and to have what the Church offers. This desire is apparently the link between the exclusiveness of the *extra ecclesiam nulla salus* and the potential inclusion of *some* who are *extra ecclesiam* within the embrace of grace.

We are concerned here particularly with implicit desire, since this could describe some outside the Roman Church who have no conscious desire to be within it, and in fact wish explicitly and emphatically to stay outside of it. Can the notion of "implicit desire" contribute anything at all to the relationship between the Roman Church and other churches? Can it provide a new tack for the Roman Church's judgment on non-Catholic *churches?* Catholics insist that *invincible ignorance* can be a complex fact within non-Catholics; various reasons can be found why given non-Catholics are unable to recognize Rome as the true Church. And this complexity opens the door to further possibilities for those outside the doors.[47] But the notion of *implicit desire* is even more difficult since it must be assumed to be present under certain specific conditions. And the problem for the Roman Church is to delimit and define the conditions under which it can judge implicit desire to be present in someone who would himself perhaps deny its presence.

Regardless of the internal problems that the implicit desire clause creates for Rome, what interests us is the fact that with it greater breadth is created and insisted upon within Catholicism and the corresponding fact that Rome has to relate this breadth with its traditional exclusiveness. Whatever the problems the Roman Church may have with the relation between the allowances of implicit desire for the Church and the dogma that outside the ark as such all men drown, the fact that rigoristic exclusiveness is being forsaken is of enormous significance. In spite of the Church's inability to deny the dogma, the dictum that no salvation exists outside the Church has lost the "appearance of a

---

[45] M. Schmaus, *Katholisches Dogmatik*, II, 1, 1952, p. 157.

[46] Denzinger, 1677. In the encyclical *Quanto Conficiamus Moerore.*

[47] In a very important article, Karl Rahner says that the Church does not sacrifice the principle of its "summons to conversion" to Rome, but is trying to interpret the *extra ecclesiam* in a way that does not suggest a simplistic proselyting ("Einige Bemerkungen über die Frage der Konversionen," *Catholica,* 1962, pp. 1-19).

monstrous and exalted posture over against countless men and women who though outside the Church and outside Christendom demonstrate a sincere desire to live as unto God."[48] The Roman Church also declined the Boston gambit that tempted the Church to enter a course that would have unproblematically assigned outsiders to perdition. Perhaps the Church followed its intuition here more than its logic, but in doing so it did point to a possible new approach to those who are outside, and particularly to the "separated brethren" swimming outside the ark.

* * * *

The possibility of salvation outside the walls of Rome is closely related to the problem of *membra ecclesiae,* the real members of the Church. This matter was involved in what is at least the indirect purpose of the Second Vatican Council — reunion with the separated brethren. The relationship between Rome and non-Catholic Christians has for some time not been the same as it was at Florence, for instance, where the Church was distinguished from heretics and schismatics as sheep from goats. The post-Pius IX era also reverted to the hard-line policy as is seen in the character of the First Vatican Council.[49] Pius IX's restrictions on the *extra ecclesiam* dogma were neglected, while the traditional line was underscored. For this reason, Rome's first response to the ecumenical movement was very negative.[50] Rome has traditionally insisted that Christ does not support and nourish other churches alongside of His mystical body, the one true Church. Yet, it has gradually come around to another look at the ecumenical movement. Its second look at ecumenicity is motivated not so much by a relaxation of its conviction of being the one true Church as by a growing awareness that this conviction carries a tangle of problems along with it.

At present the trend is to soft-pedal the exclusiveness of Rome and to emphasize the reasons for people's estrangement from Rome. Instead of pontificating on its own priority, the Roman Church is eager to analyze the conditions under which others remain apart from her. And this approach rules out a simple "return to Rome" attitude. Acknowledgment of mutual responsibility for the division, the confession that the Roman Church as it lives and moves in the actual world is often unworthy of belief,

48 Rahner, *Schriften zur Theologie,* p. 52.
49 See Chapter 1.
50 The negative response is very clearly reflected in the 1928 encyclical, *Mortalium Animos,* On the Promotion of True Religious Unity.

the necessity of making the gospel more convincing through the renewal of the Roman Church are symptoms of the new disposition. We do not hear a simple warning that to refuse conversion to Rome is to forfeit salvation. Not even the invincible ignorance clause suffices any more to deal with the complex situation. What we witness in Catholicism today is an intense self-examination, a probing effort to understand the situation in the light of the gospel. With this, a more serious attempt is made than has ever been made before to come to grips with the problem created by the Church's claim to be the only ark and the fact that many outside are not drowned in the floods of divine judgment.

The solution mentioned sometimes is that there is a sense in which people can be *membra ecclesiae* — members of the Church — *in a certain sense* without being members of the institution. They can be, perhaps, members of the mystical body while outside of the organization in the sense that they belong to the soul while absent from the body. The distinction that is made here between the soul and the body of the Church has, however, met with criticism. To make such a distinction implies that the body of the Church is not necessary to salvation. And the Catholic Church is not prepared to say that its visible, juridical, hierarchical, and sacramental aspects do not belong to the essence of the Church. To say that one can belong to the soul while not a member of the body hints that only inward and spiritual belong to the essence of the Church's reality. After all, the Cyprianic dictum was directed against those who did not belong to the *visible* Roman Church. And Pius XII's encyclical *Mystici Corporis* insisted that the entire Church with all of its machinery and hierarchy was the mystical body. Little room, then, seems left for a workable distinction between the soul and the body of the Church; the whole Church had to be seen as "one indivisibly unified" body.[51]

The lapse of the soul-body distinction only served to underscore the persistency of the problem. If the Roman Church and Christ's mystical body were one and the same, coterminous, then the problem of the division of the churches seems to scream for honest

---

[51] M. Schmaus, "Die Kirchengliedschaft nach Honoré de Tournely" (1658-1729), *Festgabe für J. Lortz*, 1958, pp. 463ff. Tournely uses the distinction between the soul and body of the Church, but Schmaus insists that the encyclical does not allow this as an option. It does speak of the soul of the Church, but means by it the Holy Spirit. Congar says that the distinction is neither ancient nor fortunate (Congar, *Chrétiens désunis*, 1937, p. 281). The Commission for the preparation of the First Vatican Council rejected the distinction as being scholastic and novel.

study at a time when those divisions are recognized as the complex things they are. The Holy Office's letter on the Boston heresy paved the way for further reflection by calling for an understanding of the Church's real intent in its dogma of exclusive salvation. In the light of this, we can take another look at Pius' *Mystici Corporis* according to which those who do not belong to Rome are not members of the mystical body. According to Pius, it would seem, the mystical body of Christ reaches no farther than the farthest Roman altar.[52] Does he, then, close out all genuine and liberal willingness to honor the existence of room within grace for outsiders? His encyclical has in fact spurred a new look at the identification of the mystical body with Rome.

Out of the intense preoccupation with this problem have come such notions as are involved in Congar's interesting description of the "Church of Abel." The "Church of Abel" is the Church in pre-Christian times, even pre-institutional times. Congar recites the Church Fathers in their readiness to speak about the Church in ways that do not fit the Church as it now exists in its visible form. He thinks that modern theologians have neglected the fact, as the Fathers did not, that the Church once did exist in a way not conformable to the New Testament structure. The "Church of Abel" is an example.[53] The fact is remarkable that, even though Congar's point had no direct bearing on the Church's disposition toward outsiders, it drew immediate fire from critics. Though it was formally granted that Congar did not want to relativize the hierarchical form of the Church, his appeal to the "Church of Abel" could suggest that the Church in the form established by Christ was not inherently necessary and could be altered without touching the essence. Congar's stress on the *history* of salvation in the Church — the critics charged — could lead to a weakened vision on the necessity of the Church in its present form. If it changed in previous stages of history, the conclusion could be that it could change now. In fact, Congar was actually trying to defend the external aspect of the Church as being essential to the Church, and this makes the criticism levelled against him the more remarkable. Congar's critics are obviously wrong in accusing him of incipient ecclesiastical "spiritualism." His accusers in their turn fail to recognize the full seriousness of the problem created by the identification of the Roman Church with Christ's mystical body.

---

[52] Cf. the opening phrase of the encyclical, "On the mystical body of Christ, which is the Church."

[53] Y. Congar, "Ecclesia ab Abel," *Festscrift für Karl Adam*, 1952.

Rahner is closer to the truth when he says that *Mystici Corporis* allows for an honest discussion of a broader concept of the mystical body than simple identification with the Roman institution. "Careful differentiation" will have to be made in the future, Rahner writes, and he is probably gauging the Catholic situation accurately.[54] On the other hand Congar's thesis about the pre-Christian Church being of different form than the Pentecostal Church does not undo the fact that *Mystici Corporis* was speaking only of the latter when it identified the mystical body with the Church of Rome. In view of this, it does not make a real theological contribution to the ecumenical discussion, for the ecumenical discussion is between Protestant churches and the *Roman* Church, not the "Church of Abel."[55]

Another distinction that is used to get at the problem is that between a true and complete membership in the Church and a membership of inferior grade. According to this distinction, those who have received the baptism of regeneration, have made confession of the true faith, and have not torn themselves apart from the body of the Church, are full members.[56] Are there then members who are something less than "genuine" or "full" members? The term "genuine" is a common translation of the Latin *reapse*, but this suggests that the alternative is "not genuine," or false.[57] What is actually intended is to suggest that an alternative to "genuine" can be "less than complete." *Mystici Corporis* rules out the possibility of another kind of member than that of membership in the Roman Church. There has, at least, to be some connection with the Church, as in the case of a catechumen who is neither fully a member nor is wholly outside the Church. *Mystici Corporis*, on the other hand, does speak favorably of those who "are inclined to the mystical body of the Redeemer by way of an unconscious desire or longing." But this again is not meant to suggest that a person with implicit desire has a membership in the Church qualitatively different from

---

[54] K. Rahner, *Schriften zur Theologie*, II, p. 73.

[55] Rahner says that the complete identification of the Church with the Christian form of the Church has an eye only for the *Christian* way of salvation in this world (*ibid.*, p. 73). But it is clear that the real problem lies precisely here.

[56] Cf. *Mystici Corporis*: "The Spirit *refuses* to dwell with His saving grace in those who are completely cut off from the body."

[57] Cf. S. Tromp, *Litterae encyclicae* 26, 1958, p. 91: *Reapse: id est re, in oppositione ad voto*" (*reapse* means *to be* in distinction from *to will*. Dietzenfelbinger says that the word *reapse* has "sucked a veritable comet's tail of interpretations behind it" (*Die Grenzen der Kirche nach römisch-katholischen Lehre*, 1962, p. 29).

him who is fully within the Church. So, those with inferior associations with the institution (catechumens, people with "implicit desire") are not members of "another kind"; they are only less complete members. The only members of the Church there are are genuine members. And so the problem of the *extra ecclesiam nulla salus* and the possibility of being members of the Church *extra ecclesiam* of Rome remains an ennervating one. It is ennervating because while several distinctions are tried and found wanting as solutions, they are tried in an awareness that the Church is involved in a tension-filled existential situation with great ecumenical bearing.

* * * * *

The discussion of this problem at the Second Vatican Council took on unique significance in view of the importance fixed to the presence of the non-Catholic observers. The phrase "true and proper" membership in the Church appeared in the first schema on the Church. But the second and briefer schema dropped this and, with a gesture toward the familiar *extra ecclesiam nulla salus,* used the phrase "genuine and unequivocal" membership. Those who lived in ignorance, it was said, could enter salvation, but only in a manner different from "genuine" membership in the Church. The same problem is brought to the fore here. Obviously Rome sees itself somehow bound to non-Catholic Christians and recognizes that the Spirit is somehow at work among them. But an adequate definition of Rome's position *vis-à-vis* those outside is terribly hard to come by. Somehow, in the Catholic view, the outsiders must be recognized as *membra ecclesiae,* as members of the Church, if they are to be recognized as *Christians.* But then what of Rome as the only Ark of the Covenant?

The question of whether there are Christians outside of the Church is not the ultimate problem that Rome is wrestling with. The personal possession of grace on the part of outsiders is not in the crucible. The question settles on the nature of the Church and of whether the Christian reality of outsiders can be fixed in some churchly sense. The second schema speaks generously of the faith in Christ, the love of the Lord, even the preservation of some sacraments, and the sanctification through the Spirit that is evident in non-Catholic Christians. The question is whether in view of this recognition of Christian grace outside of Rome the existence of other *churches* outside of Rome can also be conceded. When the ancient Church made a decision about the legitimacy of heretical baptism, it made a gesture toward recognizing the validity of an objective sacramental act among non-Catholics. True, the early Church was not immediately involved with this as an ecclesiological problem, but it was involved with something more than a recognition of a lively personal and individual faith. The early Church did not draw the same conclusion as to heretical baptism from Cyprian's dictum that Cyprian himself drew.[58] The early Church obviously recognized a certain Christian bond between those within and those outside the Church, even though it too faced the problems involved in the relationship between baptism, the Church, and the work of the Spirit.

The recognition of heretical baptism was never withdrawn by the Roman Church. Whether it was always honored in practice is another question. The answer to this question of practice depends on historical research of the contexts within which heretical baptism was practiced. Was baptism in a given church practiced as a sacrament instituted by Christ and invested in the Church, or was it practiced in a church which was rapidly on its way from heresy to apostasy? But this further question, the answer to which depends on historical research, underscores the fact that when non-Catholic baptism is honored by Rome, it is honored as a genuinely Christian and objectively valid instrument of salvation. And this makes the problem such an acute one for Rome with its assumption that it is the one true and only Church.

❋   ❋   ❋   ❋   ❋

When Paul VI opened the second session of the council, he addressed himself to "the *other* Christians" and to "Christian communities" who "believe in Christ, but whom we to our great sorrow cannot number among ourselves in the perfect unity of Christ."[59] He acknowledged a genuine Christian heritage preserved among the separated brethren, a heritage which they have developed as authentic treasures of truth and spiritual life. In such terms, Paul

---

[58] The Council of Arelas (314 A.D.) said of the baptism of (Donatist) heretics: "it has been decided that, if anyone from a heretical sect comes to the Church, he should be asked his creed, and if it is perceived that he has been baptized in the Father and the Son and the Holy Spirit, only the hand should be imposed upon him. . ." (Denzinger, 53). St. Innocent (401-417) writes: "That those who come from the Novatians or the Montanists should be received by the imposition of the hand only, because although they were baptized by heretics, nevertheless they were baptized in the name of Christ" (Denzinger, 94). The Council of Trent issued this canon: "If anyone shall say that the baptism, which is also given by heretics in the name of the Father and of the Son and of the Holy Spirit, with the intention of doing what the Church does, is not true baptism: *let him be anathema*" (Denzinger, 860).

[59] *The Pope Speaks*, Vol. 9, No. 2 (1964), p. 135.

VI was only underscoring again the problem of the Church as Rome faces it: the problem that rises against the background of Rome as *the* ark, *the* sheepfold, to which all others are urged, as Christ's straying sheep, to return.[60] E. Schlink, speaking at a gathering of German bishops in Rome, stressed the evangelical difficulty with Rome's dilemma in recognizing non-Catholics as Christians while not recognizing non-Catholic churches as genuine churches.[61] Schlink was quite right in underscoring the dilemma. The schema quotes many Catholic sources in which non-catholic groups are referred to as "churches." But this is done with reservations, since the fullness of salvation is still said to be found only in the Roman Church. And the fact that the fullness of salvation is found only there implies that the one true Church is the Roman Church alone.[62]

The fullness of salvation is bound up with the unity of the one Church, and this is the reason why, in spite of its grateful recognition of Christian graces among non-Catholic people, the Roman Church still addresses Protestantism from the platform of the one and only Church. It is just possible that Protestants may interpret Rome's glad admission of non-Catholics into Christian reality as a surrender of its position as the *unica ecclesia,* the one true Church in exclusive identification with the body of Christ. Making this mistake, we would lose sight of Rome's own deep problem and inner tensions; we would lose sight of the fact that Rome's new ecumenical encounter is experienced against the background of the inflexible tradition that it is the only true Church of Jesus Christ. The decisive question is not whether Rome acknowledges other Christians as real Christians. The decisive question at this point is whether Rome will acknowledge other churches *as real churches.* Voices at the council were heard asking that non-Catholic "fellowships" be granted the *title* of Church. But even if this were done, the question would still persist as to the significance and extent of this semantic concession. Would it be only a recognition that non-Catholic groups are *analogous* to the Church? Or would it be a real recognition of them as genuine churches? If the latter, Rome could be shaking its own dogmatic structure to the foundation.

[60] The Pope spoke of "other communions which take their name from Christ and are called Churches" (*ibid.,* p. 131).

[61] Cf. E. Schlink, "Themen des Zweiten Vatikan. Konzils in Evangelischer Sicht," *Kerugma und Dogma,* 1963, pp. 187ff.

[62] Paul speaks of the "perfect unity" that is the Roman Church and of the sheep which "properly and completely" make up Christ's flock.

We would only be avoiding the hard core of the problem if we were satisfied that reasonable ecumenical progress could be made on the basis of Rome's recognition of vestigial characteristics of the Church in non-Catholic communions. To be content with Rome's acknowledgement of the so-called *vestigia ecclesiae* — traces of the true Church — would only be to run up against a new problem as we avoided the other one. We would then have to ask what these traces were, what they meant, and what bearing they had on the more profound ecclesiological questions.[63] Giovanni Megge was right when he insisted that the *vestigia* notion offered no real solution to the ecumenical question.[64] Certainly the Orthodox churches do not see a sign of hope in Rome's acknowledgement that traces of the Church remained in the Eastern communions. When Paul VI went about as far as he could under the circumstances in recognizing elements of the true Church in the Orthodox communions, the response from the East was subdued to say the least. The *vestigia* concept leaves the real problem untouched. For the authentic form of the Church is in question. And the core of Rome's problem in its relation to other churches still lies in its own pretensions of being the Church established by Christ and maintained under the government of His Vicar at Rome.[65]

The real problem is put on the table when Paul VI speaks of the sheep that are wandering *outside the sheepfold*. Is such a distinction biblically allowable? *Does the Lord have sheep who are not part of His flock?* Could John the evangelist conceivably have had in mind sheep who were outside the door? His very definition of the sheep includes the fact that they are *inside* the door, that they *hear*

---

[63] Calvin acknowledges the existence of vestiges of the Church in Rome, vestiges such as baptism and other "peculiar prerogatives of the Church," adding: "And just as often happens when buildings are pulled down the foundations and ruins remain, so He did not allow His Church either to be destroyed by Antichrist or to be leveled to the ground . . ." (*Institutes* IV, ii, 11). Calvin is not willing to concede the title of "*the* Church" to Rome but does not "for this reason impugn the existence of Churches among them" (IV ii, 12). "I call them Churches to the extent that the Lord wonderfully preserves in them a remnant of his people. . . . and to the extent that some marks of the Church remain. . . ." (*ibid.*).

[64] G. Megge, "Vestigia Ecclesia. Signes de l'Eglise dans les Eglises," *Verbum Caro*, II, 1957, p. 211.

[65] The problem comes to sharp focus in O. Semmelroth, "Kirche und Kirchen" *Fragen der Theologie Heute*, pp. 366ff. Semmelroth says that the vestiges of the Church are authentic Christian values, "goods of an ecclesiastical character," or "something of the reality which is the peculiar attribute of the Church" or "elements of the Church." And he says that he can ascribe to the "separated brethren only vestiges of the Church, a fragmented reality" of the Church.

the Shepherd's voice and *follow* Him, that they are the sheep for whom the Good Shepherd lays down His life (John 10:1-18). The picture of sheep that are outside the sheepfold — i.e. the Church — is, biblically considered, an inner contradiction.[66] The Shepherd, the sheepfold, and the sheep are so uncompromisingly united each with the other that to use the dialectic of sheep inside and sheep outside the fold is to use a biblically unwarranted device. The image of the sheepfold is parallel to that of the ark, both of which are equally sharp and clear. One can only be inside or outside the fold, inside or outside the ark, and to be inside is to be saved and to be outside is to be lost.

To employ these images within the ecumenical problem is to cast that problem into a mold from which there is no escape. We must admit that a really workable and acceptable solution has never been offered. For, in the context of the Bible, no form can be given the formlessness created by the divisions of the churches. And the awful burden of guilt for the divisions only seems the more unbearable in the light of this. Neither the clear-cut conviction that one church among all others is the only Church, nor the vague notion of the pluriformity of the churches illuminates the separate ways the pilgrim Church walks. We have seen that the history of the *extra ecclesiam nulla salus* dictum only illustrates how thorny with problems this apparently clear-cut solution is. Even the more flexible interpretation of the dictum given in recent years has not really solved the problem. But it is a problem that has become terribly existential in times when the divisions of the Church can no longer be tolerated with an easy conscience, a problem that pierces the conscience of us all whenever we recall the words of our Lord: there shall be *one* flock and *one* Shepherd (John 10:16).

✻ ✻ ✻ ✻ ✻

In the light of the New Testament, the *original* (!) intent and inner motivation of the dictum *extra ecclesiam nulla salus* is quite clear. It was meant to echo the deep conviction that the Church was one, the one ark, the one temple, the one house of God, the only bride, the single body of Christ. To set any or all of these in *plural* form would only show how ridiculous is the notion of many authentic churches. Calvin saw this too, and he meant it when he said that the Catholic Church must be one "because there cannot be two or three churches without Christ himself being torn apart,

[66] John 10:16 refers to "other sheep" but these refer to the future and to the history of salvation, and have no bearing on the sheep outside the visible Church at any given time.

and that is impossible."[67] Calvin does not see division as unfortunate or objectionable; he thinks in terms of *impossiblity*. Given the biblical self-evident unity of the Church — the one Lord, the one faith, the one baptism, the one Spirit — the formula *extra ecclesiam nullas salus* has a very biblical and congenial ring (Matthew 12:30). It carries the same radical suggestions as do the biblical images of the ark and the one sheepfold. A person is either for Him or against Him, with Him or lost apart from Him. The radical character of biblical language has been toned down as we have grown accustomed to division. The idea that "outside the ark" one's condition can be described only as desperate and hopeless has been watered down by all sorts of qualifications and interpretations. The reasons are obvious and understandable. We meet so many people who love the same Lord and confess the same basic faith that we push the stark ecclesiological problem into the background as we honor the spiritual fellowship we share. But the ecclesiological problem with its sharp focus looms as a disturber of the joy of spiritual kinship with Christian brothers.

This is really the problem that vexes the Second Vatican Council. The more flexible, large-hearted interpretation of the Cyprianic dictum *extra ecclesiam nulla salus* has definitely won the field. But the traditional image of the ark and the one flock still has a vested status. And herein the knot is uncut. When *Humani Generis* (1950) warned against making the *extra ecclesiam* an "empty formula," it was telling the Church that there were still boundaries surrounding the Church. It was serving notice that any broader interpretations of the *extra ecclesiam* had to be set in the context of the *one* ark and the *one* flock. That Catholicism should be experiencing theological and ecumenical tremors is not surprising in the light of these two poles of Church experience. One pole is the traditional conviction of the one true Church being identical with Rome. The other pole is the broadened personal contacts with non-Catholics, the improved insight into the deep religious motivations of the Reformation, and the discovery of many Christian legacies in the non-Catholic communions. Into this situation, Paul VI set out the aim of the council as "complete and universal ecumenicity. That at least is what it desires. It is praying for it, preparing for it."[68] But it is also in this situation that the problem of the sheep and the one fold is urgently pressed. Rome still identifies Christ's mystical body with the Roman Church even while it recognizes the bond of faith

[67] *Institutes,* IV, i, 2.
[68] *The Pope Speaks,* Vol. 9, No. 2, 1964, p. 135.

between it and the "separated brethren." Neither of these can it abandon. We would be doing the Roman Church an injustice if we did not take its problem in this complicated situation with utter and sympathetic seriousness.

✻ ✻ ✻ ✻ ✻

The identification of Rome with the body of Christ provides enviable security and composure to Catholicism. It need not mean a glorification of itself and its members. But it does seem to provide a guarantee that no problem can render invalid. The Catholic "knows" that the Church, with its mysterious hold on the Spirit, is in fact secure as it goes on its pilgrim path. That he "knows" does not betray romantic illusions about some ideal Church that has no connection with the actual Church. He is now very aware that the Church is passing through genuine danger zones. He is aware that the Church is realistically called to be alert to genuine threats. Even its own history warns him. But the question that haunts the evangelical is how fully and profoundly this warning can possibly be heard once one has identified his *institution,* his historical and empirical organization, with the indestructible body of Jesus Christ. Can the urgent *warning* and the absolute *guarantee* function together in the real life of the Church?

To get at this question in depth, we must first listen to the warnings that the Lord does sound to His Church in the New Testament. Israel, as the people of God, was constantly pressed by dangers to its existence. Paul cited Israel as an example and from it culls a warning for the New Testament Church: "Let him who thinks he stands be careful lest he fall" (I Corinthians 10:12). The New Testament Church, the Church of end-time, is warned the more urgently just because it does approach the end of the age (I Corinthians 10:11).[69] Again in Romans 11 Paul warns the Gentile congregations not to be proud, but to be afraid, and to stay within the mercy of God lest they be cut off like a dead limb from the fruitful olive tree (Romans 11:20). The book of Hebrews recites the threefold warning of Psalm 95: "Today, if you hear his voice, harden not your heart as in the days of bitterness" (Psalm 95:8; Hebrews 3:8, 15). The New Testament Church is frequently put in the same situation with Israel, surrounded by very real threats and ominous dangers (I Corinthians 10:6, 11). The people are called

[69] Cf. the warning in I Thessalonians 5:22 and Titus 3:10 where the schismatics are singled out.

brothers and saints, partners in the heavenly calling (Hebrews 3:1). But they *are* warned.

Where the Church is stressed as the eschatological people of God the warnings sound the more critical. The Spirit must not be grieved (Ephesians 4:30), nor must He be quenched (I Thessalonians 5:19). And there is a real possibility that He can be. Without a hint that salvation, the new and better covenant, the coming fulfillment of the promise to which Hebrews so often points is thrown into the cauldron of uncertainty or desperation, the New Testament presses homeward the terrible existential possibilities that threaten the Church. The urgency for the Church hits a climax when it is told that the judgment must begin at the household of God (I Peter 4:17, 18). The joy of the promise is not darkened, but false security in it is shaken (I Peter 1:8). The Church is put to the test, and one form of the test is the question of whether the sufferings of the Church prove that the Church shares in the sufferings of Christ. When the Church suffers in the right way and for the right reason, it has its only guarantee that "the Spirit of glory and of God rests upon you" (I Peter 4:14). To realize that the judgment should begin at the household of God belongs to an awareness of the eschatological hour. Even the Church, says a Roman Catholic interpreter, "lives under judgment."[70] As the judgment began at Jerusalem in the Old Covenant (Ezekiel 9:6), and as God threatened to "search Jerusalem with candles, and punish the men that are settled on their lees" (Zephaniah 1:12; Amos 1-2:9) so the call is given to the Church to guard herself against the threats and dangers surrounding her lest she forfeit her place as the true Church. The very critical warnings issued by the New Testament to the Church are often jammed by our preoccupation with the riches and security promised to it. We are summoned to understand that the promise of salvation in Christ may never be mistaken for taps that sound an "all is well" to resting Christians.

The Roman Catholic hold on the *guarantee* need not be understood as a faithless and simplistic illusion about the inevitable perpetuity of the Church and of salvation in it. Evidence piles up that Catholics want to take the struggle and the warning and the dynamic of New Testament Church life seriously. But a nuance takes place at this point. The warnings are applied clearly to individual Christians while they are only qualifiedly applied to the Church. Catholic theology of recent times has recognized a problem

---

[70] K. H. Schelkle, *Die Petrusbriefe, in loco.*

here. Rahner points out that the decisive and eschatological work of Jesus Christ provides the Church with untouchable security and indestructibility.[71] The Church cannot lapse into the position of the synagogue; its own position is secured, not because of its own strength but only because of Christ. Rahner recognizes that this guarantee of the Church's indefectibility is a major issue at stake in the controversy between Rome and the Reformation. To be sure, he does not mean to set the whole of the Church's life within this impregnable sanctuary; he distinguishes between those acts of the Church which do and those which do not share in its essential indefectibility. (Though he recognizes that a clear distinction between them is not possible for us to make, he insists that the distinction exists.) The Church is still a pilgrimage of faith and hope and it cannot live without tension and strife nor without self-criticism and self-correction. Both the Christian person and the Church must both hold fast in the end to the one thing needful: "trust in the grace of God alone." But while the individual believer must keep alive to the danger and possibility of apostasy, the Church essentially stands under the light of its own indefectibility.[72]

The indefectible nature of the Church has been stressed by Reformation churches as well as by the Roman Catholic Church. Is it not true that the Bible affords this perspective of the Church, an assured continuity to the end rooted in God's corrective intervention into human guilt and failure? Does not Christ provide the Church with a guarantee that cannot be invalidated? Did He not build the Church and did He not assure it that the gates of hell will not prevail against it? (Matthew 16:18). The Belgic Confession assures us that the Church will abide to the end since Christ the King will never be without subjects.[73] The Augsburg Confession,

---

[71] K. Rahner, "Kirche und Parusie," *Catholica*, 1963, pp. 113ff. R. Schnackenburg writes: "The Church *in toto* will never again desert God. The universal saving power of Christ's death and the Holy Spirit provided by Him will prevent it. This does not rule out the possibility that individual members may forsake Him and be shut out of the Kingdom" (*Die Kirche im Neuen Testament,* 1961, p. 139).

[72] Rahner, *op. cit.,* p. 126. See also M. J. Scheeben, *Katholische Dogmatik,* I, p. 104ff. It is remarkable that Scheeben says that indefectibility is "not as absolute as the infallibility." There is a "minimum below which the Church cannot sink and from such a falling away the substantial continuity of the Church and the deposit of truth within the Church are preserved." That the Church is always kept above this minimum required for it to be the true Church is the essential idea of indefectibility.

[73] Belgic Confession, Article 27. Cf. The Scottish Confession, Article 16.

too, confesses that one holy Church is to continue forever.[74] A remarkable parallel appears between these Protestant confessions and Rahner's insistence that the Church will never defect into apostasy in view of the definitive character of Christ's saving work. The big question is how this motif shared by Catholics and Protestants is worked out in more concrete form. We have seen that the Roman Catholic stress on the indefectibility of the Church refers to the one Roman Church in its actual historical form. This institution called the Roman Church is the Church which alone is protected from apostasy by the word of promise. The indefectibility of the Church is given another slant in Reformed theology. Here, the Church's continuity is correlative to its own faith and obedience and to its will to abide in the Lord. We are kept from thinking of the guarantee given to the Church in abstraction from the correlative connections that make up the mystery of the Church. Christ is present in the Church, but in the Church that is *gathered in His name* (Matthew 18:10; 28:20), that keeps His commands (John 15:10), and that listens to His Word (John 14:23).

The assurance that the Church has for the future is expressed in conditional terms. And these conditions point, the Church to the *kind* of protection that is guaranteed to it. It is equally correct to speak of the Church being preserved as it is to speak of the Church preserving itself.[75] To speak of the Church being built and to speak of the Church building itself are both true and both necessary. Together they make up the route which opens up the sure perspective on the future. The way is travelled through abiding in Christ's word[76] (John 8:31), in His love (John 15:9), and in Himself (John 15:7). The Church *must* remain true. God remains true. These two facts are bound together in a living correlativity, and it is only in such a correlative situation that the Church is assured of its continuity. This kind of continuity is unique, *sui generis;* it has no real parallel anywhere. The continuity promised to the Church is not one that is self-evident from the nature of the Church as seen in its structure. It is one that occurs in the life of the Church as it is put to the test of its life with Christ.[77] To be gathered "in His name" is

[74] Augsburg Confession, Article VII.

[75] Jude 1 and 20.

[76] Cf. John 5:38 and II John 9.

[77] John writes that with the anointing of the Holy Spirit, one needs no man to teach him. But this does not imply an automatic guarantee of truth, for the anointing is connected with the condition expressed in the words, "If what you have heard from the beginning abides in you, then you will abide in the Son and in the Father" (I John 2:24).

correlative to Christ's promise of His presence. In the same way, the promise that the Church will never defect into total apostasy is correlative to the Church's walking the way of faith and obedience.

This was an important point with the Reformers. The continuity of life promised to the Church cannot be objectified into an automatically sustained piece of existence. It can only be grasped in faith as the Church walks into the danger zones of its earthly life, and can be discovered as strength and comfort *on the way*. This is what is expressed in the Reformed confessions. Calvin speaks about the eternal life of the Church and about the impossibility of interrupting the work of Christ. But he does not say this as a simple proposition of the brute fact of the Church's continuity nor as an observation about the Church's structure. Whether the Church as a concrete institution is participating in the promise of continuity must be made evident in its real life of faith and obedience.[78] The controversy between Rome and the Reformation is not one between a church that is sure of its indefectibility and a church that is not sure of it. Bavinck stresses the indefectibility of the Church and, in view of the promises given to it, speaks of a guarantee of the Church's continuity.[79] But this guarantee would be grotesquely misconstrued if it were lifted from the actual life of the Church as it is constantly put to the test, a test met within the context of the promise.[80] To apply the continuity and indefectibility of the Church only to the invisible Church would also be false.[81] It applies to the very visible Church as, grasping the promises in faith, it walks the way of faith and obedience through the fires of severe testing. The Church in all its earthly reality is the Church to which the eschatological warnings about the judgment that begins at the

[78] Calvin, *Institutes,* II, xv, 3.

[79] H. Bavinck, *Gereformeerde Dogmatiek,* IV, pp. 308f.

[80] Calvin sought continually to point out the correlative character of the promise. The truth of God has never been extinguished because the Church is its faithful custodian, but this depends on the faithfulness of the prophetic and apostolic ministry. If one speaks of the inability of the Church to lapse into ultimate apostasy, he must also speak of the Church's responsibility to remain in the Spirit. As it meets its responsibility the Church may rely on the "fullness of the promises." That the Church cannot err is true "in so far as the Church, having forsaken all its own wisdom, allows itself to be taught by the Holy Spirit through God's Word" (*Institutes,* IV, viii, 13).

[81] The notion of an "invisible" Church is first of all meant as a *critical* concept, though it has undeniably often been used as an escape from ecclesiological problems. See H. Berkhof, *De Katholiciteit der Kerk,* 1962, pp. 14ff. Also, H. Bacht, *Die Sichtbarkeit der Kirche in kontroverstheologisch Gespräch,"* in Ratzinger and Fries, *Einsicht und Glaube,* 1962, pp. 447ff.

house of God are directed. It is the same Church that received the promise. And the mystery of the Church is manifest here as over against mechanical and objectified notions about the preservation of the Church through history. And at this point it also becomes clear that we cannot squirm out of the mystery by separating individuals (who are in danger of apostasy) from the Church (which is secured against apostasy).[82] The Church as a whole in its entire existence as the eschatological people of God lives here and now under the light of the coming dénoument.

Speaking about the coming of Christ in connection with the unity of the Church, Schlink writes: "The first real break-through toward Church unity will take place when we all become aware, not intellectually alone but to the point of inner fear and trembling, and when we proceed from the fact that all of us are put under a radical and inescapable question mark by the Lord of the Church."[83] With this, Schlink rightly tries to pull the Church out of an introversion and self-contemplation that finds its security for the future in its own identity apart from the test to which it must be subjected. The Church has no brute factuality that guarantees its inevitable continuity. The preaching of the coming of the Lord snatches away all "static pretensions of perfection."[84] For the Lord's coming is connected to the Spirit's presence as comfort *and* warning and, in this way, opens up the perspective of the final victory. The Church can go out to meet its Lord only in fear and trembling, in constant prayer for divine underpinning. For the way on which it goes to meet Him is the way of danger and threat. And so the mystery of the Church touches on the entire human nature of the Church, including its offices and its total ministry. We stand here at the threshold of the crucial point in the entire ecclesiological problem. When Paul VI asked the Church what it thought of itself, he was not asking an introverted question. His question can be answered only as the Church keeps its eye turned to the heavens from whence the Lord will come. And the question cannot be soft-pedaled by an

---

[82] The following sentence shows how aware certain Catholics are of this fact: "The acts of the Church are not to be isolated from the acts of men in the Church" (W. Joest, "Die Kirche und die Parusie Jesus Christi," *Gott in Welt, Festgabe fur K. Rahner*, I, 1964, p. 549).

[83] E. Schlink, "Pneumatische Erschütterung," *Kerugma and Dogma*, 1962, p. 234.

[84] W. Joest, *op. cit.*, p. 548.

appeal to the guarantee the Church possesses, for the critical seriousness of the question points the only way on which this guarantee can have its real meaning.

The critical aspect of the Church's faith, within which the indefectibility of the Church must be understood, is of weight for any right approach to the unity and holiness, the apostolicity and catholicity of the Church.[85] These are usually called the attributes of the Church. But we have to be careful lest we attribute these qualities to the Church in the same sense that we attribute roundness to a circle or height to a mountain. We must not suppose that a careful analysis of measurement of the Church as an objective thing will reveal these as its qualities. A peculiar problem is involved in theology's talk of the Church possessing these four attributes. They are often described in a way that smacks of observable, demonstrable, and verifiable facts manifestly true of the Church. Roman Catholic ecclesiology has often worked with them in such an empirical manner. That it has is demonstrated by the significance it gives to *proofs* for these attributes.[86] We are not concerned here with the Roman Catholic doctrine of the Church's attributes, but there is one point which we cannot neglect. This is the factual demonstrability of the attributes. It is of importance because the evidence for the attributes is closely related to the credibility of the Church and because the credibility of the Church is being discussed in a new way by recent Catholic theology.

The background to the problem comes out in the First Vatican Council's reference to the Church as the "motive of credibility." The Church in its concrete reality and factuality is the basis for expecting men to believe. The council calls attention to the Church's growth, its fruitfulness in good works, its holiness, unity, and stability, all of which are irrefutable witnesses of its divine

---

[85] Cf. Küng, *Strukturen*, for an extensive Catholic discussion of this point.

[86] In a letter of the Sacred Office to the bishops of England, dated September 16, 1864, we read: "The true Church of Jesus Christ . . . is known by a fourfold mark, which we assert in the Creed must be believed; and each one of these marks so happens that that Church which truly is, and is called Catholic, should at the same time shine with the prerogatives of unity, sanctity, and apostolic succession" (Denzinger, 1686). The First Vatican Council declared that "God, through His only-begotten Son, has instituted the Church, and provided it with clear signs of His institution, so that it can be recognized by all as the guardian and teacher of the revealed word" (*ibid.*, 1793).

mission.[87] The Roman Church as it exists visibly before men constitutes a clear and unquestionable reason for believing its message. In our day, however, the credibility of the Church is broached, not as an obvious and discernible fact, open to natural reason.[88] It is seen more as the challenge and calling of the Church; it is not what the Church *per se* is, but what the Church is *summoned to become*. That is, the actual Church is summoned to be the *real* Church so that the image of its Lord may be reflected through it. The questionable side of the Church is too vivid to prevent a qualification of its so-called self-evident attributes. The attributes cannot be a simple description of what the Church has always been; they must be a reminder of what the Church ought to be. Clear evidence for the Church's credibility is not at hand; it is not demonstrable in the pages of the Church's history. The evidence that the Church is indeed worthy of belief must be sought and found in the daily will to respond to the calling to represent faithfully the one holy, apostolic, and catholic Church *in* the *actual* Church. The question of whether the Church is in fact worthy of belief is a most critical one for contemporary Catholicism. And instead of listing proofs for the Church's credibility, Catholics are now putting its credibility in the form of conditions.[89] The Church as the "reason for believing" and the "attributes of the Church" are swiftly being taken out of the area of apologetics and put in the area of pastoral responsibility.[90]

[87] "For, to the Catholic Church alone belong all those many and marvelous things which have been divinely arranged for the evident credibility of the Christian faith. But, even the Church itself by itself, because of its marvelous propagation, its exceptional holiness, and inexhaustible fruitfulness in all good works; because of its catholic unity and invincible stability, is a very great and perpetual *motive of credibility,* and an incontestable witness of its own divine mission" (Denzinger, 1794).

[88] "Invincible ignorance" becomes a problem in connection with the "evident credibility" of the Church. How can anyone's ignorance be "invincible" in view of the unmistakable evidence of the church's credibility? Cf. K. Rahner, "Was ist Häresie?" *Schriften zur Theologie,* V, 1962, pp. 527ff.

[89] The presence of a condition can indeed subjectivize salvation, but it can also, as in the New Testament, point the *way* in which salvation is received and respected as God's gift. Herein lies the cardinal difference between the correlation of faith and promise and subjectivism. Cf. K. G. Steck, *Lehre und Kirche bei Luther,* 1963, p. 94.

[90] According to Bavinck, Rome allows for no distinction between the attributes and the marks of the true Church (Bavinck, *op. cit.,* IV, p. 304). His contention is supported by numerous Catholic theologians. Cf. B. Bartmann, who says that the marks of the Church are "likewise in the first instance essential attributes of the Church" (Bartmann, *Dogmatik,* II, p. 178). Cf. also J. V. de Groot, *Summa Apologetica de Ecclesia Christi,* 1906, p. 148, "a mark is a property of the church." And many others.

The mystery of the Church is set in the dynamic context of both "gift" and "responsibility," of comfort and warning. The Church's "authenticity as a witness" is not so much "proved" or demonstrated any more as it is accepted in terms of a "burden of responsibility."[91] If the Church is to be worthy of belief, it must be worthy in act, as is implied in the call to renewal and self-criticism made by both John XXIII and Paul VI. Compared with the static apologetic approach of the First Vatican Council, the credibility of the Church is now seen as conditional, as a critical challenge and as dynamic movement.[92] It is not self-evident; it is true only in terms of responsibility within the life of the Church on its way toward the fullness of Him that fills everything and is in everything.[93]

The history of the Church raises a warning finger, as Küng has emphasized. This warning has a parallel in the "spiritual trembling" that Schlink recommends in the face of the Church's failures. Both of these are now allowed to play their role in the Catholic motif. The Church's human groping through history, a groping that has shadow sides as well as light, speaks relevantly to the Church's notion of its own credibility.[94] The anti-triumphalist mind prevailing in the Catholic Church at present is not about to let the notion of credibility lapse into a static and self-evident one. The guidance of the Spirit is recognized in a more dynamic sense. "The Holy Spirit," it is said, "is not caught prisoner in the Church, nor is He identified with the Church's spirit as though the Church has con-

---

[91] H. Küng, *Strukturen*, p. 55. H. Urs von Balthasar says that the marks of the Church which were formerly connected with the hierarchy "have lost some of their apologetic force to the increased significance seen in the one central mark: holiness." The unity, catholicity, and apostolicity have effectiveness only as they are subordinate to the holiness of the Church (von Balthasar, "Kirchen-fahrung dieser Zeit," *Sentire Ecclesiam*, 1961, p. 756f.

[92] See M. J. Scheeben, *Handbuch der Katholischen Dogmatik*, II, pp. 332ff. Scheeben strongly emphasizes the factuality, the supernatural manifestation of God in the Church. Cf. in this regard Küng's citation of Volk to show that the credibility of the Church has not been overwhelmingly great if judged by the increase in the number of Catholics during the years 1880-1958. He mentions a growth of 0.14 percent (Küng, *Strukturen*, p. 49).

[93] The concept of "fullness" looms fairly large in current discussions. Cf. J. L. Witte, "Die Katholizität der Kirche," *Gregorianum*, 1961, pp. 206ff. Witte reflects the Catholic problem of "gift" and "responsibility." Catholicity is a gift, yet it is not complete or "full." The "fullness" (*pleroma*) has already been given to the Church, yet it is the Church's task to strive for it. It has been given to the Church in the form of "a kind of inchoate fullness."

[94] Cf. H. Küng, *Konzil und Weidervereinigung*, 1960, pp. 60ff.

trol of Him; no, He blows where He wills."[95] The pneumatic aspect of the Church is correlated with the calling and the responsibility of the Church. None of this betrays a Catholic doubt about the continuity of the Church; but it is a strong hint that Catholics are on their guard against the perversion of the Church's credibility into an illusion that the Church is worthy of being believed simply because it is an institution called the Roman Catholic Church. It is also a hint that Catholics are calling the Church to be a Church ready and willing to be reformed so that it can be credible.

❀ ❀ ❀ ❀ ❀

This new and dynamic insight into the nature of the Church's credibility, coming as it does from evangelical motives, is now brought into direct relationship with the guarantee of the actual, presently existing Roman Church. And with this a real tension is created. Must not the actual, presently existing Roman institution, believed to be the same as the mystical body ("which is the Church"), limit and contain the dynamic approach to the Church's credibility as a calling and responsibility? Does not the *a priori* guarantee claimed by the visible institution in its actual structure weaken the summons to self-criticism and the need of putting itself to the test? On the other hand, if the call to watchfulness belongs to the essence of the Church — to the structure of the ecclesia — must not the guarantee possessed by the Church be conditioned by the love, faith, and walk in the truth that the Church is commanded to demonstrate? If this is so, can we speak of the relationship between Christ and His Church and between the Church and the Spirit in any other way than as revealed by the testing of the Gospel? The emphatic word of promise cannot, if this is true, be objectified into an announcement that the future is secured to any actual institution.

We are reminded here that all churches must make a radical distinction between the biblical reliance on the promise of the Spirit and a human pretension of possessing the promise simply by being the institution that it is. The New Testament warns the Church with the example of Israel's apostasy. Israel became apostate as it transformed the promise of God into a self-glorifying pretension. It appeared to be making a legitimate deduction from divine promise to human security. But in reality it forgot the promise in its original form and in doing so it lapsed into the same position as the Philistines; each had its exodus and each was the

[95] Küng, *Strukturen,* p. 59.

same in God's sight (Amos 9:7). The significance of God's acts in and with Israel was not undone by putting Israel and Philistia on the same level. Rather, the real significance of God's works was protected against terrible perversion by Israel. When the time was ripe, and the promise of the Spirit and of the presence of Christ was given to the Church, the example of Israel could be set before the Church as a warning in its own eschatological situation. The Church has been clearly told that the reality of salvation cannot be automated. Only as it is lived out in faith and obedience does this salvation remain the inheritance of the Church.

The new Catholic theology is protesting against the identification of the promise of the Spirit (and its "guarantee") with an automatically secured continuity. The very urgency of this protest, so closely related to the anti-triumphalist movement, signals a fairly new and important point of contact for ecumenical dialogue. The Reformation was not at all of a mind to overlook the promise of the Spirit and of Christ to the Church. It did not look on the Church's history as a series of discrete contingencies in each of which the salvation that Christ won was hanging uncertainly from the hands of believers. The Reformation did not see Church history as an uncertain experiment. But, with the sure promise in the near background, the relation between the Church and the Spirit's presence was seen as related to the preaching of the gospel, prayers for the Spirit, the challenge to abide in love, to walk in the obedience of faith, and in short, to the *mystery* of the Church's continuity. Today, Roman Catholic ecclesiology too is warning with an increasingly urgent tone against confusing the Lord's guarantee with self-sufficiency and automated perpetuity. The mystery of the Church is such that the Church's attributes cannot be turned into static and observable categories.

In view of Catholic calls to humility and Catholic insistence on a right to criticize the Church,[96] may we expect a new view of the credibility of the Church? Since the actual existing Church has been drawn into the question of its own credibility and since the attributes of the Church are seen more as the goal than as the obvious possession of the Church, may we expect a changed insight that will move the Catholic Church closer to other churches?

---

[96] B. Schneider contests the view that the Church's history is a "photostatic copy of the ideal Church, free from failures and undisturbed by shortcomings" ("Bemerkungen zur Kritik an der Kirche," *Gott in Welt,* II, p. 251). He refers to the "ultimate heresy against the real Church" that is expressed in such a notion of the actual Church.

This movement is in fact observable on many fronts, be it with tensions and against protests.[97] The new movement toward other churches is manifest in a changed attitude toward them. The spiritual relationship to other churches has outpaced, it is true, the dogmatic-ecclesiological expressions. This is due in part to the sense that the problem of the credibility of the Church is shared by other churches. The terminology is following the spiritual institution, however, as is witnessed by Cardinal Alfrink's reference to other churches as "instruments of divine salvation."[98] While the conviction that the Roman Church is the one and only Church remains officially untouched, the anti-triumphalist trend has led by degrees to a sense of common testing and confrontation among the churches. The change that has taken place in Catholicism on the point of the Church's credibility has implicit consequences that have already come to life in more than cautious statements. No one has a right to draw conclusions that the Roman Church must draw for itself, certainly not those which the Roman Church does not wish to draw. But we can say that its evangelical-critical approach to the credibility problem has dynamic and explosive potential. We must, of course, be careful lest we fall into a Protestant triumphalism; the Church's life under divine searching is too serious and too radical to allow for any new pseudo-Reformed triumphalism. As we try to live in a conscious reliance on the gospel, the door to self-glorification and pretension is shut to us. For pretension is a denial of the real sort of glory the Church has. Reformed theologians have talked about "more" or "less" pure churches and about the *vestigia ecclesiae* in other churches as though they had forgotten that comparisons are never bases for boastfulness and pretension. A Church's "pure confession" can have relevance only as a call to greater responsibility for the total life of the Church. All the words we have learned to use for the Church — "one holy, apostolic, catholic" — get their meaning only

[97] Karl Rahner recalls how Pope Pius XII read Hugo Rahner's speech on "The Church, God's Power in Human Weakness" without protesting but also without feeling any inner sympathy for it. One of Rahner's associates told him: "Yes, for the Pope the Church of Glory is much closer than the Church of men." Karl Rahner tells this story in connection with his discussion of the "sinful Church of sinful men" (Rahner, "Dogmatische Randbemerkungen zur Kirchenfrommigkeit," *Einsicht und Glaube*, 1961, pp. 771ff).

[98] The reference was made in a letter to the General Synod of the Dutch Reformed Church on the occasion of Princess Irene's conversion to Catholicism. The Cardinal spoke about the respect for "the other Christian Churches" that is demonstrated in acceptance of their baptism.

as the Church really does reflect its Lord. The Scriptures' "if," echoed in Luther's "insofar" and in Calvin's constant warnings to the Church, recall the Church to the awareness that it is tested all along the way of history and in all its particular forms; it is tested for credibility and incredibility, for truth and heresy, for unity and schism, for faith and unbelief, for love and lukewarmness to the Lord. It is tested for any effort on the part of the Church or its officers to be "great" in a way that casts a shadow over the image of Him who once and for all revealed beyond any possible misunderstanding what true greatness must mean for the Church (Mark 10:43).

*   *   *   *   *

Roman Catholics have raised the question of whether the promise of the Spirit and the resulting indefectibility of the Church has any bearing at all on the concrete, historical Church as it has taken shape before us, and whether this Church does after all reveal the mystery of the body of Christ, if not the oneness of the Church. Outside the Catholic Church, too, the New Testament acknowledgment of only one Church has led to doubts about the notion of the Church's pluriformity. The trouble with this approach is not that it makes use of the obvious New Testament assumption of the Church's unity. The trouble with it lies in the temptation to fasten the attributes of the one Church to one's own Church, forgetting the share in guilt for the divisions that each Church bears. There is an acute danger that in speaking of *the* Church, one forgets that he is talking about the one body of Christ and begins to secularize the concept "Church." With this, one falls easily into the trap of introverted ecclesiology that in fact forfeits true catholicity. In our day, the realization has grown that catholicity is a critical concept and that it must function as a critique of the actual Church. If one is conscientious about catholicity in this critical sense, he will avoid the simple expedient of covering the whole problem of the division of the churches with the mantle of pluriformity. The concept of pluriformity too quickly extracts from our consciousness all sense of responsibility for and burden of conscience about the divisions. The world around us ought to be able to recognize in the Church what unity and unbreakable fellowship can be. And no cliché ought to be allowed to rob us of our responsibility toward the fulfillment of the words of our Lord: "As thou, Father, art in me, and I in You, that they may be in us, so *that the world may believe* that thou has sent me" (John 17:21).

Concretely, all that is going on in the Catholic Church means for us a continuation of the dialogue and a critical testing of *ourselves* in the light of the gospel. The way ahead is hard and sometimes seems to offer little perspective. But His scepter is lifted above us. We must believingly perceive that the mystery of the Church is *not* the "mystery of its divisions." The divisions are only a *riddle* in the critical light of the one Shepherd, the one body of Christ, and the one bread. The ecumenical movement is always threatened by the danger of compromise in its confession of the Name of Christ. But it is also evidence that the Church is disturbed by the riddle of the division. This is the same disturbance that Paul felt and expressed in his haunting question: "Is Christ divided?" (I Corinthians 1:13). Paul's question echoes through the history of the Church. It is not to be tossed around lightly. But when taken seriously it forces us to new thoughts and new sense of responsibility to the gospel, especially as we stand at the crossroads where Christians go their separate ways. The question Paul asks corresponds to the categorical statement of Jesus: "There shall be one Shepherd and one flock" (John 10:16). There are many questions and many facets of the great mystery of the Church. But there is also a biblical obviousness, a biblical unambiguity: the one Shepherd and the one flock.

As this chapter ends, we may be well served by recalling the images and analogies that reflect the mystery of the Church: the temple, the people of God, the sheepfold, the bride, the body of the Christ. In their fascinating variety they all point to the one reality of the Church. The essence of the riches of the Church reflected in the harmony of all these images contradicts in clear terms any pretentious sense of the Church's riches.[99] The Church's true riches can be recognized only as the Church is truly worthy of being believed and it is in turn credible only as it is transparently nothing other than the Church of the Lord who commanded love to each other in order that it would be clear to all that "you are my disciples" (John 13:35). The present controversy that involves the churches is carried on against the background of our Lord's command. This defines the urgency and the responsibility of these discussions. For what is above all important is that the Church should be visible as the Church of Christ's disciples and that its

---

[99] Cf. P. S. Minear, *Images of the Church in the New Testament*, 1961, pp. 221ff. Cf. Revelation 3:17: "I am rich, I have prospered, and I need nothing," which is a caricature of Psalm 23:1: "I shall not want."

light shine to the glory of the Father.[100] Following this line, the important question cannot be whether a soft or hard line is used in interpreting the *extra ecclesiam nulla salus*. The important question is whether the witness of the humble people of God is being heard, the people who sense that they have been called out of darkness into the wonderful life of the Savior.

We do not need any idealizing of the Church. But to pray and speak of her as the people of God, on their pilgrimage as one body, witnessing as they go to the wonderful works of God, is not to idealize the Church. For this is its "reality"as described in the New Testament. It is the Church from which all offenses — including the offense of its divisions — must be removed except the offense of the cross (I Corinthians 1:25). Only then will it make deep and earnest sense to point to the boundaries of the true Church. And only as we keep our eyes open to the *mystery* of the Church will the divisions of the Church not paralyze us, but drive us on to the responsible course within the controversy. What apart from the mystery of the Church would be pointless polemic, can in view of it be of service both to the Church and its Lord.

[100] Cf. Matthew 5:14-16; Philippians 2:15.

Mary

DURING AND PRIOR TO THE SECOND VATICAN COUNCIL consideration was given to a further elaboration of the dogma of the Virgin Mary. The proclamation of Mary's assumption in 1950[1] stimulated a powerful new interest in the veneration of Mary and Mariology. Pius XII was especially active in the promotion of Marian devotion, devoting a few encyclicals to it,[2] giving special attention to Lourdes,[3] and in general indicating enthusiasm for increased devotion to Mary. Since Pius XII felt that Mary's assumption to heaven was the "crown and perfection" of her original privilege, the immaculate conception, one could conclude that further de-

---

[1] In the papal bull *Munificentissimus Deus*. Delius says that the composer of the bull was G. Filograssi, professor at the Gregorian University. I have not been able to corroborate this.

[2] *Fulgens Corona* (On the Marian Year — 1953), and *Ad Coeli Reginam* (On the Coronation of Our Lady — 1954). See besides, his encyclicals, *Mystici Corporis* (1943) and *Mediator Dei* (1947).

[3] The Pope issued an encyclical (*Le Pèlerinage de Lourdes*) on the occasion of the Centenary of the appearances at Lourdes in 1858. In this encyclical, Mary's reported statement, "I am the Immaculate Conception," is cited once more as miraculous support for the dogma proclaimed in 1854. Lourdes is called the "seal of her infinite goodness."

velopment of Marian dogma is unnecessary. The question of whether the Church ought to say anything more to elevate Mary's position was pertinent, moreover, in view of the council's indirect purpose of creating the possibility of reunion with the "separated brethren." The Catholic leaders were sensitive to the reaction that the spurt of Mariological action under Pius XII had evoked in the Eastern and Protestant churches.[4] Therefore some Catholic spokesmen, feeling that the ecumenical situation did not provide the proper occasion for a new formulation of dogma, were very lukewarm to any further Mariological statements. Others, on the other hand, insisted that Catholic relations with non-Catholics should not cause Catholics to have reservations about confessing the full truth.

The keynote message of John XXIII supported the pre-council feelings that a further statement on Mary was unlikely. John made a point of saying that the primary task of the council would not be to discuss "specific articles of Church doctrine," but to apply the unwavering truth of the Church to our times in a way that would let its power be seen and felt anew.[5] The paths that Catholic theology was taking during the years preceding the council also cast doubt on the likelihood of further elaboration of Marian dogma. The trend seemed to be towards an honest and candid review of the past development of the dogma and a re-evaluation of the Reformation's motives for rejecting it.[6] At a time when biblical studies have become very prominent, attention ought to be given, it was felt, to the Protestant insistence that the Marian dogmas of 1854 and 1950 were without scriptural support. This argument received an additional impetus when the doctrine of the double source of revelation was debated so heatedly at the sitting of November, 1962. As the point was made that there was really only *one* source of revelation, it also became clear that the proponents of this view were not about to argue the legitimacy of the Marian doctrine by pointing to tradition as its source.

The reaffirmation of the notion that there was only one source of the apostolic witness created a new demand for showing that the Marian dogma was founded in Scripture. This came on top of the clear trend in Catholic theology for seeking new ways of interpreting the traditional teaching of the Church. As we have seen, the new interpretations are sought by getting at the deepest intentions of the Church in the formulations it made under limiting his-

---

[4] The reaction in the Eastern church was based not so much on the *content* of the dogma as on the fact that it was issued in the *authority of the Pope.*

[5] *Gaudet Mater Ecclesia.*

[6] Cf. H. Küng. *Konzil und Wiedervereinigung,* 1961, p. 160.

torical and polemical situations. Recall again the recent interpretations given to Trent's decrees on justification and human merit and on tradition. The question relevant here is whether the Church's former assertions about Mary are also amenable to such revised interpretations and whether any new interpretation could have a constructive bearing on the ecumenical dialogue.

Any revised interpretation of the Mary doctrines would seem to be extremely difficult to come by since they are statements of fact about events — her immaculate conception and her assumption into heaven. Moreover, these have to do with essential points of Church doctrine.[7] Can these be interpreted in a way that would make the Church's intent clearer and, perhaps, less objectionable to non-Catholics so that some of the painful points of the controversy could be dulled? Or is the dogma of Mary so fixed that it must remain one of the biggest obstacles in the way of mutual understanding and closer contact? Are the new and unquestionably important new interpretations Catholics are giving to Catholic doctrine overshadowed by this one immutable doctrine of Mary? In brief, is there any possibility for new light on the Marian dogma such as would open up a new ecumenical perspective on what otherwise seems closed territory? Or has Roman Catholicism reached the point of no return in its Mariology?[8]

* * * * *

Roman Catholics do not exclude the possibility of a new approach to Marian dogmas and they offer a number of arguments to support their contention.[9] In view of this, we should orient ourselves somewhat in the area of contemporary Mariology. There has been a noticeable effort on the part of Catholic theologians to remove the foreign quality that non-Catholics sense about Marian doctrine. To do this, a critical eye has been turned on the development of Marian devotion. It is admitted that popular devotion has sometimes taken bizarre forms. And the objections to it on the

[7] Cf. the papal bull of 1854 which says, concerning those who would question the immaculate conception, that "if any should presume to think in their hearts otherwise than as it has been defined by us, which God avert, let them know and understand that they are condemned by their own judgment; that they have suffered shipwreck in regard to faith" (Denzinger, 1641). The papal bull of 1950 says that to doubt or deny the assumption of Mary is to fall utterly away from divine and Catholic faith.

[8] Karl Barth says that the dogma of Mary is "the critical central dogma of the Roman Catholic Church" with which everything else stands or falls (*K.D.*, I, 2, p. 157).

[9] Cf. A. Fiolet, "Oecumenische Bezinning op de Mariologie" *Tijdschrift voor Theologie*, 1962, pp. 375ff.

part of non-Catholics are conceded as justified. In fact much criticism of Marian devotion within Catholicism today sounds like an echo of Protestant objections in the past. There is an honest recognition that Marian devotion contains a real danger of obscuring the glory of Jesus Christ. Catholics are not content merely to answer Reformed charges by saying that Marian devotion, far from robbing Christ of His due, actually honors Christ, Mary's son. Today they are more likely to admit that *in fact* popular piety has indeed tended to let Mary overshadow the mediatorship of Christ. One hears Catholic theologians criticize Mariologians for ascribing a function to Mary in the work of salvation that has already been completed by Christ. They go so far as to say that some forms of Mariology have introduced a new gospel in her name.[10] This is especially the case in the matter of Mary's cooperative role in the accomplishment of human salvation. While the pious cliché — "there can never be enough said about Mary" — still is used in some circles, it is fenced in tightly by the newer theologians.

The phenomenal appeal of Mary is explained by some in terms of the Church's tendency to dehumanize Christ. P. Rusch contends that the christological controversies ended by laying such stress on the uniqueness and divinity of Christ that a deep gulf was created between the ordinary believer and his Lord. The distance between Christ and simple piety created a vacuum that was filled by Mary. "As Christ the Redeemer disappeared from view, the very human and intimate and religiously appealing figure of Mary drew near to take His place."[11] In the West as well as in the more speculative East, "the mediatorship of Christ declined in the popular religious consciousness," and the image of Mary grew correspondingly large.[12] The Counter-Reformation gave a new impetus to Marian devotion as did the spectacular phenonenon at Lourdes in 1858. Rusch is highly suspicious of any Mariology that offers a compensation for what the pious fail to experience in Christ. Mary set as the "mother of mercy" as over against Christ the Judge offers a dangerous and false alternative.[13] Rusch reminds his fellow Cath-

[10] Cf. F. W. Künneth, *Maria, das Romisch Katholische Bild vom Christlichen Menschen,* 1961, pp. 61ff.

[11] P. Rusch, "Mariologische Wertungen," *Zeitschift für Katholische Theologie,* 1963, p. 131.

[12] *Ibid,* p. 133.

[13] *Ibid.,* p. 135. Pope Leo XIII issued an encyclical in 1891 called *Octobri Mense* (On the Rosary) in which he said on one hand that we must all fear the Lord our Judge, but on the other hand assured Catholics of the invincible power of the prayers of Mary on their behalf.

olics that the New Testament gives no excuse for suggesting that Mary can appeal to simple trust better than Christ can as though Christ were "too divine."[14] He appeals to I Timothy 2:5 to show that Christ is mediator between God and man, "the only mediator of salvation," and expresses a feeling of uneasiness in the face of what he senses is a popular "dishonoring" of the only mediator.[15] Rusch is not the only one to warn against the dangers implicit in Mariology; many Catholics are asking for a fresh restudy of the "basic notion of the Mother of God" in the light of the gospel. And wherever this critical sound is heard it is accompanied by a negative reaction to further development of Marian dogma, particularly of a development in the direction of Mary as "co-redemptrix."[16]

Even before Rusch published his article, Fiolet had made a comparison between the devotion given to Mary and the humble position which the Scripture assigns to her role in the salvation purchased by her Son. He pointed out that Mary did not stand alongside of Christ in the redemptive mystery, but on the side of men.[17] The Reformed Christian is right, he admits, in protesting the picture of Christ and Mary standing together in the mystery of redemption. For anything even suggesting that Christ and Mary occupy the same plane is not merely misleading but clearly distorts the biblical witness concerning Mary. The rightness of the Reformation response to Mariology on this point, says Fiolet, opens up the possibility for "an ecumenical discussion on Mariology."[18]

In such frank talk there is no criticism of the dogmatic definitions of the Church. What these critics want is "another tone, a different atmosphere, and different proportions." They are warning against exaggerating the image of Mary out of proportion; they are accenting the unique mediatorship of Jesus. They want Catholics to demonstrate by *word* and *deed* that devotion to Mary

---

[14] Rusch, *op. cit.*, p. 140.

[15] *Ibid.*, p. 141, 145.

[16] A. Müller, "Fragen und Aussichten der heutigen Mariologie," *Fragen der Theologie Heute,* 1957, p. 314.

[17] Fiolet, *op. cit.*, p. 378. The so-called Collyridians, a female sect of the 4th century, offered sacrifices to Mary as being "alongside of God." The conservative Catholic dogmatician Diekamp refers to their devotion to Mary as "a pagan worship of Mary" (*Dogmatik*, II, p. 388). The entire problematic in Catholicism is concentrated on the fact that Mary is a human being, a "pure creature," and on the question of her status as a human being.

[18] Fiolet, *op. cit.,*, pp. 375f.

does not in fact minimize Christ's position as mediator between God and man. In this way they hope to close part of the deep gulf that exists between the churches at the point where Mary appears. This approach is given the unimaginative name, *minimalism*. It does not suggest that Catholics should speak as little as possible about Mary. It calls for a critical view of some excessive devotion to and speculations about Mary. And it asks the Church to be alert to the heresies that can and actually have crept into the Church by way of Marian excesses.

The papal encyclicals about Mary reveal little of this concern. They do stress that devotion to Mary takes nothing away at all from the honor due to Christ,[19] and they point for proof to the formulation given the doctrine in 1854.[20] The encyclical *Inter Complures* of 1954 illustrates the tone papal letters display. Pius XII here gives a passing nod to the middle position that Marian dogma takes between denial and excess, and then goes on more extensively to contend that fear of giving Mary too much honor is an unreasonable fear since "the Son would never begrudge honor given to His mother whom He Himself covered with so much grace."[21] The encyclicals are too general in their suggestions of possible excess in devotion to Mary and too lavish in their enthusiasm for Marian piety to communicate any real concern. But in today's Catholic theology this has changed. Now piercing warnings are heralded and protests are sounded concretely against what is called "Marian heresy."[22]

The "minimalist" approach to Mariology bears a strong exegetical stamp. Catholic theologians veer wide of forcing texts to fit Mariological dogma. And with this a very important point is made that came up at the council in respect to the Scripture as the unique source of divine revelation. Compared to former use of Scripture to substantiate Marian dogma, today's emphasis marks a definite shift. Encyclicals that dealt with Mary appealed to Scripture in a remarkably superficial and almost playful way. For instance, we are told that Noah thought about Mary as he entered the ark, just as did Abraham when he was told not to slay his son, Jacob in his vision of the ladder, Moses at the burning bush, David when he moved the ark, and Elijah when he saw the cloud

---

[19] Cf. *Fulgens Corona.* Here the Pope answers the charge that "we would thereby in any sense derogate from the worship it is our duty to bring to God and to Jesus Christ. On the contrary . . ."

[20] *Ineffabilis Deus.*

[21] *Fulgens Corona.*

[22] Cf. H. Küng, *Konzil und Wiedervereinigung,* 1961, pp. 157ff.

rising from the sea.[23] There is a remarkable nonchalance in explaining certain texts: "everyone knows," for instance, that the woman clothed with the sun of Revelation 12:1 is Mary.[24] Scripture passages are borrowed from the fathers to demonstrate the assumption of Mary: for instance, Psalm 132:8 ("Arise, O Lord, into thy rest; thou, and the ark of thy strength") and Isaiah 60:13 (". . . I will make the place of my feet glorious.").[25]

These encyclicals are free from any hint of independent biblical study. They reflect only what was said of Scripture in former days, without so much of a hint that exegesis may have anything new to say for the understanding of Scripture.[26]

Back of this uncritical use of Scripture lies the generally accepted thesis that the decisions about Mary made in 1854 and 1950 are not directly or explicitly revealed in the Bible. There is a general agreement that they are implicit in Scripture, though in a "hidden and shrouded way, so that they must be pointed out by tradition." In view of this, the new appeal to Scripture becomes particularly relevant to Mariology, for since tradition is said to be non-creative, the Scripture must be translated and interpreted in such a way as to make the Mary doctrine clearly a biblical truth. With the new stress on Scripture as the only source of revelation, the interpretation of Scripture's teaching about Mary becomes a most important Catholic task. The "consciousness of faith" may be significant,[27] and the teaching authority of the Church may be important, but neither of these can take the place of establishing the dogma of the Church in revelation. In times when the apostolic norm for the faith of the Church is given special emphasis, as it

---

23 *Ad Diem Illum* (On the Fiftieth Anniversary of the Definition of the Immaculate Conception — 1904.)

24 *Loc. cit.*

25 *Munificentissimus Deus.*

26 Pius XII said that theologians use a "certain freedom in citing events and texts from Scripture in order to illuminate their faith in the assumption" (*ibid.*).

27 M. D. Koster says that "the simple sense of faith can be not only the only support for the tradition of faith, but can even contradict the dubious witness of Scripture, the bishops, the liturgy, the fathers, and the theology of the Church" (Koster, *Volk Gottes im Wachstum des Glaubens. Himmelfahrt Mariens und Glaubenssinn,* 1950, p. 128). Carl Feckes writes in regard to Mary's assumption: "The primary norm of my faith is by no means Holy Scripture but the living consciousness of the present day Church . . . . The Church therefore does not need in principle Holy Scripture." Cited by R. J. Ehrlich, "The Protestant-Roman Catholic Encounter," *Scottish Journal of Theology,* 1963, p. 28. There would be no norm by which the "consciousness of faith" can be held up to criticism, if such statements as these were the consensus of Catholicism.

is today, biblical exegesis is likely to place a large role in further discussion about Mary.

*   *   *   *   *

In a speech broadcast to the international Marian Congress, on October 24, 1954, Pius XII declared that Mariology had to be based on solid foundations. He mentioned the wonderful things that the Scripture expressly declared about Mary, her virgin motherhood and her immaculate conception. Though it is true, he said on another occasion, that the nobility and exaltation of Mary cannot be fully recognized without the aid of tradition and authority, the assumption of Mary is *based* on Scripture and even the proofs from the fathers are ultimately grounded in Scripture.[28] In view of the Pope's appeal to Scripture, it is not surprising that Mariological discussions are centered increasingly around the doctrine's Scriptural basis. And today there is a great deal more care taken before a text is cited as a "Marian text." Much attention is given to those passages in which the natural relationship between Jesus and His mother is relegated to the background and where Mary is found "as part of the faithful congregation" in Acts 1, as well as to the fact that after Pentecost she does not appear at all. Moreover, Catholic exegetes are facing up without embarrassment to the words Jesus spoke to His mother at the wedding of Cana, "Woman, what have I to do with you?"[29]

A reaction has set in against the fanciful exegesis of past Marian enthusiasm. Catholic exegetes are slow to see implications for Mariology in many texts which not so long ago were commonly produced as obvious support for Marian dogma. Even passages which were traditional mainstays are now read with new slants. Genesis 3:5, for example, is approached very hesitantly. Does this text really provide us with a clear and transparent divine statement to the effect that both Mary and Christ will be antagonists of the serpent, and does it reveal that Mary — with and through Christ, of course — will rise triumphantly to crush the serpent's head with her unsullied foot?[30] To whom does the woman of Genesis 3:15 refer? The Vulgate translated the text as "*she* will crush your head." But the Vulgate is doubted by many. De Fraine says that the word *she* (rather than *he* or *it*) betrays the influence of the

[28] *Munificentissimus Deus.*

[29] Cf. J. Michl, *Biblica,* 1955, pp. 492ff., and P. Glächter, *Maria im Erdenleben,* 1954, pp. 171ff.

[30] *Ineffabilis Deus.*

Marian tradition on the Vulgate.[31] Renckens adds that no one has ever successfully associated Mary with Genesis 3:5, neither literally nor typologically.[32] This is enough to suggest the tensions that have become apparent between traditional ways of finding Scriptural bases for dogma and specific fruits of current biblical exegesis. The tensions are not reflected in the official proclamations, however. In *Fulgens Corona* (1954), Genesis 3:5 is cited again as though there were no doubts about its bearing on the Marian dogma. And the total image of Mary still defines much official interpretation of the sense of Scripture.[33]

Revelation 12:1 provides another example of problems that Catholics are having with the interpretation of Scripture. This is a text that commonly appears in encyclicals about Mary's heavenly glory. But Pius IX's remark that "everyone knows" that Revelation 12:1 refers to Mary is not reflected in later Catholic exegesis. The awareness of the peculiar apocalyptic literary genre has led to more reservations about the references to Mary that people used to see in John's Revelation. Some Catholic exegetes baldly say that the Marian interpretation of this text is simply false. In his commentary on the book of Revelation, the Catholic exegete Wikenhauser flatly says that the Marian interpretation of Revelation 12:1 has been "abandoned by modern scientific exegesis." More commonly, the woman in this verse is said to refer to the Church, but even then Mariological elements get involved. That they do is related to the strong desire in current Mariology to find as much reference to Mary in Scripture as possible. And this, according to Michl, goes hand in hand with a growing inclination toward pneumatic interpretation of the Bible.[34] And thus, the hermeneutical problem that has always stood in the shadows of traditional Catholic exegesis comes out in the open. In face of this hermeneutical problem, the exegetes are veering away from the analogies and types that have long been seen in Scripture and are fastening on the passages that deal with Mary directly, particularly the stories of the birth of Christ.

31 J. de Fraine, *Genesis*, 1963, p. 58. De Fraine insists that the Mariological exegesis was unknown to most of the fathers.

32 H. Renckens, *Israel's Visie op het Verleden*, 1956, p. 234.

33 "When the text itself does not prohibit such a rendering, it may be interpreted in the light of its fulfillment rather than according to the words of the text itself" (M. Schmaus, *Mariologie*, 1955, p. 159).

34 J. Michl, "Die Deutung der apokalpitschen Frau in der Gegenwart," *Biblische Zeitschrift*, 1959, p. 301. Cf. A. Th. Kassing, *Das Verhaltnis von Kirche und Maria im 12. Kapitel der Apokalypse*, 1958, Chapter VI.

Two lines have become apparent in current Mariological discussions: those customarily indicated by the names *minimalists* and *maximalists*. Both sides accept fully the dogmas about Mary, but this fact should not obscure the importance of their divergence. The intense controversy that has been going on between minimalists and maximalists reveals that both are conscious of an important theological difference between them. Each warns the other in most solemn and urgent terms. Minimalists warn against exaggerated Marian devotion. Maximalists ascribe to others a "most deeply regrettable minimalism." Against this background, the Second Vatican Council's treatment of Mary becomes especially important.[35]

✦   ✦   ✦   ✦   ✦

The subject of Mary came before the council soon after the Pope, on November 21, 1962, interrupted the discussion on the sources of revelation only a matter of days before the ending of the first session on December 8. Cardinal Ottaviani proposed on November 28 that the schema on Mary ("On the Blessed Virgin Mary, Mother of God and of Man.") be discussed at that time. He took the occasion to point to the many things that the Roman Catholic and Eastern Church had in common in regard to Mary. He said that, after the tension-filled discussions of recent days, it would be profitable to turn to a subject in which unanimity would be manifested. "We are united in our love for her. After discussing various points of difference, it is well for us to remember that she can serve to unite us."[35a] But Ottaviani's proposal was rejected by the chairman when it became clear that it would not have passed as a motion.[35b] The chairman ruled instead for the subject of the *Church*.

Actually, Ottaviani had misjudged the situation, for it was apparent in the discussion of his proposal that the schema on Mary would have evoked as much controversy as the one on the sources of revelation. And when the chairman decided against introducing the subject of Mary at the close of the first session, there was no doubt that it would come up at a later session. It reached the

[35] Cf. G. B., "The Theology of the Blessed Virgin Mary at the Council," *The Ecumenist*, Vol. II, No. 3, 1946, pp. 33ff. See also R. A. Newman, "A Protestant Note on Saint Mary," *The Ecumenist*, Vol. II, No. 2, 1964, pp. 26ff.

[35a] From X. Rynne, *Letters from Vatican City*, 1963, p. 202.

[35b] A. Wenger, *Vatican II. Premiére Session*, 1963, pp. 147ff. The schema on Mary was not very long; it discussed the bond between Mary and Jesus, Mary's position in the economy of salvation, her titles and privileges, Marian devotion, and Mary's bearing on Church unity.

floor in 1963. And we must recall that it came up as the subject following the doctrine of the *Church*. On a given morning, unexpectedly for most, the chairman asked whether Mariology should be discussed in connection with the separate schema on the subject or whether the council wished to discuss it as a subheading of the doctrine of the Church. The chairman's question was very crucial. Two speakers were given opportunity to argue opposite sides of the question. First, Cardinal Ruffini J. Santos of Manilla gave a strong plea for a separate consideration of the Mariological issue. Then Cardinal F. König argued for incorporating the doctrine of Mary into the schema on the Church. Santos was careful to say that he did not deny the relationship of Mariology to the Church, but that to include it within the doctrine of the Church would be to reduce the significance of Mary. He added that if Mariology were taken separately, its relations to christology and soteriology would reveal that Mary is certainly a member of the Church, but that she, in certain senses, is above the Church and therefore distinct from all other members of the Church. Cardinal König, in opposing Santos, brought in theological, historical, pastoral, and ecumenical reasons for discussing Mariology within the context of the Church.

The suggestion was strong that if Mariology were discussed as a separate subject, the council would be indicating its inclination to prepare a new dogma on Mary. But actually the Church was the central theme of the whole council, and there seemed to be sound reason for including Mary in the discussion of the Church to show her intimate relation to the Church. The ecumenical argument was that the non-Catholic Christians would be more easily persuaded that the doctrine of Mary was based on the witness of Scripture as well as tradition, since the council would stress that "Mary, the people of Israel, and the Church" are all bound together in the light of Scripture.[36] A vote was taken immediately after both speakers had finished, with Cardinal König winning by a small majority.[37]

Much more was at stake here than a procedural issue. The relationship between Mary and the Church had been at issue for some time in Catholic theology, and the procedural vote was a

---

[36] It is possible that an allusion was made here to the studies by Max Thurian, who was present at the council. His *Marie Mère du Seigneur. Figure de l'Eglise,* 1962, stressed the same thought. Thurian also wrote an important article on Mary's assumption: "Le dogme de l'Assumption," *Verbum Caro,* 1951, pp. 2ff.

[37] The vote was 1174 to 1074.

token of where the council's sympathies lay in the material issues. Müller has said that "the problem of the relation between Mary and the Church has risen like a comet out of nowhere" in the past few years.[38] The patristic and biblical traditions carry suggestions of the relationship between them, but since the fourth and fifth centuries Mary has been seen primarily as the bride and associate of Christ.[39] And from this the line has been drawn to the idea of cooperation between Christ and Mary and from that to the present trend to proclaim her a co-redemptrix.

Recently, however, Catholic theologians have felt for going back to the older emphasis on Mary as part of the Church, a feeling that was shared by the majority of the council. The smallness of the majority hints that many of the council fathers feared lest Mary might be given too minor a role if the doctrine about her was placed as one section under the broader doctrine of the Church. The situation was complicated by the fact that many privately written schemata were being passed around that could have influenced the opinion of some council members. Against the confused background of all kinds of privately printed schemata on the subject of Mary, the feeling may have grown that the subject simply needed separate treatment, a feeling reflected in the large minority that voted against including Mariology in the treatment of the Church.[40] It was an understandable response. Would the inclusion of Mariology within and as a subordinate part of Ecclesiology lead to a Church-dominated Mariology that would then leave insufficient leeway for the broader and profounder perspectives that were considered necessary for an adequate Marian piety? Regardless of this attitude among the minority, the majority decision did open the door to a new approach to Mariology while it seemed at least to close the door to additional Marian dogma. The ecumenical situation doubtless was behind the majority vote.

* * * * *

The emphasis on Mary's station as a member of the Church is associated with a corresponding emphasis on Mary in her human situation and especially in her historical association with the peo-

[38] A. Müller, *Fragen der Theologie heute,* p. 308.

[39] Cf. Müller, *Ecclesia Maria. Die Einheit Marias und der Kirche,* 1951, p. 309.

[40] R. Laurentin mentions certain Mariologists who claimed that the council's placement of Mary within the schema on the Church was really a vote against Mary. Laurentin speaks of a propaganda move to influence the voting, and regrets that the Mother of unity had become a banner of conflict (Laurentin, *L'enjéu du concile. Bilan de la deuxième session,* 1964, pp. 100f.).

ple of God in the Old Testament and the Church of the New. The question of her place in the economy of the history of salvation is what is involved here. Strikingly, she is compared with Abraham as the father of believers. Abraham, we are told, became the "father of us all" by his faith. He who "against hope believed in hope . . . staggered not at the promise of God through unbelief; but was strong in faith, giving glory to God" (Romans 4:16-20). Abraham exhibited the abandon and the perseverance of faith that made him a model within the history of salvation. *In this sense,* Abraham forms a parallel with Mary. His kind of faith was Mary's kind of faith.[41] And so Mary is seen standing on the side of believers. Like Abraham, our model, she accepted the promise though evidence pointed to the contrary, and in accepting the promise gave God the glory. Her response was directed to the divine mystery. We would misgauge the situation, however, were we to jump to the conclusion that Mary is now being levelled off to the stature of Abraham. For *her* faith is directly related to the mystery of the Word become flesh, and this context makes Mary unique.

❖   ❖   ❖   ❖   ❖

The incarnation remains the center of Mariology. That even the minimalist Mariology keeps this fact in the foreground is not surprising. Bavinck, trying to keep Mary's role in the incarnation in perspective, says this: "Mary is the most blessed among women; she received a privilege which is given to no other creature. Through unmerited grace she is elevated above all men and angels. Rome has rightly maintained this, and anyone who denies it is not taking the incarnation of God seriously."[42] The Reformed theologian is here steering clear of docetism; he wants us to accept the incarnation and Mary's role in it with all its implications. But the question is, what are the implications of Mary's involvement in the miracle of redemption?

These implications, whatever they are, are drawn variously by the two wings of Roman Catholicism, the minimalists and the maximalists. The maximalists conclude that Mary's role is co-operative; she is a co-worker in redemption. Mary is not merely passive and receptive; she involves herself in a unique role — a

41 We find the same thoughts in Protestant writers. See Calvin's exegesis of Luke 1:38ff. Cf. H. Vogel, *Gott in Christo,* 1952, p. 619, where he refers to Mary as a "type of faith." And W. Tappolet, *Das Marienlob der Reformatoren,* 1962, p. 174.

42 H. Bavinck, *Gereformeerde Dogmatik,* III, p. 261.

Marian role, shared by no one else. She was more than the mother of the Redeemer. Her entire life is bound up with that of her Son. She participates, as God wills, in the mystery, not merely by way of helping in the applying of salvation to men's lives, but in the objective achieving of it for men. Without standing on a par with Christ — she remains dependent on Him — she is *mediatrix*.

Mary's so-called *fiat* is said to illustrate her cooperation in the work of gaining salvation for men. The miracle of redemption happens *through* Mary's response; it does not occur above the human level. Therefore, argue the maximalists, the notion of co-redemptrix is not a hobby of a certain group of Catholics. It belongs to the essence of Mariology. And it could well be fixed as a Catholic dogma. The controversy centers on this point. Would not the official formulation of Mary's vital role as co-redemptrix be consistent with the place she occupies in the whole redemptive program? Does not the history of Mary's place of honor in Catholic piety and theology lead irresistibly to this climax? Marian devotion is not merely a matter of popular piety, granted that it is sometimes excessive and even distorted in a way that elevates Mary to the rank occupied by Christ alone. Papal encyclicals have seemed to point in the direction of the Church's recognition of Mary formally as co-redemptrix. Benedictus XV said that Mary together with Christ has redeemed the human race.[43] Pius XII more recently said that Mary was most closely associated with Jesus in bringing about the work of redemption, that she had an extraordinary part in our salvation and contributed to it in a very special way.[44]

Understandably the maximalists appeal to such encyclicals and claim to discern in them at least the clear implication of a co-redemptive role for Mary. They do not deny that she is a "member of the Church." But they do stress the same points the encyclicals make about Mary's royal prerogatives. The encyclical issued on the occasion of the Feast of Mary the Queen went a long way to support the maximalist line, for in it Mary is portrayed as the "consort" of Christ, she in her royal capacity as Queen alongside of Christ who as God and Redeemer is King. Logically, there seems to be no more than a single step from Mary the Queen of Heaven

---

[43] "So did she suffer with her suffering and dying son, and almost die . . . that it can properly be said that she with Christ redeemed the human race" (Denzinger, 1978, note 2). Again, "The Virgin participated with Jesus Christ in the very painful act of redemption" (*ibid.*).

[44] *Ad Coeli Reginam* (On the Coronation of Our Lady).

to Mary the co-redemptrix. But that step has not been taken. Pius XII carefully avoided the term, in spite of the stimulus of the excitement about Mary at the time of his encyclical. And as time has gone on, the resistance to establishing Mary — dogmatically — as co-redemptrix has grown stronger.[45]

The resistance is explained not only by the question of how Mary could be co-redemptrix in gaining the salvation that she herself needed. This is a problem that has always been implicit in Catholic Mariology. The minimalist fear of the co-redemptrix notion stems from a fear that the unique role of Jesus Christ will be undone if Mary is made a partner in it. If the role that Mary played in redemption is going to be based on her *fiat*, will that not mean that divine redemption was *dependent* on her agreement and her cooperativeness?[46] And would this not mean that redemption stems from two components — the act of God in Christ *and* the act of Mary? (The Catholic minimalist and the Reformed theologian raise the same questions at this point.) And what then of I Timothy 2:5 — the "one mediator between God and man"? Quoted as frequently as ever, perhaps, could it ever again have the same force if the team Christ-Mary are co-redeemers? And since Mary remains human, would not her status as co-redemptrix mean that salvation has an earthly source? And is this not the Mariological heresy?

Protestant criticism of Catholic Mariology tends to see the notion of co-redemptrix as the inevitable and intended climax of the whole doctrine of Mary. Barth provides an example of this when he typifies the Marian dogma as the core of Roman Catholic teaching. Barth uses the German Catholic M. J. Scheeben as an illustration to show that, according to Catholicism, Mariology is the "one heresy of the Roman Catholic Church which explains all the rest. The 'mother of God' of Roman Catholic dogma is quite

---

[45] The idea of Mary as co-redemptrix was sharply critized by Bartmann, (*Dogmatik* I, pp. 442ff.) as early as 1932. Cf. Karl Rahner, *Maria, Mutter des Herrn*, 1956, pp. 98f. The problematics involved in the idea of co-redemptrix came out when a plea was made for the title priestess (Sacerdotissima), based on her share in Christ's sacrificial work. The suggestion was rejected by the Holy Office in 1927. But Pius IX had approved a book in 1873 which supported the title. In 1913 the Holy Office prohibited statues of Mary in priestly garb. The suggestion was still alive after 1927, however.

[46] Cf. the encyclical *Octobri Mense*: "The eternal Son of God, when He wished to assume the nature of man . . . and for this reason was about to enter upon a kind of mystic marriage with the entire human race, did not do this before He received the wholly free consent of His designated mother . . ." (Denzinger, 1940).

simply the principle, type, and essence of the human creature co-
operating servantlike in its own redemption on the basis of pre-
venient grace, and to that extent the principle, type, and essence of
of the Church."[47] Clearly, the controversy will not gain much head-
way merely by having Catholics point to Mary as the type of the
Church, as the prime example of the possibility of human cooperation with grace. Barth's criticism of Scheeben is aimed precisely
at the synthesis made by Catholicism between the synergism of
Mary's co-redemptive work and the example Mary provides of the
believer's cooperation with grace.

Sometimes Catholics have insisted that there is no synthesis here;
the typological role of Mary, they say, is not intended to suggest
her having a co-redemptive function. Rather than emphasizing
Mary's active *fiat*, they lay stress on Mary's *faith*, which associated
her with the sovereign and gracious saving acts of God. Schillebeeckx, for example, disowns the idea that Mary adds a complementary function to the incarnation such as would suggest that she,
as a human being, participates actively in the work of salvation by
adding something to the work of Christ.[48] Were Mary truly active
and creative in this sense, says Schillebeeckx, human cooperation
would be an ontologically necessary component of the incarnation.
And we would be ascribing to Mary the human being what was in
fact accomplished by Christ. But this cannot be the import of Mary's
position in the work of salvation, for if it were, the suggestion would
be unavoidable that Mary provides the human side of salvation
while Christ provides the divine side — and this leads to the heresy
of monophysitism. For monophysitism creates a vacuum where the
humanity of Christ should be — a vacuum too easily filled by Mary.[49]

In fact, the humanity of Jesus has been part of the concern in
the minimalist criticism of maximalist Mariology. They frequently
refer to monophysitism and docetism as dangers implicit in the
co-redemptrix notion. Many facets of the emphasis on Mary as type
of the Church become clearer if we keep the concern for the complete human activity of Christ in mind. If it is clear that Mary's role
as type or example is not understood in the sense of an example of
human cooperation in the work of salvation, we can better appreci-

---

[47] K. Barth, *K.D.*, I, 2, p. 157.

[48] *Theologische Wordenboek*, II, p. 3146.

[49] This is in my judgment the core of much criticism levelled against the
maximalists. Cf. K. Rahner, "Probleme heutiger Mariologie," *op. cit.*, pp. 89ff.,
where Rahner accentuates this point. Mary the epitome of humanity—"as though
Christ is not truly man!" Rahner also speaks of monophysite tendencies in the co-
redemptrix notion.

ate the fact that new approaches are being sought to Mariology.

The idea that Mary is a type of the Church, in contrast to the maximalist co-redemptrix notion, leans heavily on the simple stories of Jesus' birth. Minimalists stress the important place that Mary is given as Mother of the Lord, pointing to her unique connections with the great mystery of godliness. There is no difference of opinion anywhere on this point, since her place in the context of the incarnation is beyond dispute. The heresy of docetism underplays the real role of the human here in order to concentrate exclusively on the divine, the docetism is out of favor everywhere. Mary appears as an active, participating person in the entire drama. The climax comes, not with Mary pushed out of the picture, but with God setting Mary on the stage with a marvelous benediction. She is not only introduced as the blessed among women (Luke 1:24); she is greeted by Gabriel as the woman full of grace (Luke 1:28). Through the rest of the story, she is flooded by this light. We see her arrive at the home of Elizabeth. And we hear Elizabeth marvel spellbound at her privilege of being visited by the mother of the Lord (Luke 1:43). Elizabeth blesses Mary (Luke 1:45). And Mary echoes this blessing around the world in her own Magnificat: "from henceforth all generations shall call me blessed" (Luke 1:48). What Luke gives us is not a vision of divine invasion with no human involvement. Men are not pushed into the shadows when Christ comes. Mary is in the spot-light, her faith is illumined, her joy and her songs of praise fill the stage.

One recalls the woman of Bethany who emptied the costly vial of oil on Jesus' feet as her act of devotion. Her act was so loving and sacrificial that Jesus promised that wherever the gospel was preached her memory would be kept alive (Matthew 26:13). But the honor that all men ascribe to Mary is different. For Mary is not simply an example of love and goodness toward the Lord. She is *involved* in the great things that the Almighty has done for her (Luke 1:49).

There can hardly be room for difference of opinion on whether Mary is a leading figure in the birth of Jesus. The miracle of redemption, the coming of God, sweeps Mary into the drama *via* the annunciation *and via* her response, her readiness to be the servant of God. The act of God in the work of the Spirit overshadowing her is at center; but her answer of faith is just off center: "Behold, the handmaid of the Lord; be it unto me according to thy word" (Luke 1:38). When Simeon was almost blinded by the light that had arisen over Israel, he was not so overcome by the act of God that he could not see Mary or forget to bless her; nor could he restrain from telling her what his mind saw of things to come: "a sword shall pierce through your own soul" (Luke 2:35).

The gospel is not too timid to give Mary all the prominence of being the Mother of the Lord. But all that is said about her is part of the witness of the gospel to the divine mystery and all that shall be said about her by "all generations" is meant to witness to the mercy of God.

The signs pointing to divine redemption show that the great mystery occurs in a correlative bond with Mary's faith and surrender. Christmas preaching must, unless it is an abstract doctrinal dissertation on the incarnation, deal with Mary seriously if it is to be gospel preaching. For if we de-historize the gospel stories of Jesus' birth in an effort to stress the divine character of redemption, we can only fall into a docetic emasculation of the mystery. Fear of this led Bavinck to say that Reformed objections to Catholic Mariology must not lead us into the trap of a docetic incarnation doctrine. The Reformation did not attack Catholic Mariology in order to dehumanize the gospel. Reformed christology does not want to say that God acts only "immediately," without means, shaking off human involvement so that God can be transcendently alone in His redemptive acts.[50] The controversy about Mariology does not pit on one side those who say that God works by Himself and on the other side those who say that God uses creatures like Mary.

The Reformation was not against giving due attention to Mary's role in the incarnation. It was the *nature* of her role that was at stake. Was she a kind of *mediatrix* or not? We need not be reminded that Rome emphatically separates veneration of Mary from any worship.[51] For the controversy is not whether Rome intends to deify Mary. It does not. But the controversy has to do with her disputed function as co-redemptrix, a function ascribed to her to this day. Nor is the personal character of Mary a point at issue. Catholicism finds no discrepancy between the personal humility of Mary and the Church's veneration of her — nor is there any discrepancy from the Catholic standpoint. The issue, from our point of view, is whether Mary's very real activity, her most exemplary faith and humility, and everything else about her are taken up as part

---

[50] M. Schmaus has interpreted the Protestant criticism of Catholic Mariology as though the Reformation felt that all divine use of man in His service was a threat to His own glory. Cf. Schmaus, *Mariologie*, p. 312.

[51] Every Catholic dogmatics distinguishes between worship *latreae* (given only to God), worship *duliae* (given only to saints), and worship *hyperduliae* (given only to Mary).

of the gospel *witness to* the salvation that came into the world with Christ.

In view of this issue, we cannot help wondering whether the various titles assigned to Mary serve a useful purpose or whether they actually mislead. We are quite aware that none of them is intended to deify Mary; we are asking the question in the context of Mary's human role in the salvation event. She is called "mediatrix," "reparatrix," and "Queen of Heaven." Even granted a studied effort to place Mary subordinate to Christ, does not this kind of language unavoidably suggest a kind of duplication in the work of salvation? The question is not a betrayal of a desire to maintain a Reformed monergistic transcendentalism. We are not dealing with a matter of ontological possibilities. We share the Catholic minimalist concern to keep Mariology on a non-metaphysical level. What we are dealing with here is primarily a soteriological matter: What function does Mary have in the work of redemption?

The problem as we see it comes down to this, that Mary's role is often delineated by Catholicsm in a way that the Gospels ascribe exclusively to Christ. We recall the fact that believers are awakened to trust in Mary, in her power and in her enormous goodness, and in the Spirit whose help her prayers obtain for us.[52] Meanwhile we are assured that her intercessions turn the favor of God toward us.[53] We are told to ask Mary to "pray for us to God as it were in our name" because her prayers have greater effect on God than do ours.[54] For the "mediatrix of our salvation is as powerful as she is kind."[55] These titles do not necessarily fit into the area of Mary as co-redemptrix, since Mary's function *within* the Church is being underscored for the most part.[56] But even in view of this we are forced to ask whether the same problems do not rise in connection with the subjective aspect of Christian experience of redemption that are present in the objective sphere of God's redemptive acts. For in Christian experience too the active role of Mary brings into question the role of Christ and the Holy Spirit. Obviously, Catholicism does not mean to minimize Christ's own intercessory prayer or the Spirit's "groans that cannot be put into words." Nor does it neglect the reality of the Comforter's presence. But it casts an ob-

---

[52] Cf. the 1895 encyclical *Adiutricem Populi* (On the Rosary).

[53] Cf. *Laetitae Sanctae* (On the Rosary), 1893.

[54] *Iucunda Semper*, 1894.

[55] *Ibid., Conciliatri salutis nostrae aeque potens et clemens.*

[56] We do meet statements in the encyclicals on the rosary that suggest it. For instance, in *Iucanda Semper* we read about the "part that Mary played in the redemption of mankind."

scuring shadow over these treasures of salvation by placing the Marian mediation between them and the Church. The fact that Mary's mediation has a long tradition does not help clear up the obscurity. The mediation of Mary — not her deification — is the real area of difference. The minimalists' insistence that nothing may be brought into Mariology which threatens the unique mediatorship of Christ has cleared up the situation to this extent at any rate, that we can now seek together the limits beyond which devotion to Mary does indeed cast a shadow upon the glory of the one Savior, Jesus Christ.[57]

     ✱   ✱   ✱   ✱   ✱

The striking parallel between the Reformation polemic against Mariolatry and the Catholic minimalists' concern to protect the uniqueness of the one Mediator, gives the conciliar discussion of Mary extra importance for us. Now that the council has determined to subordinate the discussion of Mary within its discussion of the Church and has thereby made clear that it has no intention of proclaiming a new dogma of Mary as co-redemptrix, we are excited about the course that the discussion may take. The question is how the minimalists will succeed in arriving on *their* way at Roman dogma. Maximalists give the impression that the minimalists will arrive at Roman dogma only by a leap; their premises, it is said, will never lead naturally to the Catholic truths. No one accuses the minimalists of forsaking the Marian dogma; it is only claimed that they have to accept it by making a leap, not by the irresistible logic of their thinking. The implication is that the minimalist Mariology is intrinsically an aberration in Catholicism. How, it is asked, can it be shown that the immaculate conception and the assumption into heaven are implicit in the idea of Mary as type of the Church? But on the other side are heard warnings against isolating Mary from the common lot of mankind, elevating her to equal status with Christ, and making salvation a fruit of two sources, Mary and Christ. The controversy has given no signs of letting up.

     ✱   ✱   ✱   ✱   ✱

The readiness of the minimalists to accept the Marian dogmas is not a peripheral issue. The parallel between Abraham and Mary as examples of faith does not exhaust the idea of Mary as a type of

---

[57] An illustration of how modern Catholic warnings against exaggerated Marian devotion represent a change is Croonenburg's uncritical remark in 1945 that the great surge of devotion to Mary has not in the least "put Christ into the background" (E. J. van Croonenburg, *Kritiek der Maria-verering*, 1945, p. 104).

the Church. However important Mary's exemplary role may be, the unique mystery of the incarnation in which Mary is involved means that Mary's place in the whole divine dispensation for and in the Church is of cardinal interest. The minimalists too see a line drawn from the mystery of godliness to Mary as mediatrix. They work with the privileges given to Mary as expressed in a long tradition of pious language. Marian devotion has led to a growing hope that the pious language about Mary would be expressed in dogmatic form by the Church. Many of them have been, and the lines between Marian piety and Marian doctrine are interwoven. The dogmas proclaimed in 1854 and 1950 expressed formally a long tradition of pious devotion.[58] And as such they keep their significance for the minimalists.

At the same time, the minimalists shy away from deducing one privilege given to Mary from another, as though one good thing must logically imply another. Congar, for example, complains that concluding from one privilege given to Mary that another is necessarily implied in it is bad theology. Max Thurian agrees with Congar, but points out that this is exactly how the assumption of Mary into heaven was arrived at.[59] The assumption is recognized as implicit in the immaculate conception and is seen as the "crown and perfection" of the first privilege given to Mary.[60]

Do these dogmas allow for an interpretation which would protect against heresy and at the same time stay clear of the notion of co-redemption? According to minimalism, they do. And minimalists believe that Reformed thinking has been unduly influenced by reaction

[58] Cf. *Ineffabilis Deus* and *Fulgens Corona.* Both of which speak of the great desire of the people for the proclamation of Mary's assumption.

[59] Congar's criticism agrees substantially with that expressed by A. Müller: "A metaphysical analysis of concepts without constant analysis of revelation is not an adequate theological method." Müller has the deductions drawn from Mary's motherhood of Christ in mind here (A. Müller, "Maria als Bild der Gnade und Heiligheit," *Begegnung der Christen,* 1959, p. 594).

[60] Cf. *Munificentissimus Deus* and *Fulgens Corona.* A good deal of debate was carried on prior to 1950 on the subject of whether the assumption was indeed a necessary inference of the immaculate conception. Cf. B. Altaner, who contended that the first did not necessarily imply the second (Altaner, "Zur Frage der Definibilität der Assumptio B.M.V.," in F. Heiler, *Das neue Mariendogma,* 1951, pp. 49ff.; see also J. Coppens, *La definibilité de l'Assumption,* 1947, pp. 26ff. The question of whether Mary had died prior to the assumption was part of the discussion. This question was never resolved by a papal statement.

closed mind to a legitimate appreciation of Mary.[61] Moreover, they insist that everyone ought to recognize that the typological significance of Mary has an ontological *aspect* to it; after all, she *is* the mother of our Lord.

* * * * *

By taking a longer look at the "crown" of all the privileges given to Mary, the assumption into heaven, we may be able the better to understand the minimalist appeal. The first question that we ask about the assumption is whether it signifies the anticipation of our own glorification; is it the "pre-glorification" of the saints? This is the eschatological side of Mariology, and it is heavily emphasized by the minimalists. It is not a deduction from the dogma of her immaculate conception nor from that of her role as Mother of God. Here Mary's assumption is the anticipated eschaton and its implication for our comfort and encouragement.[62] We are dealing here, then, not simply with the fact, but with the meaning and purpose of the assumption. Pius XII suggested it back in 1950 when he underscored the significance of the assumption as a physical reality. To him this implied a protection against materialism, decay of morals, and the reckless destruction of human life. More than that, the assumption sets before the eyes of all men the "glorious final goal to which both our soul and body are destined."[63] Since 1950, Mary's assumption has been frequently put forward by Mariologians as the kerugmatic dogma which proclaims our faith in the resurrection of the body.[64] Salvation came into the world through the Word become flesh, and this was magnified in the immaculate conception as God's "Yes!" to human kind. The same "Yes!" of divine grace is manifest anew in the assumption of Mary as it signifies the total redemption of mankind from physical death. The assumption is a form of realized eschatology.

The minimalists do not approach the eschatological import of

---

[61] "The Reformers were prisoners of their own logic and so did not know what to do with Mary" (M. Winowska, *Die Jungfrau der Offenbarung. Maria gestern und heute,* 1950, p. 114).

[62] We cannot enter into a discussion of the implications of Mary's virginity at this point. But we may note that in our day the logical deduction and what Congar calls metaphysical or gnostic concepts do not loom large. Rather, we hear more about the significance of the virginity of Mary as an eschatological sign, as augur of the final fulfillment. Cf. K. Rahner, "Virginitas in partu," *Schriften zur Theologie,* IV, pp. 195ff.

[63] *Munificentissimus Deus.*

[64] Cf. *ibid.,* where we read that faith in Mary's assumption "strengthens and fructifies our faith in our own resurrection to glory."

Mary's assumption as an inner ontological implication of her status as Mother of God or co-redemptrix. They see it more as a gift of grace, as a privilege; it is the love of God genuinely revealing itself, not "as a volcanic fire which flows over the empty field of nothingness to the glory of a lonely but absolute deity"[65] but as blessing and mercy to humankind to the end of the age. The eschatological view has a quite distinct ring to it, different from the notion that the assumption of Mary carries us to its next logical step, the proclamation of Mary as co-redemptrix. The assumption, seen as the anticipated destiny of the believer and as a gift of the grace that stems from redemption, leaves room for a forceful warning against heresy. The message of grace is heard here more clearly than when Mary's assumption and eventual status as co-redemptrix is deduced from her closeness to God. The notion of co-redemptrix puts a decided stamp on christology and soteriology through Mary's function within the work of redemption. But in the eschatological approach, grace to Mary and to us all comes out more clearly. It signifies that grace which truly triumphs over sin and death and for that reason proclaims that God has really begun realizing His salvation and is on the way toward presenting "to himself a glorious Church, not having spot or wrinkle" (Ephesians 5:27). Thus, says Rahner, the "Church greets Mary as its own example, its own future in the resurrection of the flesh."[66]

But even in this relation between the expectation of faith and the sign of the future (I believe in the resurrection — the assumption of Mary), the question is whether Mary's assumption does not still have the marks of a complement to the work of Christ. If she is not here the co-redemptrix, is she not an assistant in giving the grace of assurance concerning the coming salvation? Consider the relation of Mary's assumption to the glorification of Jesus as our assurance of one day "being with Him." Of course, the Catholic minimalists do not deny that Christ is our assurance and guarantee. But Mary does form a complement to Him. Let us listen to the possible line of thought in consideration of Christ, the Son of God, as our assurance. "Christ is ascended, yes. He is God. What can this say to us? Yes, we have learned that we shall join Him. We believe that. But how wonderfully is our personal hope commended, enlightened, and filled with tenderness by the fact that Christ has al-

[65] K. Rahner, *Maria Mutter des Herrn*, 1962, p. 43, and "Zum Sinn des Asumpta-dogmas," *Schriften zur Theologie*, I, pp. 242ff.

[66] K. Rahner, *Maria Mutter des Herrn*, p. 95.

ready given to Mary a share in His own destiny."[67] The thought is that Christ's ascension is associated with His divinity, but Mary's assumption and glorification is altogether human. And this provides a better reason for assurance. There is something of a contrast made here, with Mary providing a compensation for Christ's great superiority.

The compensation motif is much older than 1950. It is observable in the later middles ages in the person of Gabriel Biel who taught that Christ's ascension did not speak to men as directly as Mary's assumption did since Mary was *only* human.[68] Heiko Oberman is right in ascribing a docetic trait to Biel, since Biel was unable to find a really significant place in this thinking for Christ as man. Finding the significance of Mary's assumption to heaven in the fact of her pure humanity offers an interesting parallel to the human role that Mary is said to play in salvation as co-redemptrix. In both cases, Mary's humanity offers a complement to Christ's divinity. The question we are forced to ask at this point, then, is whether the minimalists do not face the same problem as do the maximalists. At least it offers something worth thinking about. The minimalists want to ward off the docetic penchant in the co-redemptrix notion, but do they escape the problem themselves when they interpret the assumption of Mary kerugmatically as the message of special eschatological assurance to men? Do they not suggest that Christ's own ascension and glorification is somehow too remote to be of effective assurance to those who hope to share in His victory? And if they say that it is Mary's pure humanity that makes the difference, are they not overlooking the true humanity of Jesus? And do they not suggest the same kind of duplication of work in regard to the eschaton as the maximalists do in regard to the work of salvation?

Paul sees in Christ the complete assurance of both salvation and eschatological hope. For He has made us alive in Him and provided us a sure place in heaven (Ephesians 2:4-6). Our faith is set on the grace of God with its power to make dead men come alive. And this grace is centered in Christ who rose again in the flesh and became the "guarantee" of our faith (I Corinthians 15:20-23).[69] Christ

[67] Maltha, *De ten hemel Opneming van Maria*, 1950, p. 29.

[68] Oberman writes that to Biel Christ "was not *pure* nature because his humanity was united in a hypostatic union with the Godhead" (H. A. Oberman, *The Harvest of Medieval Theology*, 1963, pp. 313f.). It is this distinction that puts a stamp on the confidence that people are led to place in Mary, and which is accented in the idea of Mary *as mediatrix*.

[69] Cf. Romans 6:9f.; Colossians 3:1-4.

in His resurrection and ascension is the one assurance of our parti-
cipation in His future. In view of this, does the special significance
attached to Mary's assumption as our assurance of like experience
suggest that somehow Christ's ascension does not quite serve the
purpose? It seems to me that as Catholic minimalists emphasize
the eschatological and kerugmatic importance of the truly human
in Mary's assumption they will be faced with several unavoidable
problems.[70]

Some of these problems will be of an anthropological nature,
especially in reference to the body-soul dichotomy that seems pre-
supposed in the assumption doctrine.[71] Along with this, there is the
problem of the relationship between time and eternity; if eternity,
as is contended in some Catholic writers, is not infinitely extended
time, how does the assumption of the human Mary fit into the new
ideas on what eternity is?[72] But the most profound of the problems
is that created by the new theology's effort to re-emphasize the
true humanity of Christ. Theology is alive with new approaches to
the humanity of Christ the divine Redeemer, but as yet there has
been no real attempt to relate them to the dogmas of Mary. It is
fascinating to hear Schillebeeckx contend that the doctrine of Mary
can be purified if full weight is put on the Savior's humanity, "for
in earlier days Mary tended to fill the vacuum left by the lacunae
which seemed to exist in Christ's humanity."[73] Schillebeeckx makes
this comment by way of criticism of the complementary notion of
Mary as co-mediatrix. But it seems to me that his argument could
also be turned against the notion that Mary's assumption affords a
guarantee that Christ's ascension cannot. I do not mean to say that
the new concentration on the humanity of Jesus will bring about a
crisis in the Catholic attempts to point out the significance of Mary's
assumption into heaven. But as the current Catholic studies of
christology tend to brush aside the traditional distinction between
Christ as God-man and Mary as wholly human, we wonder whether
the kerugmatic-eschatological interpretation of the assumption of
Mary will be able to stand. The foundation of the assumption
dogma is the pure humanity of Mary in distinction from the divine-

[70] The 1951 encyclical *Sempitermus Rex Christus* (On the Fifteenth Centenary of the Council of Chalcedon) warned against excess in this tendency
to emphasize the kerugmatic over against the ontological meaning of the
assumption.
[71] Cf. K. Rahner, "Das Leben der Toten," *Schriften zur Theologie,* IV, pp.
429ff.
[72] Th. Sartory, *Die Konfessionen und das II Vatik. Konzil,* 1963, p. 37.
[73] Schillebeeckx, *Tijdschrift voor Theologie,* 1960, p. 29.

humanity of Christ.[74] Once the re-emphasis on Christ's complete humanity — His divinity nonetheless complete, of course — gains a solid foothold, the foundation of the minimalist teaching about the assumption of Mary will be weakened if not undermined. One can also put the question in another form. Does the sharp criticism levelled by the minimalists against co-redemptrix Mariology because of its docetic tendency carry the seeds of destruction for the minimalist eschatological Mariology?[75]

❆ ❆ ❆ ❆ ❆

We have been trying to sketch the situation in today's Mariological discussion in connection with the council's decision to contain the discussions about Mary within the discussion about the Church. The council's decision opens the possibility that the kerugmatic and pastoral purpose of the dogma will be discussed along with its implications for the ecumenical situation. There is no way of predicting what the results of the trend toward seeing Mary as a type of the Church will be. It could even be turned into a basis for a new synergistic Mariology in which Mary as *example* will be given a creative role in the work of redemption. On the other hand, various statements in papal encyclicals that have come very close to setting up Mary as co-redemptrix could still play a role.

Now that a strong current of resistance to the co-redemptrix idea has set in, and now that the council apparently has no inclination to proceed with a statement to that effect anyway, and, further, now that the notion of Mary as type of the Church has established itself within Catholic respectability (though not without severe and continued resistance), it has become clear that the whole controversy converges on the renewed emphasis on the "true humanity" of our Lord. Each side, Rome and the Reformation, laid the charge of creeping docetism at the feet of the other. Each accused the other of giving inadequate weight to the real humanity of Jesus Christ. According to Catholic Mariology (both minimalist and

[74] F. X. Arnold says that the form of Christ was misrepresented as "purely divine" by a strong anti-Arian trend and that His unique human mediatorship was watered-down by the tendency to give Mary and the saints an independent place in popular devotion. This would not have happened, according to Arnold, "had the significance of salvation of Christ's human nature and His unique mediatorship been given as clear a place in pastoral care and popular piety as was given to His deity" (F. X. Arnold, *Chalkedon*, III, 1954, pp. 314 and 316).

[75] The sign of the virgin's assumption has no special moral force in view of the New Testament moral appeal to Christ's Lordship and His indwelling Spirit. Cf. I Corinthians 6:13f. and 15:33f.

maximalist) the Reformation refused to allow the complete implications of the incarnation to come to fruition; and this is why the Reformation has never been able to recognize the value and legitimacy of a proper veneration of Mary. The Reformation theologians have accused Rome of giving Mary such a prominent role in the Church that she appears to duplicate the work of the Savior at important points. They have accused Catholics of a failure to recognize the total sufficiency of Christ's humanity for the accomplishment of all that needed to be done for our salvation and our future; and this is why Rome's Mariology introduces Mary as a needed complement to the work of Christ. In this unusual situation — with each side fearful of incipient docetism in the other — we want to emphasize that the Reformation repugnance to Mariology did not in fact stem from docetic tendencies but did stem from a suspicion of docetic tendencies in Rome, tendencies that affected its soteriology as well as its christology. There was indeed no tendency in the Reformers to cast all redemption into an exclusively divine mold. This comes out in the attention they gave to Mary. They respected her role short of anything that could lead to her ascendance to the status of mediatrix. They were convinced that any mediatorial role ascribed to Mary would detract in that proportion from the exclusive mediatorial work of Christ; the very nature of the incarnation was such that an ascription of the work of mediation in any part of Mary would overshadow the total significance of the fact that the Word did indeed become *man*.

Docetism in Mariology is not theological denial of the complete humanity of Jesus Christ. It is not to be equated with the ancient heresies that did deny a full human nature to Jesus. The issue here is whether the humanity of Jesus was adequate for the *work* of redemption, and whether the assistance of Mary was necessary or not. The question is *not* whether Mary deserves honor and praise or not. We need not take sides in the condemnation of the Jansenist statement that "the praise given to Mary, as Mary, is vain praise."[76] The real issue lies in the *kind* of praise given her. The New Testament often gives honor to human beings. The glory of God is too tremendous that it can be threatened by a glory that belongs to man. Christ Himself has promised that those who serve Him will be honored by the Father (John 12:26). The Christian demand for humility need not negate the place of honor due to human qualities of worth. But the moment we have said this we must call ourselves to careful consideration of the kind of honor given to any human

[76] Denzinger, 1316.

being. Recognizing that the deepest motives in Mariology do not lie in the direction of her deification, but in the unique relationship she bears to the work of salvation, it becomes clear that the difference between Rome and the Reformation cannot be that one side honors Mary and the other side refuses to honor her. The Reformation *is* not docetic or unhistorical; it knows how to preach on Christmas. The difference lies in the *function* ascribed to Mary, and this difference defines the difference in the respect paid her.

The historical development of Marian dogmas reveals that the idea of Mary as co-redemptrix in the work of salvation and the idea of Mary as mediatrix in the application of salvation are very intimately related. Her association with the earning of salvation has occasioned ascriptions of praise to her which caused concern even within Catholicism. And it stimulated new study of the New Testament concept of "praise" as a way of warding off honor to Mary as a duplicate mediator. In such resistance to excess lies the possibility of a new consideration of the true humanity of Christ in connection with the certainty of salvation earned in the past and fulfilled in the future. The issue in this consideration will be whether, in view of the one Mediator, true man as well as true God, the proper dissociation can be made between a legitimate role for Mary in God's work of salvation and a co-redemptive role. Mary's own hymn of praise to God for His great mercy, even to her, will have to loom large in our consideration. The salvation won by the one Mediator is so full and complete, so real and certain, that the only co-worker it leaves room for is the Holy Spirit (John 14:16), the same Spirit for whom Mary waited in expectation along with her fellow believers (Acts 1:14), and the Spirit whose presence neither detracts from nor relativizes the unique mediatorship of Christ, but rather witnesses to it (John 16:13). For He comes from Christ and, through Him, points the way to all truth. There is no need for the interjection of a co-redemptrix in the light of the fully human Savior's completed task. And if the growing resistance to what is suspected of being a docetic track in Catholic Mariology continues, we shall watch with intense interest in how the Catholic theologians who point the way to the kerugmatic and eschatological interpretation of Mary's significance deal with the docetic dangers implicit in their own construction. And we shall watch with equal interest how the council deals with the role of Mary as the type of the Church that waits for the day of redemption when it will share in the glory given by the Father to . . . . our Brother, Jesus Christ.

Epilogue

9 WHAT OF THE FUTURE FOR THE VATICAN COUNCIL AND for the Catholic theology? The unwary may be tempted to substitute vague desires for cautious analysis, or give a superficial prognosis in order to avoid open-end questions. Even if in our long discourse we have gauged the present somewhat correctly, we cannot suppose that the future lies in the present as the flower in the bud. The ways of the past have been too illogical to expect that future developments must follow a straight line from events of the present. Prediction is as dangerous in Church affairs as it is anywhere. And looking at the council from the outside as it were, we must be extra careful not to let our own pessimism or, if that is the case, our own optimism to run over into pseudo-responsible prognosis. This does not mean, however, that we cannot raise the questions about the future. The very mystery of the Church invites, rather compels us to ask about the perspective ahead for the difficult way of estrangement and rapprochement, of dialogue, contact, controversy, and for the ecumenical striving to overcome the divisions of the Church.

We would be irresponsible if we let our concern for the future be a disguise for a flight from the present. The Church as it is now, with its tensions and problems, its guilt and dividedness is the

Church for which we share responsibility. New Testament eschatology — pointing as it does to the Church's final victory — is charged with a sense of urgency as it calls us to do for the Church what our hands find to do here and now. It is no accident that Christ's prayer for the unity of the Church in John 17 includes a prayer that the Church may be kept from the Evil One. So, our thoughts about the future of the Church must come out of tensions in the present, tensions that must creatively produce watchfulness, prayer, faith and commitment, love for truth *and unity,* love for unity *and truth.*

While the council was in session, Yves Congar addressed a side meeting with a warning against a polite ecumenicity that always underestimates the problems and road-blocks in the way of unity and is intoxicated with a romantic vision of the Church's possibilities for unity, an optimism which is bound to be sobered by ultimate disillusionment. Congar was speaking for the realistic ecumenicity that is necessary for a discharge of responsible churchmanship. On the other hand, we would add that realism about ecumenicity is something different from a fatalistic view of the future. We must not rule out the possibility of surprises; the mystery of the Church forbids us to be fatalists. Realism will keep us from misjudging the present situation, but it must not keep us from a believing consideration of the unity of all believers in Christ, of the reality of the One Shepherd and the one flock.

* * * * *

The interpretation of the Church's past, getting at the Church's real religious intent in its polemics and dogmas, could lead to relativity and with it a levelling out of all genuine differences. When this happens, hermeneutics, the science of interpretation, is often waved as a magician's wand that can solve all problems, whereas it can and does sometimes confuse the issue so profoundly that believers do not even know at what points they are really one, to say nothing of the points on which they are divided. This is a very real danger at present. Interpretation, getting at the kernel of things within the dogmatic and historical husks, can indeed reduce the gospel to a vague and common denominator notion, and lead people to assume that all of the controversies in the Church are based on grotesque misunderstandings.

We have reason for thanks that the Second Vatican Council, including its ecumenical aspects, has steered clear of such simplistic thinking. There is a strong feeling for getting at the real meaning of past controversy so that popular caricatures that each side holds of the other can be corrected. But the desire to get rid of misunderstandings is motivated by an equally strong will to get at the real and abiding differences. And it is at these points of difference that the ecumenical dialogue comes alive with both urgency and desire.

There are several problems faced by Catholicism that turn out to be problems faced by Protestantism as well. The more Catholics and Protestants confront each other in utter seriousness, the more they become aware of a communion in problematics. Confrontation that is both serious and relevant reveals that both sides face the same problems in meeting the new responsibilities of a new day. The questions placed before theology by modern science surge through all churches as all sides become aware that they can no longer divide the estate of life between science and theology. In both camps these questions have raised an uncertainty. And in both sides there are many who rightly sense that we cannot take flight into a religious inner life, isolating ouselves from the *tensions* of today in radical irresponsibility toward the generation tomorrow. We need mention only the problem of evolution, the many questions thrown up by anthropological studies, the deep searching into the meaning of human life, its origin and destiny. Add to these the issues presented by modern psychology and sociology, and finally the challenge of the prevailing sense that human life is subjected to forces political and demonic over which human beings have no control.

Not the least of the problems we share is that of *continuity* amid the powerful forces of change surging in the variableness of human life. This problem takes on unique relevance for the Church, for here the decisions of faith made in the past are binding decisions, making the past in some sense determinative of the future. Are these decisions irrevocable in every sense, or are they so historically defined that we can shake ourselves loose from them in the face of each new insight and challenge? Is the Church, like every other institution, caught up in the relativity of historical thought, and must it accept all the radical consequences of this relativity for its faith and life? We know something these days of situational ethics. Is dogmatics also situational? Or are whatever changes that do occur in dogmatics merely innocent variations of form as compared to the light of unvarying truth that sheds an undeviating illumination over the Church?

If the Church is determined to avoid capture by historicism, if it says no to the notion that *all* of life is prisoner of the capricious but hard taskmaster of restless history, even then it cannot escape problems inherent in the fact that the *Church* is historical and that even divine revelation is incarnate in human and historical forms. No one can rest with a *deus ex machina* view of revelation. No one today can accept the kind of "supranaturalism" that nineteenth-century Christians often held to. We are done with separating God from history in such a way that His relation to it is only by way of occasional wonderful incursions. We are better aware today than many were in the past of the reality and significance of the horizontal dimension of human life as it is taken up in the service of God's revelation and providence.

Respect for the full-dimensional humanity of the Church is reflected in a revived respect for the stress on the true humanity of Christ in the ancient christological creeds of the Church. This is not a covert distrust of the doctrine of Christ's deity; it is a desire to guard the humanity of Christ against an exclusive devotion to His deity, a misguided devotion that rubs off the sharp contours of His image and leaves a vague projection of distant divinity. The same mind is discerned in the concentrated attention given these days to the full humanity of the Scriptures. Again, this is not necessarily a covert unbelief in their divine origin; it is a desire to guard the real humanity of the writers of Scripture against an exclusive devotion to the divine inspiration of the Bible, a misguided devotion that obscures the mystery of hearing the Word of God through human words. And even while this is happening, new and urgent problems are being forced upon the churches, problems that bear hard upon everything the Church is and does. The biological definedness of man, the demythologizing of Scripture, the program of Bultmann and Tillich for pressing the ultimate implications of the irrelevance of what they call dualistic supernaturalism — these are only a few of the pressures placed on *all* the churches.

Not surprisingly, questions are being asked of Church leaders that strike at the heart of piety and faith. What about miracles? What about the effectiveness of petitionary prayer in times when the hope of divine invasion into a naturally determined life is almost passé? And so the controversy between Rome and the Reformation is affected by problems that confront both sides because both sides are part of the modern situation. Much has changed since the dialectical theology of the twenties and thirties led many to suppose that the vertical dimension is the only dimension with which theology is engaged. Christian faith is now confronted by the horizontal dimension of life and cannot flee from a responsible encounter with it. This is a confrontation compared to which the crisis of ninteenth-century theology in its encounter with natural science was child's play.

＊　＊　＊　＊　＊

In the light of this common confrontation with modern problems, do the historic differences between the churches loose their importance? The question is most understandable. Yet, we must give a negative answer to it for the reason that there is a vital relationship between the problems within the Church and the problems that confront it from the outside. The questions put to the Church from the outside force the Church to ask the basic question of its listening to and preaching of the gospel. The divisions of the Church are forcing the churches to get at the root question of their existence and task. The root question takes various forms, but it always confronts the Church the moment the Church faces the questions rising from science and culture, believing or unbelieving. For this reason it would be irresponsible to shove the questions that divide the Church aside or to give them a simple answer that only camouflages the fact that they have not been answered at all. We cannot make believe the differences do not exist. This would be too high a price to pay for a common front against the problems that confront us commonly. To do so would be to deny the very importance of the Church in the modern situation.

We must add that for those who together confess Christ as Lord of their lives and Lord of the world, who have a common stake in the cause of Christ in face of the urgent modern problems forced on all who join His cause, for all who want to go into the world with its radical doubts to give witness of their faith — for these the issues of the day will affect their approach to the issues that divide them. The problems are too pressing and the need for a clear answer is too great to allow for a naive relativizing of faith's answers. The mind that takes the problems seriously also takes the question of faith and its content seriously. But for the sake of this mind, we must also ask whether separate traditions have hardened into positions that have their origin, not in the gospel, but in historical situations and the limited human insights that have gradually distorted the truth on both sides.

Herein lies the radical difference between a common-denominator ecumenicity and a serious inquiry into the true nature of unity in Christ and how it came about that this unity was broken. The question implied here summons us to tireless concern and effort. One can avoid the ecumenical responsibility only if he assumes that the gospel is so unclear that it is open equally to anybody's interpretation. If the adventure of ecumenicity is going to have real relevance to our world, the question of the gospel and the unity of Christ must be both honestly and stubbornly faced as *the* important issue. The Roman Catholic Church in its relation to other churches is not the only one given this responsibility. The other churches must accept it too. The presence of non-Catholic observers at the council from widely differing groups was a remarkable reminder that the problem of division is not simply one between the Roman and the non-Roman sides. The observers had a non-Romanism in common, but their own great diversity and divisions were never out of sight. And it served only to press home the inescapable duty of us all to subject ourselves constantly to the touchstone of the gospel that is meant to lead us all on one pilgrimage in one faith toward the future that will reveal the one truth to us all.

✻   ✻   ✻   ✻   ✻

The internal questions of the churches and their common confrontation with the problems of modern times are closely related. That they are is evidenced by many parallel situations which all the churches encounter. Take the presence of conservative and progressive wings within the Church. Our study of the council and Catholic theology revealed that forces within Catholicism, if not pulling in opposite directions, are pulling in different directions. And parallels to the Catholic tensions between conservatives and progressives are found in almost every Church. But to characterize the two forces as conservative and progressive explains almost nothing at all. The factors in each are terribly complex, and they include psychological, characterological, and sociological factors as well as theological. All these factors play a role in the variant ways in which men construe their own calling and the calling of the Church in changing times. And the tensions are dangerous because each side can come to think that its perspective is absolutely imperative and that the question of "to be or not to be" ends with the decision of the Church to follow its way. And with this conviction, tensions turn into conflicts.

The tensions can create a wall of division within a given Church, with those on each side of the wall thankful that it is not like those on the other. Pride rears its ugly head, and pride always makes for estrangement between men. And where pride is bolstered by conviction it leads to almost incurable estrangement. The contrast between the conservative and progressive wings of the

Church is defined in many ways. One is described as "closed mindedness" and the other as "open mindedness." Or, the contrast is made between timidity and courage, escapism from new problems. Clearly, there is a pressing urgency for keeping these tensions from mastering the Church. The Roman Church is facing this urgency today; so are most other churches. And what makes the tensions so difficult to live with is the fact that each side is convinced that only by conformity to its mind can the Church truly be of service to the gospel and to the world.

In the Roman Catholic Church the tensions are centered on what it means for the Church to be the guardian of the truth as expressed at the First Vatican Council. The "progressives" are surely not of a mind to break with the past of Roman Catholicism. They are making a plea for applying the old to the new, the teachings of the Church formulated in the past to the new situations and ideas of the present. To them, for the Church to be the guardian of the truth does not mean that the Church must keep the truth locked up in a set of untouchable definitions. It means that, because the Church has the truth, it must have the courage and the openness to let the truth be manifest in new forms as the Church confronts new times. The "conservatives," being less impressed by the impact of history upon doctrinal truth, want to accent the immutability of truth in the face of historical relativism, to accent the Church's duty to encounter the changing times with the *one unchangeable* truth. At first glance, this would seem to be merely a difference in accent; preservation of the truth need not contradict a call to the Church to face the problems of present times. Yet, in fact the representatives of each side see profound implications in the position of the other side.

The tensions in Catholicism may remind us that no "position" or "mind" ever is free from danger of perversion. One side runs the greater danger of static irrelevance to the times, of traditional*ism* and confessional*ism,* and of seeking to put the Church under the control of a school of theology, notwithstanding the assumption that the particular "school" identifies itself with the gospel. For the Church to be guardian of the truth could be twisted so badly that the Church would lose perspective for the future, lose power to test the gospel in new situations of life, and lose the willingness to attempt new answers to new questions. The other side runs the danger of being so open and fearless in the face of the problems of the time that it does not sufficiently honor the critical, testing power of the gospel. It faces the temptation to engage the issues of the day so openly that it neglects to bring the power and hence the blessings of the unchangeable gospel to bear on the situation.

A study of Catholic responses to the Church's guardianship of the truth makes it clear that this is an ecumenical problem. The Church is custodian of the truth. But what kind of custody does it have over the truth? The question sounds through the walls that divide the churches and forces itself upon all as a universal question carrying universal responsibilities with it. Many Protestants are amazed that a Church with such a unified structure and with its dogma of infallibility should reveal such divergencies within itself as the progressive and conservative wings that are present at the Vatican Council. It would, naturally, be untrue to the council to suggest that all of its discussions are defined in terms of the tensions between the progressives and conservatives. But the tensions are present in that form, and they do help shape the image the Church shows to the world today. The tensions are the more striking just because the progressives and conservatives are not distinguished by having youth on one side and age on the other. The fact that both generations are represented in both camps underscores the vital nature of the problems that the tensions pose for the Church. The Roman Church is faced, not with the question of which side will prevail, but with the challenge of getting at the depth dimension of the tensions. For almost all the problems around which the tensions are felt have to do with the Church as the people of God, its humility, its obedience and freedom, its laity and its offices, its charisma and its ministry, its relationship to other churches, and all these in relation to the assured results and the limitations of science, biblical criticism, natural evolution and its effect on morality, and the calling of the Christian in the world.

In most periods of crisis the Church hears the call to face the new times with a new mandate. John XXIII sounded this call in his opening message to the council. He set out the challenge within the conviction that the truth the Church guards is "ever the same," but in the conviction that this truth has to be made relevant. His appeal was bound to remind the council that the so-called "separated brethren" are trying to find their way through the times in faithfulness to the truth and are hearing the same call to responsibility and are facing the same problems that this responsibility brings along with it.

The progressives have been characterized by the old story of the Lapland deer which, according to legend, had to drink the water of the Polish Sea once in their lifetime. Among the herd there was always one who, restless and furtive, would lift his head high, sniff the North wind, begin to move and to set the whole flock in motion behind him as though driven by a secret power and guided by a secret compass. But the image is far too romantic and naturalistic to fit the picture within the Church. It makes it sound as though the Church is involved in a romantic experiment that can be finished successfully by following an instinctive drive to the future. The Church is not involved in an experiment. Indeed, the matter of its own unchangeability and continuity is the issue. And for this reason the Roman Catholic Church is faced with tremendously important decisions, decisions that must be made with intelligence and faith, decisions that will set the compass for the Church's way into the times ahead. Even if the council does not provide concrete answers to the several problems it faces, the problems themselves will keep pressing until they are given an answer in the route the Church actually takes. And the answer will not be private Catholic answers, for the problems are not private Catholic problems. They touch the depths of the one Christian faith and affect the churches that ought to be and are not visibly the one flock of the one Shepherd, that ought to be and are not giving witness to that one faith with one voice and with a single power.

Along with the doctrinal challenges comes the challenge for the Church not to lose its joy and certainty of faith in its confrontation with the world. Joy and certainty of faith are being tested at their roots today.

The recent history of the Church shows that the process of elimination and the search for common denominator ecumenicity is a fruitless way to seek unity. But it is no compromise of the faith to point to a common call to discipleship of Jesus Christ and to the gospel Paul preached, Jesus Christ and Him crucified. Enmeshed in the polemics of Church history, Paul's word can be made to sound like the word of a man ready to compromise his convictions for the sake of unity. But the Church of the Cross is bound forever to this message, and whatever reduction of the Church's speech takes place must be a reduction to the content of the kerugma, the Cross of Christ. In fact the Church at present is being tested down to the last phase of its life precisely on this point. Does the Church, in its faith and its credibility, its acts and its words, its listening and its learning, its controversies and its problems, does the Church have its sights on the one message that it has for the world? John XXIII pointed to the one thing that has stayed the same throughout almost two thousand years of change and crisis in the Church:

Jesus Christ, the center of history and life, the center of the gospel that the Church must guard for the purpose of giving it to the world. Standing under the Cross, the Church need fear no problem, not even problems it will see as through a glass darkly until the end of the age. Standing under the Cross, the Church also places itself within the grace and under the judgment of Him who through His Cross has become the one Shepherd of the sheep. The Shepherd will not let the Church escape the question of its divisions, will give the churches no rest as long as they are guilty of dispersing His one flock and of making a travesty of His one sheepfold. But standing under the Cross, even the guilty churches are granted the assurance of His presence on their pilgrimage. It is an assurance that is valid only as the churches do indeed stand under the Cross, listening to the Word of the God of peace, and only as they are established forever by Him who establishes us all "in good works to do his will, working in you that which is well pleasing in his sight, through Jesus Christ; to whom be glory for ever and ever."

Index

INDEX OF NAMES

261